NO MORE ~~BOARD~~ BORED ROOMS®

Accompanying you on your collaboration adventures

A complete companion for your journey to highly effective meetings

Martin Peterson

Copyright © 2023 Martin Peterson. All rights reserved.
First paperback edition printed in 2023.

A catalogue record for this book is available from the British Library.
Published by Successfactory™, Chester, United Kingdom.

ISBN - 978-0-9931390-5-5

Although every precaution has been taken in the preparation of this book, the publisher and author assume no responsibility for errors or omissions. Neither is any liability assumed for damages resulting from the use of this information contained herein.

Illustrations by Martin Teviotdale.
The moral right of the author has been asserted.

Contents

Introduction 04

Types of Meeting 12

Here's a Quick Win For You 14

My Lessons Learnt 18

How The Book Works 30

To guide you through the book 31

Section 1 – The Meeting Environment 33
    Part 1 – The things you can see 42
    Part 2 – The things you can't see 82

Section 2 – The Inspired Meetings Framework 107

Section 3 – Tools For Meetings 149

About the Author 224

Recommended Reading 225

Introduction

On January 4th, 2006, I started a new job as a venue coordinator for Successfactory™. This was the official start of the journey leading me to be so passionate about ensuring the time people spend together is enjoyable. It should be purposeful, positive, productive, and regardless of the approach attendees should feel the meeting was worthwhile. For many years prior to this I had attended many types of meeting with various levels of success (much as I still do, despite my passion and knowledge). But the environment, people and processes followed at Successfactory™ events showed me exactly what could be achieved. You'll hear about some of the most memorable in this book. My work has been in many different settings, from retail, hospitality, the military, finance, science and technology, and outdoor pursuits. Some of which had five employees, and others had thousands, each had their own unique culture therefore the effectiveness of meetings varied.

A few examples of past meetings in my working life have been: team sales meetings, which were just like a 'bashing' because the local manager had received the same from the area manager. Half-day appointments at a sales showroom to learn about the next seasons' mountaineering equipment, where we regularly had lots of coffee and cake with a few rucksacks and tents thrown in, but these were so memorable and effective. Command group meetings with the power lined up at one end of the table, then everyone else descending in rank to the opposite end of the table where the lowest and newest team member sat next to the secretary and so often the noise heard was people banging on the table in disgust and control when a more junior officer had a better idea than a senior one. There have also been idea and good practice sharing workshops that gave responsibility and accountability to everyone in the room and the trust that they could share their ideas without fear of ridicule or being cut off. Regardless of positive or negative impact I've always left a meeting asking myself 'what ideas can I take away?' and 'what would I never repeat or want to inflict on anyone ever again?'

Many of the meetings I have been part of could very well have been the reason some of the following quotes were created, but I want to change this.

"A MEETING IS AN EVENT AT WHICH THE MINUTES ARE KEPT AND THE HOURS ARE LOST."

AND

"I'VE SLEPT WITH EVERYONE IN MY OFFICE. WE ALL ATTEND THE SAME MEETINGS!"

UNKNOWN

"NOW, IF ANYONE HAS ANY QUESTIONS, QUIETLY RAISE YOUR HAND AND PLACE IT OVER YOUR MOUTH"

ANON

This is why I'm so passionate about effective meetings and have been for a long time and why I decided to write this book to share my insights and experiences.

2020 was the beginning of a challenging time for us all (sorry about the understatement). What I did get from this awful time was time, and it made me realise the benefits of writing this book. I was able to go deeper in my research and consolidate my existing knowledge in order to present the most comprehensive guide possible for you. During these toughest of times we had limited opportunities to be face-to-face with friends and colleagues, very few chances to travel for business or pleasure and lots of choices when it came to working online with people. But in what also feels like a very short time since the Covid-19 pandemic and at the time of writing this book, so many people have ridden the rollercoaster of Zoom fatigue whilst trying to continue to earn a living, keeping vital work going and, more importantly, maintaining relationships with friends and family whilst not being able to be physically present with them. In brief periods where restrictions were lifted everyone did their best to spend some time together experiencing full-bodied interaction such as handshakes, eye contact and very limited hugging. But also, to pick up on a wider range of body language than just head and shoulders, to feel and experience the empathy, warmth, and intuition that you only get when you walk into a room with others and equally important to chat at the coffee machine to fill the white space and help you connect so much more deeply with friends, colleagues and clients.

This tough time has allowed us to learn some of the best ways to use the many online platforms, the tolerances of people from both a physical and mental health point of view in relation to time spent meeting online and helped us find ways of collaborating more effectively when not together. It also taught us, in many cases without realising it, how much more effectively our brain can work when active as we took our calls in our headphones on our daily permitted exercise. Not to mention realising that we do need physical time together, and when we can do it, it must be so much more effective that it used to be.

It is my hope that every aspect of this book is of use to someone. We are all different, and we have different roles to play as leaders and participants in meetings, but we should all strive to make sure every meeting matters and do so by being authentic and emotionally intelligent. I'm sure you have heard the phrase, 'Always treat people the way you want to be treated.' Well, I think in the case of meetings, we should actually 'treat people the way they want to be treated.' This way, you connect with them personally and work to get the best out of them. This is the reason why I don't just share my experience and, in some cases my opinion, but also, I share options. There may be short meetings with a few people where two paragraphs from this book are relevant, or there could be conferences and workshops which will succeed due to the application and use of the many, many insights and techniques I share. This is why I have created a comprehensive guide to meeting effectiveness and will provide many approaches and tools for you as you craft each meeting solution.

After spending so much of my time over many years in the great outdoors and continuing to do so, I felt it appropriate to draw on this time to help share metaphors and examples with you. As with many parts of life, our experiences in different areas can influence and help us learn for other areas. Not only have I done some of my best thinking during my outdoor pursuits, but I have been able to connect it with the environment of meetings, which will become apparent in this book, but more of that later.

I want to be clear that this IS a leadership book. But I am not going to explore leadership as a topic. Instead I will delve into a key aspect of what I call leading self, teams, and individuals. That is the topic of meetings and how whether leading them or taking part in them, we must act in a manner that demonstrates how important they are.

Many leadership theories, manifestos and frameworks often refer to meetings, either directly or through an aspect of the model. Here are some examples from my teaching or from clients and organisations that I have worked with:

Leadership Laid Bare – Graham Wilson
In this book, Graham explains how great leaders 'Create a high-performance environment where success is inevitable'. In further detail his Leadership Truths explore principles such as Inspiring Action, Unleashing Innovation, Creating High-Performance Teams and Helping People and Organisations learn. Whilst these are not just about meetings as they involve culture, strategy, and personal authenticity, often these truths come to fruition in meetings and collaboration opportunities.

The Army Leadership Code
The British Army's top level-document, The Army Leadership Code, uses the acronym LEADERS to encourage a set of positive leadership behaviours. This breaks down into:

L	Lead by example
E	Encourage thinking
A	Apply reward and discipline
D	Demand high performance
E	Encourage confidence in the team
R	Recognise individual strengths and weaknesses, and
S	Strive for team goals.

The areas of encourage thinking, recognise individual strengths and weaknesses, and strive for team goals will often require collaboration during coaching, reviews and feedback sessions and goal setting workshops will undoubtedly involve meetings.

Action-Centred Leadership – John Adair
In his tried and tested model, John Adair's Action Centred Leadership drills down into the roles, tasks, and functions of a leader in relation to the Task, the Team, and the Individual. All three areas provide opportunities for people to get together to be successful. Whether that's coaching the individual, setting objectives, allocating tasks or building the team.

As you can see, meetings, whether implicit or explicit in your approach, are a fundamental part of leadership. Be it board meetings (no, not bored) for the senior leadership and executive teams of a business, a presentation of ideas by the sales team or 1-to-1 coaching sessions and everything in between. Poor meetings can paralyse, demotivate, and frustrate people. Great meetings will inspire, motivate, and help people grow. An effective meeting will communicate a clear and consistent message that drives the right actions.

But why should we have meetings? Often meetings are to align people and create or share one consistent message. The image below represents how many ways a message can be interpreted as the numbers grow. When passing messages one to one across many people, there's a great risk that the meaning of the message can change on its journey. At least by getting everyone in the same space (online or face-to-face) they hear it once and can use the language used to decode or add meaning to the messages together. Great meetings can reduce the risk of misunderstanding or misinterpreting the message and they should create a clear and consistent urge for action. The most important part of a meeting afterall is what happens afterwards.

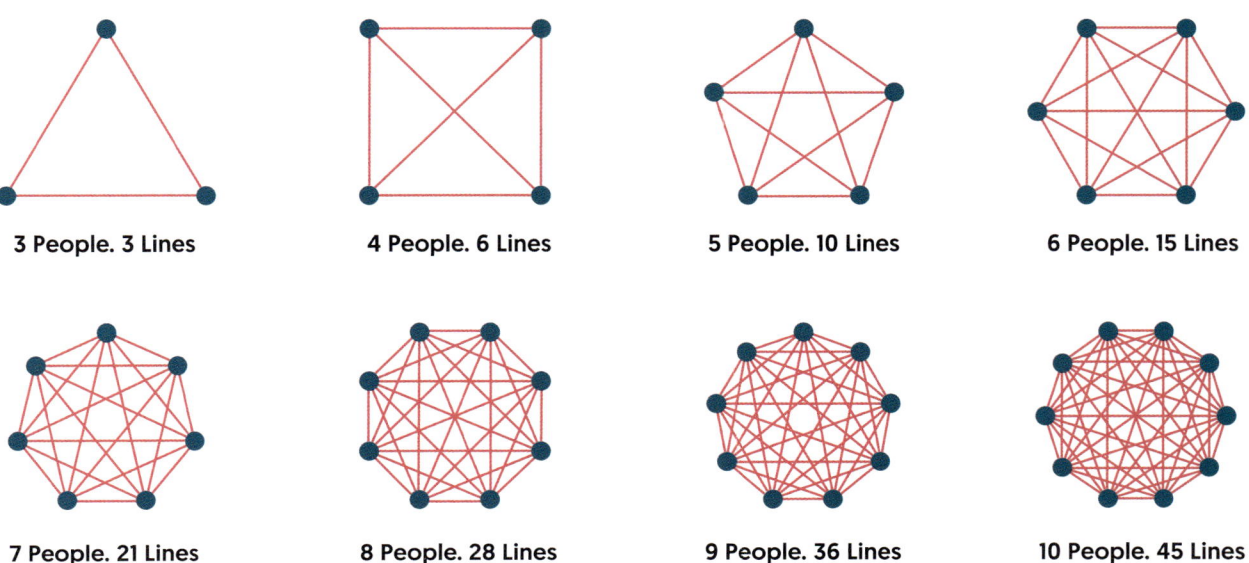

Complexity and lines of communication

Together we should work to make every meeting matter. Why? Well, it's always worth bearing in mind the real cost of the time people spend together. There is a time and monetary cost, not to mention productivity. A two-hour meeting with twelve people should be considered as twenty four hours of time or three days of productivity. But don't let this put you off having meetings. Often the time spent together just sharing ideas and building relationships can have a huge and lasting effect on team outputs which is well worth the investment.

The dictionary definition of a meeting is:
noun
- *an assembly of people for a particular purpose, especially for formal discussion.*
- *a situation when two or more people meet, by chance or arrangement.*

Dictionary definition of collaboration:
- *The action of working with someone to produce something.*

My definition of a meeting:

An opportunity for multiple people, teams, or organisations to get together, collaborate and make a positive difference.

In this book, we will explore many different types of meeting and collaboration opportunities, but for simplicity and ease of reading, I will call them meetings for the most part. I am a big fan of keeping things simple (as you will see), but there is much more information out there on many of the areas I will touch on in this book. With that in mind, I have provided a recommended reading list at the end of the book. Armed with this reading list and our old friend Google, you will be able to delve as deep as you wish. In the Tools for Meeting chapter, I have referred to the best of my knowledge as to the origin of the model or approach. The descriptions I have used are to help you to plan and adapt for a variety of meeting formats, but for many of them, there may also be further reading if you wish. The section of the book entitled 'My OCD (obsessive compulsive disorder) is so bad I've alphabetised it to CDO' will build on this and explore the benefits of the process and respecting its design.

LEADERSHIP IS ABOUT CREATING A HIGH-PERFORMANCE ENVIRONMENT WHERE SUCCESS IS INEVITABLE

Graham Wilson

Types of meeting

When working with my clients on the topic of meetings, I ask them what types of meetings they attend. A team of ten people can come up with a huge list of different meetings, which I find interesting. This book can be applied to all types. I thought it useful to connect a little by sharing a list of the common types of meetings that I hear of out there. Have a look and consider how many of them are familiar to you.

Initial Consultation
Scrum Meeting Board Meeting Weekly Check-in
Action Review Meetings Progress Updates Idea Generation
Extraordinary General Meeting
Annual General Meeting (AGM) Walk and Talk
Team Huddle Broadcast Meetings Problem Solving Meetings
Project Kick-off Meeting Information Sharing
Decision-Making Meeting Team Cadence Meetings
Town Hall Meeting Sales Meeting Crisis Meeting
Strategy Planning
One-to-Ones Governance Cadence Meetings
Issue Resolution Meetings Daily Tactical
Coaching Sessions Workshops Training Sessions
Quarterly Planning Meeting 90-day review
Sense-making
Community of Practice Meetings Morning Flash Meeting
Planning Meetings Retrospective meeting
Idea Generation Meetings
Team Building Meeting Committee Meeting
Daily/Weekly Check-in
Introductions

CONGRATULATIONS YOU'VE JUST SURVIVED A MEETING THAT COULD HAVE BEEN AN EMAIL.

Quick Win

If you're getting ready to go into a meeting or have to plan a meeting at short notice, here's some quick and easy tips that will make a big difference. Give them a try, and if you like them, do come back for more and read on.

I'm going to guess that you're a busy person; This short but game-changing guide can be used to get some quick wins and easily improve your meetings. I always challenge clients to keep things as simple as possible, which I've tried to do here. There is enormous value in taking the seemingly complex and making it simple. We often get so caught up in the challenge and the business of driving for results that we forget to ask the most important question:

"What do we want people to do after they have seen, heard and experienced the strategy, plan or briefing?"

Because of how busy you all are and the many meetings I hear you attend; I feel it is important to share these crucial principles and help you to focus on making your meetings rock!

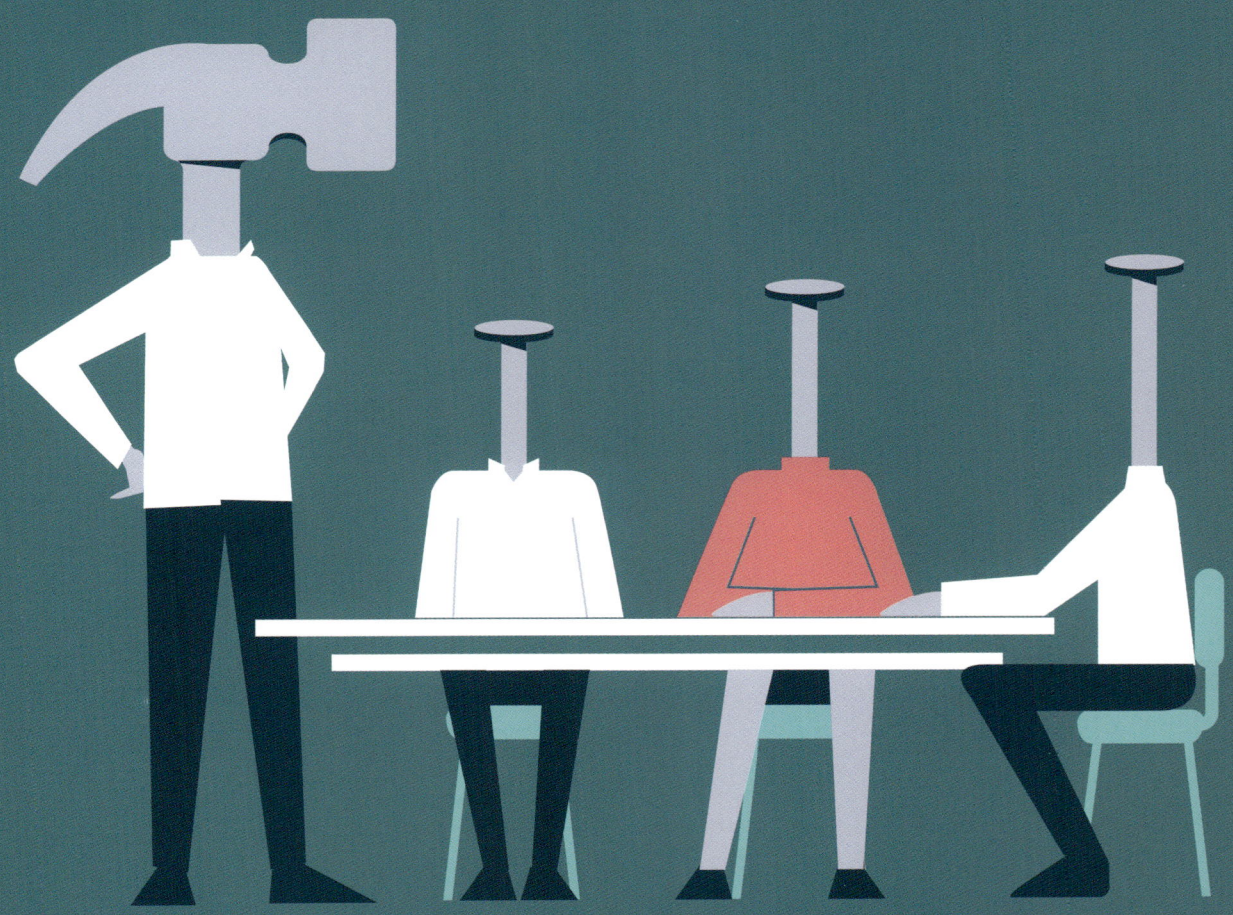

I challenge you to use the following 15 tips to change your meetings and build a toolkit that has much more than just a hammer in it. Here is a summary of what I've learnt from crafting and delivering many meetings and workshops in many different cultures on my journey so far.

1. When planning a meeting ask yourself the following questions. The starting point has to be the question, **"What is the purpose of the meeting?"** Your second question should be, **"What do I want people to do after the meeting?"** Third question, **"How do I want them to feel?"** and the fourth question, **"How am I going to inspire action?"**

2. Always have a purpose for the meeting which is aligned to the organisation's goals and values - and over communicate it. Everyone should be absolutely clear why they are there.

3. Sell the purpose of the meeting before people get there - they should want to be there and arrive curious, excited and valued.

4. Invite individuals personally to the meeting, sell the value of them being there and why they need to be there.

5. Ask yourself if the invited attendees will add or receive value. If the answer is no, don't invite them.

6. Never have Any Other Business (AOB) - find out at the beginning what peoples' hopes and fears are and kill the risk!

7. Handle any negativity at the start to give you time to raise desire and motivation for people to leave on a high.

8. Use a flexible planning approach to craft your agenda – "We want to... to achieve this we must..." and use the best tools and techniques possible when developing the 'what' and 'how' for your agenda.

9. Write agenda items as questions to get people in the right frame and get them thinking about solutions.

10. Never ask, "Do you understand?" Check for clarity and challenge people to say what they're going to do. Get playback of understanding and actions from the meeting from all attendees. Ask questions such as, "What actions have you got?" and, "What resources or support do you need to complete that?"

11. Use technology appropriately. Keep it simple and rehearse.

12. Remember, there are no difficult people at meetings, you have or are using the wrong process.

13. Actions should leave with everyone immediately, writing up actions days later is poor discipline.

14. Create the right environment for the purpose and type of meeting. Use different processes and don't be afraid to change things around. The same format and agenda for repeated meetings will stagnate quickly.

15. Make it fun, keep active, use nature, use music, keep it interactive, use visual facilitation and inspire action. Always look for ways to improve your meetings, review and learn every time.

Make your meetings rock!

My Lessons Learnt

During the last twenty-plus years, I have had many positive and negative experiences that have cemented my thinking about meetings and helped me to learn. Most of my lessons learnt have come out in this book as The Meeting Environment, the Inspired Meetings Framework, and the Tools For Meetings. However there have been some defining moments that I'd like to share the stories and lessons with you here before we get stuck in. I'm pretty confident that you will have had moments like these, but it's key to ask, "So what?", as I have done here.

I am quite the reflector; which can be both a gift and a curse. If, like me, you travel to events, courses, and meetings on your own, you will have spent lots of time in a car or on a train with nothing but your favourite radio station, a bottle of water and your own thoughts. The curse has been when I have played the event over in my head repeatedly on these journeys, asking myself what went well and what could have been even better (sometimes it's simple questions like these that open the best learning), exploring every aspect from set up, prep, resources, behaviours, and feedback. The gift is when you have the time and mindset to ask, "So what?" To stop and think, if that went well, how can I ensure I do more of it when appropriate? And if that didn't go so well, how can it be even better next time?

In these examples, I will tell the part of the story that has played out in events and meetings and follow it up by sharing my, "So what?". In essence, I have had an experience, reflected on it, learned, and connected it with my context and then acted on that lesson, just as in Kolb's Experiential Learning Cycle on the next page.

In the Tools for Meeting section later in this book, I have shared some review tools and templates, and I strongly encourage you to try each of them, on your own and in teams. Find one that you like and use it regularly to help you grow as the leader, either of a meeting or in a meeting.

Concrete experience

Reflective observation

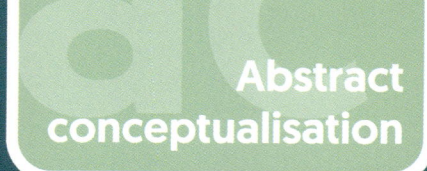

Abstract conceptualisation

Active experimentation

Kolb's Learning Cycle

Lesson 1 – The London Conference

Several years ago, quite early in my journey as a lead facilitator for events, I undertook the role of co-facilitator at a conference for all staff in a public sector organisation. The staff in the organisation were spread across the whole of the UK, and they spent much of their working time supporting parents in deprived areas, dealing with everything from financial difficulties to getting the right support for a child with learning difficulties and even helping victims of abuse in the home. They were the kind of people who gave far more to others than the average employee in other organisations. This meant that we had to make the conference impactful and a good use of their time, and they also wanted us to make it fun and rewarding for them. The organisation's main contacts (The Chief Executive and Project Director) pulled out all the stops to get the best budget they could, but that budget had to cover attendees travel and accommodation, venue hire, refreshments and 'us' to design, prepare and facilitate. They managed to get funds from different pots to club together for their conference to be held at a hotel opposite Madame Tussauds in London. Once they had made the booking and told staff the date and location details, they did exactly what they should have done and handed it over to us.

Months before the conference, my colleague had planned the programme and sent the agenda and proposal to the client. Once agreed we received confirmation of the expected numbers due to attend, which was around 125. Not a huge number, but the planning required to make the programme work with this number brought its own complexities. The date was in my diary, and we agreed to do detailed planning a month before and run it like a small project. We set a board up in our office and took the opportunity to walk our talk. We used tools such as Stick to the Plan, had regular reviews to check in, see how the plan was going and to re-distribute work if necessary. I was keen to impress and had bought in fully to the impact we had to make. Just before we were to travel to the event, we had the last meeting and everything was going to plan, there was a packing list, piles of resources mounting in our corner of the office and when we had our daily lunchtime walk, we would talk through an aspect of the day in detail.

I don't have an issue with planning in detail and have always appreciated the small things when it comes to planning, such as ensuring we packed a selection of different coloured sticky notes and that they were the super sticky variety, checking that whiteboard markers worked and that they weren't the ones that people should discover and throw straight in the bin. We planned for the attendees to be split across 15 tables and having boxes of resources such as pens, paper, sweets, bottled water, tangle toys, fidgets and inspirational quote cards. We felt in control and had all bases covered. A few days before we travelled, we had a last check through and were both happy with the plan. We were ready.

We had planned to travel the day before, to have access to the conference room to set up and have dinner with the client to ensure they felt relaxed and that we had everything under control.. So, from the heart of Cheshire, we packed up the van and headed to central London. We gave ourselves plenty of time, knowing that if all went to plan, we could catch up on other work with the remaining time and maybe even have some time in the hotel gym before meeting the client for dinner. I'm sure you can guess, but our spare time started to get eaten up. Traffic was bad on the motorways, traffic getting into London was (as usual) poor, and one wrong turn in the City led to several seemingly endless loops to correct ourselves. We got to the hotel, and all we wanted to do was unload and set up the room. Although we were later than planned, the hotel staff were only just putting out the tables and chairs in the layout we had asked for. Not that it was an issue, but I ended up helping them to move furniture around to finish their work so we could set up our kit. We had graphic facilitation boards, templates to put on them, paper tablecloths for the world café exercise, the boxes for each table, not to mention my colleague's exceptionally high standards when it came to how things should be laid out on the table. Although sometimes tiring, I got it and knew it made a difference.

A quick change and freshen up before dinner with the client, sharing tales of which Gin is best and what it should be drunk with, if anything (I'm a beer man personally, but my time in the officers' mess allowed me to join the conversation if not the libation). As we left the bar that night, a quick look into the conference room to check if we had missed anything allowed us to have a good night's sleep before an early breakfast and a quick walk-through before people started arriving.

I'm not one to eat much breakfast, especially on big days like this. Instead I use the time to get ahead. I walked through the room, set up anything I could for the early part of the session and laid out the other resources for later activities in an easily accessible and logical way. The day happened, and it went well. There were fastballs and changes to the running order, but because of our plan, process and confidence, everything happened without a glitch, and the feedback was awesome from the client. It was a long and tiring journey home, but it felt good, and we had nothing but good things to recall from the day.

So what? I'd prepared to this level for many events before this, but this cemented my need for preparation and organisation. I realised the benefits of having resources staged and ready for use. The benefits of particular types of equipment and their layout came to the fore, and clients' comments backed it up. I've put lots of effort into the small things since that day and noticed the difference when it hasn't been done. A big lesson for me was, that by unintentionally going above and beyond in the preparation and organisation, we had added goodwill and energy to the bank so that if anything was taken, we still had plenty of reserves. My later section on 'critical incidentals' is a result of events like this, where lots of tiny noticeable things have made the detail. Remember, "Perfection is no small thing, but it's the small things that make perfection."

Lesson 2 – The Imposter

Once, as the appointed subject matter expert, I was responsible for aspects of the Duke of Edinburgh's Award in my Army Cadet unit. I spent many an evening as a volunteer reading minutes from meetings that I was 'too junior' to attend. I had issues with this, in that 1) I was reading comments in the minutes that had been taken out of context about my area of responsibility and 2) far longer than many of the meeting attendees and was the same rank as some of them too. My line manager wasn't the chair of the meeting, but one of the key attendees, so I spent lots of my time explaining to him the misinformation being shared and asking for a place at the table to give my updates first-hand. I tried to ask in different styles but to no avail. This went on for some time, but on one occasion after metaphorically backing him into a corner, he managed to persuade the senior officer to let me attend. I planned my update, printed copies of the material needed, walked through it in my head many times and was genuinely interested to see how the rest of the meeting went. The evening came. I drove straight from work to the unit, got changed into my uniform to play the game, greeted a few other early attendees and got a coffee.

Shortly before the meeting began, the senior officer (who had agreed that I could join the meeting) came into the office where I was sitting near to my line manager, looked at me, then said, "What's he doing here?" A conversation about me proceeded, not a very long conversation, which led to them agreeing that I could join the start of the meeting, they would bring my item forward to the second item on the agenda and then I should leave whilst they went through the other agenda items that were specifically for the senior members of the group. I did as briefed, gave my update, asked if there were any questions (I didn't get many) and was promptly asked to leave. I had a copy of the agenda on my seat, and couldn't see anything of a delicate matter on there, I observed the very obedient and transactional behaviours of other group members ("Sir", "Yes sir", type behaviours) and noted that some newly appointed members of the group were more junior than me and new to the organisation. This frustrated me and made me feel like a complete outcast and alienated by the behaviours. I also wondered what really went on in these meetings as to why they were so secretive, especially when most of the minutes that were distributed were about cascading data and policy updates that everyone needed to know.

A couple of years later, my volunteer journey with the organisation progressed and I finally became one of the coveted members of this 'command group' where I had to attend each of these meetings. I finally learned what went on behind the curtain and what a disappointment it was. Some of the behaviours where abhorrent. Supposedly senior officers barked at each other, claiming the information being shared was false or that their idea was the only good idea on the table. The language was occasionally colourful, to say the least and some members banged their hands on the table as a show of power. I still wonder to this day where they had learnt those behaviours, but thankfully they've moved on and the meetings have changed. Many meeting attendees were often quiet with little to say other than their own updates (including mine), and lots of the information was just the reading of text that quite frankly could have been an email. Even back then, I liked to ask questions to stimulate discussion, but that often got shut down with comments like, take that outside of this meeting. Ironically, my peers at the table used to answer those questions honestly with me when we were either at the coffee machine or stood by our cars at the end of the night waiting to go home.

These meetings, held behind mystical closed-doors, were unproductive shows of power that were quite frankly a waste of everyone's time. Thankfully things have moved on in many areas of this organisation and leaders now realise that people should not be treated like that. There are now many examples of great meetings being held.

So what? As a reflector, I came to the following conclusions about these meetings that I have shared the real learning from later in the book.

1. The time has moved on from when truth does not speak to power. Great leaders will be willing to receive feedback about how meetings are run. Poor leaders will run bad meetings.

2. If a meeting needs to have input from someone outside of its usual attendee list, it needs to happen. They should be made to feel welcome and be involved in the meeting. Yes, it may be necessary for them only to attend part of the meeting, but that can be handled better than in this experience.

3. Meetings are a great opportunity for discussion, and this should be encouraged. Attendees should not take matters personally or, worse direct personal comments at attendees to provoke poor behaviour. Real meetings should not take place around the coffee machine.

Lesson 3 – Who's Idea is this anyway?

When I worked in retail, I rose to the dizzy heights of assistant manager for a specialist mountaineering and climbing equipment retail store. A great environment for a young man who loved the outdoors and was working towards gaining outdoor leadership awards. Part of my role in this particular store was working with the manager to develop our seasonal product offering and attend suppliers' showrooms, and road shows to view the range. We were also asked to keep an eye on the market for exciting new things to add to our store. As a team, we were all active users of the kit we sold, which naturally helped with our sales, but also helped us to see other products out there as we were self-confessed gear geeks. We had regular team meetings to discuss the kit we'd used and other items we'd seen on our adventures to consider as options for our range.

Over time, I had clocked a new product range being sold in increasingly large numbers of other competitor high street stores. This product range wasn't big or costly and, I thought could be a great add-on sale to many of our customers. The brand was called 'Buff' and is now synonymous in the outdoors. There are many similar products and they also offer a wide range of items. They are known collectively as multifunctional tubulars or in some cases snoods. I did a little research and in one of our team meetings shared the concept, a little about cost and products, I'd even explored who the local distributors were, and package deals available. The conversation didn't go very far (even though I thought I knew our store), as I was told it's not for our market and would be a waste of money for us. I disagreed but didn't get any further. For some time, I continued to keep an eye out for new things but felt pretty bad about the knock back as I kept seeing them in other retailers, I even bought one myself from a competitor.

In our line of work, we had to order many months ahead for the following season. Often, before the summer product lines were being delivered to us, we had placed orders for the next winter range. Around six or seven notably obvious months after my suggestion, a package arrived, and the store manager was quick to sign for the delivery. I remember to this day his words, he said, "Hey team, this is exciting. A new product range that I saw a few months ago and thought it would be ideal for us." Yes, you guessed right, he had ordered a pop-up display stand full of Buffs for us to sell in-store. Shocked, I didn't say much, looked at the range and dutifully sold them to as many customers as I could. A few days later, a colleague of mine asked me if these were the items I suggested a few months ago, to which I replied, "Yes," and he just shook his head in disbelief. At no point did I get any credit regarding this or even acknowledgement that the idea started from me. Maybe he just had a bad memory, but I doubt that, as he never forgot the odd occasion when I was late!

So what? Rightly or wrongly, I limited the number of ideas that I shared with him after that. I know it was in the businesses best interest, but team members should get the credit for their work. In meetings, behaviours that stop attendees from contributing will kill a business and switch people off in the short term. Tools identified in this book for sharing and generating ideas are a sure-fire way of involving people.

Lesson 4 – You must be quackers

I trained as a LEGO® Serious Play® (LSP) facilitator in 2017 and subsequently tried to use as much of my learning in as many different contexts as possible. On one occasion I persuaded a very sceptical group of colleagues in the Army Cadet Force to allow me to use an activity from my training as the icebreaker to an annual conference of over 100 attendees. The intention was to use the activity to encourage everyone to be creative, have fun, connect on a personal level and demonstrate that everyone sees things differently and has different opinions. This activity would guarantee that.

When I passed out little bags containing six specially selected bricks to over 100 volunteers in army uniforms, I got some very funny looks and even heard people say things like, "I've no idea what to do with these. I haven't played with LEGO® for over 40 years", "This is a serious conference, why are we playing" and even, "Does he know who I am". But I also saw huge smiles, heard lots of laughs and people saying, "Wow, this looks fun," and, "Can't wait to see what I've go to do with these."

I ran the icebreaker in two parts, as described later in this book. What we discovered was:

- When given the same resource and instructions, out of all the attendees, only two built the exact same thing. Everyone else had different ideas and interpretations. And they were happy to talk about their ducks.
- Asked to modify their duck, they got very creative and used that creativity to answer a very personal question in a non-personal or threatening way. Everyone got involved and shared.
- People were very proud of their ducks and wanted to keep them. They shared pictures on social media and they talked about them frequently during the conference.

So what? Despite their reservations and the assumption that certain types of people can't play, they absolutely can! In addition, it was clear to them at that point that they all had a voice and they were fully engaged throughout the conference. Now I'm not saying that was down to just my icebreaker, but if asked to do role play or present to a large group so early on, we may well have disengaged them very early on and not gotten the best out of them, the energy levels would have been affected, and they would have had less of a common connection to network with over the weekend.

Lesson 5 – It's all about competition, or is it?

Several years ago, I was the training officer and subsequently commanding officer for an area within the Army Cadets. This in simple terms, was to provide exciting, progressive, safe and fun training from a basic military syllabus for young people aged 12 to 18. The leadership teams of a group of areas used to attend a command meeting every other month. This meeting was to essentially update us on policy, safety and look at the 'leader boards' for each area. There was an annual trophy awarded by the commandant, based on a very over complicated set of scores for which area got the most young people through qualifications and awards. For some time, the command meetings felt like a struggle. My main focus was learning from and with others, but others, especially the senior leadership team (SLT) seemed to think otherwise and this created some interesting and occasionally abhorrent behaviours, where senior officers would shout at each other, tell each other to shut up and occasionally walk out. What surprised me the most about this was that members of this group were often former senior members of the armed forces or hold exec level positions in big corporate companies. Anyway, during these meetings, and I believe as a result of the drive for the trophy, I often found myself trying to persuade people to collaborate, examples of this were:

- An area commander had just been to a training location that I had booked, I asked her if she had any tips from her experience that would help me make the best use of the location, areas to conduct certain activities or the condition of the facilities. I even asked for a copy of some of her training plans and safety documents. General information was given reluctantly and not much of it. More strangely, she refused to share any of her documents, using the reason of – "my team worked hard to prepare them, your team should do the same".
- When it was suggested that resources should be allocated evenly across the four areas for our annual programme, on one occasion the CEO and Quartermaster (QM) said it wasn't possible on the basis of creating more work for their team. One quote I recall was, "My staff are already busy enough, they don't need this extra workload."
- In a meeting where we were planning an event where all four areas would be present, it transpired that some of the areas had deficiencies in staff qualified to run certain activities such as rifle ranges and obstacle courses. When asked to swap some staff around or simply to 'borrow' some staff, the other area commanders became a little defensive, refused and said that would help our areas to score more points. No regard to the young people missing out on opportunities.
- We were once presented with a challenge of, "As an organisation we need to reduce the time it takes to recruit and train new volunteers. Applicants are getting frustrated by the bureaucracy and not staying. How can we help?" A few of us started to contribute ideas to the discussion, where we were hit with constant replies of, "That won't work around here" and, "I tried that in my area, but it didn't work." We eventually stopped sharing our thoughts and ideas, the room fell silent and the next agenda item began. A missed opportunity, I thought.

A few years into this role, all but one member of the SLT changed and with them, they brought new ideas and behaviours. Some of them fought the culture but didn't feel they could influence quick enough, so they left. Others stuck it out and made some small incremental changes to the way things were conducted. I'm still connected to this part of the organisation and I believe that there is now much more collaboration, joined up thinking and bad behaviours are called out.

So what? Take a moment to think about the meetings you attend where multiple areas/functions are represented. Do attendees of your meetings spend their time contributing from the perspective of the team they lead or the team they are part of? Meeting attendees should be clear of their role when attending a meeting. Often I find a lack of clarity of role causes the most challenges.

If you are going to lead a meeting and ask for people ideas, firstly I would say, create an environment where people are willing to contribute – this means not cutting them off, dismissing or commenting on their ideas and most importantly, do something with their ideas so they know it was a good use of their time. Secondly, don't just ask them for ideas, create a process that allows everyone to contribute in their way, in their time, i.e., use some of the tools later in this book such as Cross that Bridge, Radiant Problem Solving and the Disney technique.

We often hear about 'best practice'. Create a culture where people are willing to share for the greater good of the organisation, not just their function or department. Huge amounts of time and resource can be saved across whole organisations (and probably wider) by offering solutions to problems that you've already solved, to other colleagues who are going through the same or similar challenge.

How The Book Works

Introduction
Setting the scene, Connecting with you and your context

**Section 1
The Meeting Environment**
Exploring the details of the environment in which we collaborate and hold meetings

**Section 2
The Inspired Meeting Framework**
Sharing the five Steps to the most effective meetings; Crafting, Aligning, Doing Agreeing and implementing

**Section 3
Tools For Meetings**
A fantastic selection of tools, methodologies and ideas to make your meetings awesome

To guide you through the book...

I want to place here some thoughts about the book and how to use it. No, not instructions, but an explanation of my intent, so that you can bear it in mind when going through the book. If you plan to read this cover to cover and want to keep going; please go for it. But if you're using it to help make a difference in meetings as and when you have a need, here's some food for thought. I have structured the rest of the book into three sections.

We will delve into the **The Meeting Environment**, exploring the things you can see and the things you can't. A bit like going for a walk in the countryside. There is so much going on. The flora and fauna, the weather, obstacles and other users of the environment, all these things have an impact on what you achieve. This will give you some insights and maybe help you get the most appropriate benefits from your meeting environment.

We will then look at the **Inspired Meetings Framework**. This section can be dipped into if you think you have a particular issue with a stage of a meeting. Don't ignore the fact that your issue may initially feel like you aren't getting commitment to actions, but it could be down to how you conduct the main part of your meeting. However, in a step-by-step guide, we will share what you should do when CRAFTING, ALIGNING, DOING, AGREEING, and IMPLEMENTING your meeting. I will also share some helpful diagnostic tools to help you explore your current situation and where to start.

If you just want to change it up a little, add a little spice to a meeting, do something different or prevent stagnation, I have put a selection of tools in the section called **Tools for Meetings**, with everything from energiser activities through to ways of generating ideas and gaining consensus to action planning and prioritising. Feel free to use these to craft a whole meeting or to use one to facilitate just one meeting agenda item.

In summary – meetings are a complex beast. They involve people. People are fragile things (some more so than others). There is no silver bullet to getting rid of 'Bored Rooms', at least not in my opinion. But there is a comprehensive book here which will give you lots of ideas, insights, and things to try, which will all make a positive difference in their own way.

Section 1

The Meeting Environment

Exploring the world in which we collaborate

The Meeting environment	36
The outdoors as a metaphor	40
The things you can see	42
One click and they've got you	44
Location, location, location	45
It's all about the experience	47
Face-to-Face vs Online	50
Trust the Process – basic facilitation	52
Call in the professionals	52
Is there an IT Wizard in the room?	54
Donuts, bacon butties and sweets, why not all?	55
Critical Incidentals	57
Have you got a notepad with you?	60
Props or No Props	61
Pens, Sticky Notes and BluTac	61
My OCD (obsessive compulsive disorder) is so bad I've alphabetised it to CDO.	64
Tech Top Tips – online and F2F, platforms, projectors, computers, and interactive whiteboards	74
PowerPoint	75
73% of Statistics are Made Up	79
The things you can't see	82
The Left and Right Brain	84
Pen Clickers or Misophonia	86
Flow	87
Pilot, Holiday maker, Prisoner and Passenger	89
100/100	90
There are no difficult people in meetings	92
Playing to strengths	96
Simplicity	101
Thunks – it's all in the questions	102
Repetition, Repetition, Repetition	104

The Meeting Environment

One of the key things about meetings is the environment in which they take place. I want to spend some time on this topic and have settled on an analogy with the outdoors. I struggled at first to come up with a good link for the section but eventually settled on this, and I love it. I started writing and creating stories, examples, and metaphors whilst out and about on local walks. I took to mulling over ideas and working them through on my walks, and then there it was! It had been staring at me for many, many thousands of miles. THE MEETING ENVIRONMENT. I hope you can connect with the analogy and link to your own meeting world.

For many years I have been an outdoor pursuits instructor, taking groups of adults and young people into the outdoors to participate in rock climbing, gorge walking, scrambling, mountain walking, orienteering and mountain biking. Each group I took had a different aim or purpose for being there. They were searching for different experiences and outcomes. They each had different perspectives and, although in the same place, often saw, felt, and experienced it differently. The reasons for this varied and were sometimes less obvious than others. This already sounds like meetings, right?

For example, a group of young people from the city attending their first country walk, having heard horror stories about strange animals called sheep and cows, were so distracted by these things that they were very narrowly focussed. At every gate and stile, they would ask, "Are there any animals in this field, what do we do if there are cows or bulls?" Very few cows were out that day and the group missed the kingfisher on the river, the salmon leaping and the wildflowers in the hedgerows. Like in meetings, we often spend time concentrating on or looking at the wrong things, and we can be very narrow in our focus and miss what's really going on.

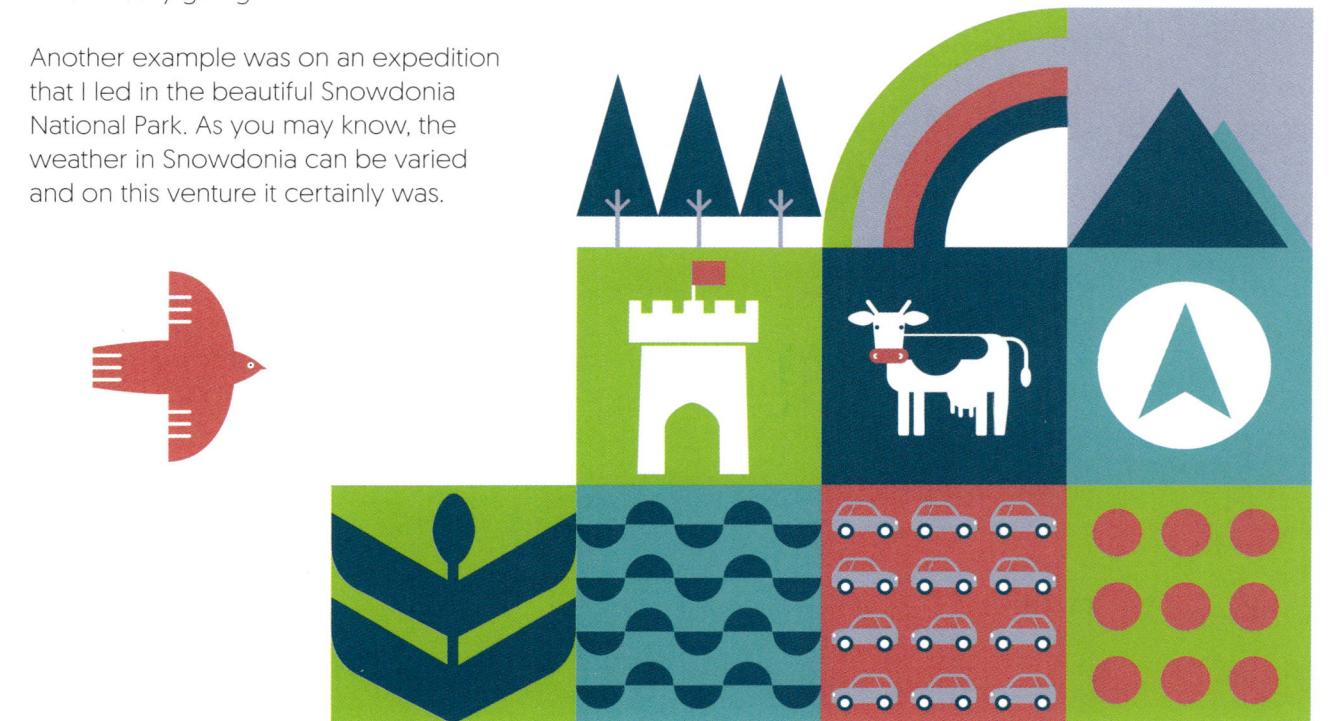

Another example was on an expedition that I led in the beautiful Snowdonia National Park. As you may know, the weather in Snowdonia can be varied and on this venture it certainly was.

Day one started early and there were already signs it would be a hot day. As the heat increased, the team focussed on themselves and rightly so, resting in the shade when they could, taking on lots of fluids and moving forward at a slow pace. A planned six hour day took them over nine hours. It was right that they looked after themselves, they took their time, enjoyed the environment, and had lots of fun together.

Day two was very different, within minutes of the team setting off from the campsite, the rain came in. It was persistent and the team put their hoods up, rain covers on their rucksacks and got their heads down to make progress. They took breaks when there was a wind break or sheepfold, they could shelter in. They couldn't see much around them, so just worked hard to navigate through the weather and the terrain to get to their next campsite. They were 30 minutes early that day, didn't see much, but got to where they were going. Some meetings can be like this. The team need to get together, solve problems, and make progress, maybe even review, but they can't be too reflective. There's a storm going on around them, a narrow tactical task focus can be appropriate, but beware of what you can't see and how it impacts the people around you. More on this as we go through the book.

I have split this section into The Things You Can See and The Things You Can't See. In each section I will share lots of my thoughts, experiences, and tips, from the choice of venue for a meeting to keeping the audience in flow. We'll not only discuss bacon sandwiches, sweets and pens, but also delve into difficult people – or will we? A little like the environment or climate, there are some things in meetings, that I believe must exist for it to be a success. There are also things you may decide are not to be afforded any attention at that time. There will be things that can receive too much focus and therefore won't help in achieving your aim. This is where your judgement is needed to get the balance right. That bit I'll leave to you.

I think of all meetings as a collective, like a global climate. Within it are lots of different environments. It's worth being aware of the different environments, things that make up that environment, what is in it that makes it thrive, the things that make it beautiful and the effects of too much or not enough of something in that environment. We should also consider the impact of certain activities on the environment. A good example could be mountain biking through a beautiful woodland. It can hack away at plants and flowers, frighten off wildlife and erode pathways – some see this as fun, others as dangerous or reckless, much like the fast pace of a tactical review meeting full of data and chest prodding when your RAG (Red, Amber, Green) ratings are all red or amber. These types of meeting too often can erode trust, frighten off healthy challenge and hack away at goodwill – unless structured and handled well. This is why I am sharing so much to inform and enable you to make the best decisions possible when planning and participating in meetings. I hope you'll also disagree with some of my views and challenge your thinking.

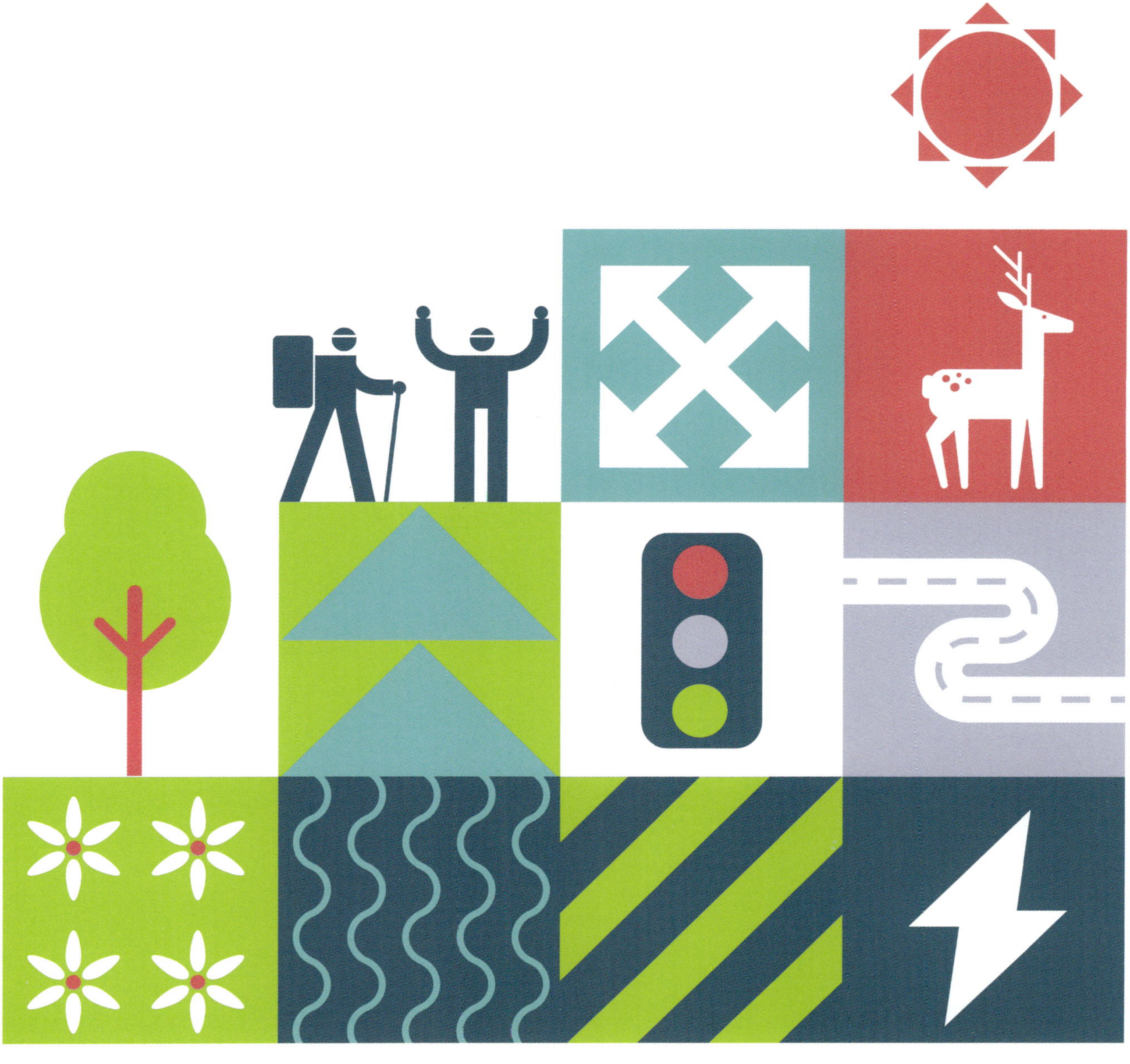

The outdoors as a metaphor

I have shared my own ideas here but consider for yourselves what each of the following could be in relation to a meeting and bear them in mind as I delve into The Meeting Environment. It might be a good idea to come back to the table as you go through this section and draw your own connections:

The Physical Environment	The Meeting Environment (mine)	The Meeting Environment (Yours)
Roads, paths, tracks, and trails	The direction your meetings can take. The options you take and their levels of ease or difficulty. How some things lead to the unknown and some go 'round and round'.	
Roundabouts and traffic lights	The rules or guidelines in place. Too many rules are like traffic lights – do this or do that. Roundabouts have a set of guidelines or principles that allow you to think.	
The Sun	This could be where the energy comes from (people or activity) a guiding light or something to celebrate. I often use a picture of the sun in meetings to anchor peoples' hopes.	
Clouds	Clouds in a meeting could cast unnecessary shadows across the room. Not allowing as much light and energy to flood in. This could be the mood of attendees, bad news or poor behaviours not being dealt with.	
Trees, flowers, and shrubs	These are the nice things to look at - something to brighten up the environment or even something that can pollinate and help to flourish. Trees could be a source of fruit or even a place to get some shade from the intensity of the weather.	
Other people – car drivers, motorcyclists, walkers, runners, climbers, fishermen, farmers, retailers, etc.	These could be opportunities to learn from others. Maybe people invited to be a guest speaker, share their experiences, ideas or contribute to part of your process. They may even be a chance for you to join someone else's meeting.	
Birds and Insects	Subtle hints, moments of beauty or realisation. Something small that just needs you to stop and recognise it.	
Farm animals – cows, sheep, chickens, pigs, etc	Some things you just need to pass through, but where some members of your team may be frightened or concerned by and not want to make progress, they may even have not seen them before and want to spend some time on them even though they are not relevant.	
Wild animals – deer, rabbits, foxes, squirrels, etc	A nice thing on the horizon. It looks good and interesting and naturally you want to get closer. But is it the right thing to do and a good use of your time?	
Heavy rain, wind, and snow	Pain and discomfort. A short time to pause, take shelter, refresh and refuel. If that isn't appropriate, you may need to need to speed up and get to the end (but plan to come back) or even stop the activity and re-schedule.	

Mountains	Big obstacles and challenges. Maybe projects that are tough and need planning. The mountains could also be something that's staring you in the face, but you don't know if it's relevant, necessary, part of the big picture or maybe just a distraction.	
Bridges and fords	Often an obstacle, that needs teamwork and skill to solve. Approach with the right people, skills and care.	
Benches and seats	Quite literally a resting point. But beware, there are some public places and parklands with benches every 20 metres, you don't need to sit at them all.	
Sea views	What's on the horizon? Stand back, take a look at the beauty in front of you. It maybe work you've created or the context surrounding your current situation.	
Woodlands and forest	Sheltered, but busy spaces. Lots of possible paths to take, many lead to the same place, but occasionally the paths lead to the wrong side of the forest.	
Wild foods and berries	Some useful information. But you must know what to do with it. Misuse, inappropriate sharing or overuse can be a risk.	
Historic buildings and places of interest	Somewhere to stop on the way. A lesson, presentation, or input from a visitor. This could be part of building a shared experience or maybe a lesson relevant to the topic.	
Fences, walls, and hedges	A handrail to follow. This could be a process to follow or tool to use.	
Stiles and gates	A feature to use marking a point in your journey. This could be an ideal time to break or change direction.	
Canals, rivers, and streams	Flow! These features need to flow. Remove any blockages to allow your meeting to flow.	
Cliffs and rock faces	Depending on the skill and will of the group, this could be something that causes a team to re-think and change direction. It could however be a project that needs time and resources to complete.	
Lochs, lakes, reservoirs, and dams	Very often a point to stop and refresh. It has great views, interesting features and helps orientate to the ground.	
Rainbows, cloud inversions, thunder, and lightning	Often something unexpected and regardless of how beautiful or fierce it can be, gives you something exciting to be thankful for.	
Wildfires, floods, erosion, and drought.	Often out of your control, a big event or activity that forces you to react. A crisis that takes up most of your meeting or maybe even stops your meeting.	

Can you think of any more?

The things you can see...

Looking around at the physical features of your meetings

The things you can see...

Imagine going out with a few friends to walk a section of a well-known long-distance hiking path. You agreed to meet at a car park, but on arrival, half of it had been dug up for development, the other half was nearly full, and there were big signs saying parking outside of the marked bays will incur a penalty charge. You shuttle friends around to find parking and eventually get going. As you start, you realise that you only have one of the correct maps you need and one of your friends says she must leave around 2 pm to go and collect her husband from the airport. You'll have to adjust your planned walk, which probably puts you on your back foot. You might be a bit grumpy and distracted, as all these things, in your opinion, could be avoided and better planned. Your walk starts, and you all get chatting. The mood warms up a little, as does the weather. Around lunchtime, you find a perfect spot where you can see across the open moorland for miles, it's stunning, calm and there are some rare species of birds nesting nearby that you watch whilst chatting with friends and enjoying your favourite hill food (for me it would be roast ham and coleslaw sandwiches, washed down with a good coffee from my favourite flask – yes, I have a favourite flask!) What's your favourite food for a day of activity? Anyway during the last bits of the walk, your group agree to schedule another date to do the originally planned walk, but as fortune goes, the newly amended route takes you past the most amazing waterfall where you see beautiful wild ponies playing on the meadows nearby.

All these things can happen in their own way in a meeting, and I have called them, "The things you can see." In my experiences, I've always had walking buddies that take our trips seriously. They plan ahead, communicate and prepare themselves well for great adventures. Why do we sometimes not do this for our really important meetings? In this section of The Meeting Environment, we will explore the things that are obvious, evident, visible, and unavoidable in our meetings and look at what we can do about them. Some of these are obvious, like having a venue (the most appropriate venue) or the right online platform and basic equipment needed. Some might appear less obvious and can often be even more important to the success of our meetings, such as the tiny yet noticeable things like sticky notes, pens, sweets and maybe even the types of data shared. My experiences have shown me that no matter how good the discussion and the outcomes, some things can make or break your meeting. They can affect how attendees engage during it and what people say afterwards. So, like your favourite hill food, here's some food for thought.

One Click and they've got you

Other than the occasional time when someone walks up to your desk or picks up the phone and talks to you before inviting you to attend a meeting, we are often hoodwinked into attending meetings with the use of diary invites through our email system. This is even worse when we get the invite to a recurring meeting, such as a weekly sprint meeting or monthly managers meeting, all of which occur on the same day at the same time with regimented frequency and are etched into our diary forever! David Grady described this in his hugely popular TED talk from 2013 called, "How to save the world (or at least yourself) from bad meetings." He labelled this condition as Mindless Accept Syndrome (MAS). Just because the invite was sent out by your boss or the CEO's executive assistant doesn't mean that you must accept it and turn up. It's likely that the only information it has on the invite is a time, date, and room number for you to attend. You are allowed (possibly not all the time) to challenge the meeting, why not try some of the following:

- Replying (only if it's true) to say I'm sorry I have something else in my diary at this time, can we change the time?
- Send an email to the organiser asking them what the purpose of the meeting is to help you prioritise your conflicting invites or other demands on your time.
- Hit 'decline' or 'tentative'. This should prompt the organiser to contact you and tell you more about why you should be there, or they may just realise you weren't needed anyway.
- Consider sending someone else to the meeting on your behalf.
- Manage your time by asking other meeting organisers if their meeting can be moved in order for you to attend two meetings or even to give you time for a well-deserved sandwich between meetings, often called a 'Lunch' break - I know you might not remember what they were called.
- Contact the organiser asking for the value that you will add or gain from the meeting and gain information to understand your part in the meeting. This will help you prepare and might even prompt the organiser to share this information for future meetings.

Location, location, location

Having spent over 12 years working at the amazing Successfactory™ venue in the heart of the Cheshire countryside in North West England, I am probably a little biased when I say that the environment in which you conduct your meetings has a huge impact on the outcomes gained (pictured here). It is key to understand that it is not just this experience that makes me say this.

The title of this book, No More Bored Rooms, epitomises what I hope to help you achieve with your meetings. Imagine (or walk down the corridor and look at) a very outdated image of a meeting room. It will likely have a large table down the middle of the room, laid out with blotting pads, name place markers to ensure people know the hierarchy and power in the meeting, a dusty conference phone in the middle of the table, bottles of still and sparkling water next to a bowl of mint imperials, only eaten by people to metaphorically get rid of the bad taste generated by bad coffee and a diatribe of unnecessary one to ones with the CEO that everyone has been forced to endure, numbed occasionally by the hum as the air con kicks in, the room is on the 15th floor of the office block where the windows can't be opened in case someone takes the meeting to heart and leaps out trying to save themselves. Is any of this familiar? Or how about the new MD that joins the company after working in what she calls 'the most engaging environment she's ever worked in'. The office is open plan, and spaces have been set up for people to have informal chats on bean bags, whilst eating mini bars of chocolate and drinking cans of soft drinks provided by the employer. The meeting rooms have tables, but they're collapsed in a corner and there's a U-shape of comfy chairs set up around the interactive whiteboard that no one really knows how to get the best out of. An environment where everyone starts happy, engaged, and productive and outcomes grow. So much so that there's a need to employ more staff, but where do the new staff go? Well, it's usually in the corner where the bean bags and drinks machine was, which now gets relegated to the back stairwell, and people start to revert to old vanilla ways of collaborating. Naturally, there becomes a little bad feeling, like benefits are being taken away from them, and the upset makes senior leaders think there's serious problems, so they invite an expensive consultant wearing a suit with a double-breasted jacket in to talk about staff engagement. To make the consultant feel at home and to look professional, they set the board room up with tables and the conference phone again. Does this one sound familiar? My point here is one of choosing the right environment to get the best out of people when collaborating and to do our best to send a consistent message.

But what is the right environment?

It's all about the experience...

Here are things attendees are looking for in conference and meeting spaces today. Before you choose your next meeting site, it's worth considering if your venue can help you check these criteria.

1. **Attendees want to be in meeting spaces that are open and have an energy about them.**
   We've all been at conference venues that feel like a dungeon and a maze. The space is uninspiring, and everyone keeps getting lost. Is that the best place to foster productive professional development experiences?

2. **Attendees want to relax and feel safe.**
   We need to ensure the space is relaxing and enables people to open up, speak their mind and enjoy being there. Formal office-type meeting spaces rarely work as well as well-designed informal environments.

3. **Attendees want good food and a ready supply of drinks throughout the day.**
   We've all been to meetings where the food is poor, and you are restricted to certain times for breaks throughout the day. It doesn't have to be like that. You want what we call brain food to keep the energy up and to break when you want to break. Flexibility is key.

4. **Attendees want the latest technology that can enhance presentations, discussions, and brainstorming.**
   Using the right technology and technology that works can really enhance meetings. You also want it all included in the day rate rather than adding to the costs. You need bright projection, great sound, whiteboards, flip charts and fast WIFI at no extra cost! Many venues hide these costs in a low day rate to get you in and then fleece you with extras!

5. **Attendees want free parking right next to the venue.**
   Nothing is worse than getting to a venue and realising there is no parking on-site, or the car park is an extra cost. Or the car park is a mile away and you must walk in the rain to get to the venue. Free car parking on-site is a must.

6. **Attendees want fun.**
   There is nothing worse than having to sit through 80 PowerPoint slides in a darkened room and being presented to. We need venues that can combine suitable activities indoors and outdoors. Meaning experiential exercises should be provided as part of the solution. Or there should be space for activities to be conducted.

7. **Attendees love getting into nature.**
   Nothing is better to stimulate learning, thinking, and connecting than getting out into nature. You want a venue with great views, the opportunity to hear the birds singing, the sun on your face and be able to walk in beautiful countryside.

8. **Attendees love the right light.**
   Lighting plays a huge role in shaping people's moods and can affect their health too and plays a larger role than you might think. If the room is too bright, people get antsy and distracted. If it's too dark, they get tired and melancholy. Experts agree that warm white light and natural light from large windows and doors are best for boosting mood and energy. To keep everyone on task, make the lights over the presentation or speaker a little brighter to direct attendees' eyes in that direction.

9. **Attendees want spaces that ease the networking and collaboration experience.**
   For many attendees, conferences are as much—or more—about the networking as the education. Will your next venue provide ideal spaces for networking functions? Does it have many different places where attendees can gather on their own?

Venue Selection Checklist

Element	Yes	No
Their website is modern, exciting and gives you the confidence that you have chosen the right place.		
The staff at the venue understand learning, listened to what you wanted and craft a solution with you.		
The booking process is simple and easy to use.		
You have a great choice for lunch and refreshments and are not restricted to set times.		
Ideas were generated and discussed, ensuring your meeting will achieve a great result.		
There is free parking on-site and a location map is available to download.		
The venue is in a beautiful location and looks amazing with awesome views.		
The décor is vibrant and stimulating.		
There is a meet and greet area.		
There is space outside to relax, network and do activities.		
The meeting room is light and airy, with plenty of natural light.		
Filtered and chilled water is provided in the rooms free of charge.		
The venue is well maintained, clean and smells amazing.		
The projector, TV, audio and screens are modern, working and provided as part of the day rate.		
Flipcharts, whiteboards and pens are included.		
There is a choice of layouts from tables and chairs to beanbags.		
There is space to put things on the wall.		
Music is provided.		
Experiential activities are available if required to energise and support learning.		
Support staff are always on hand, helpful, but not over the top.		

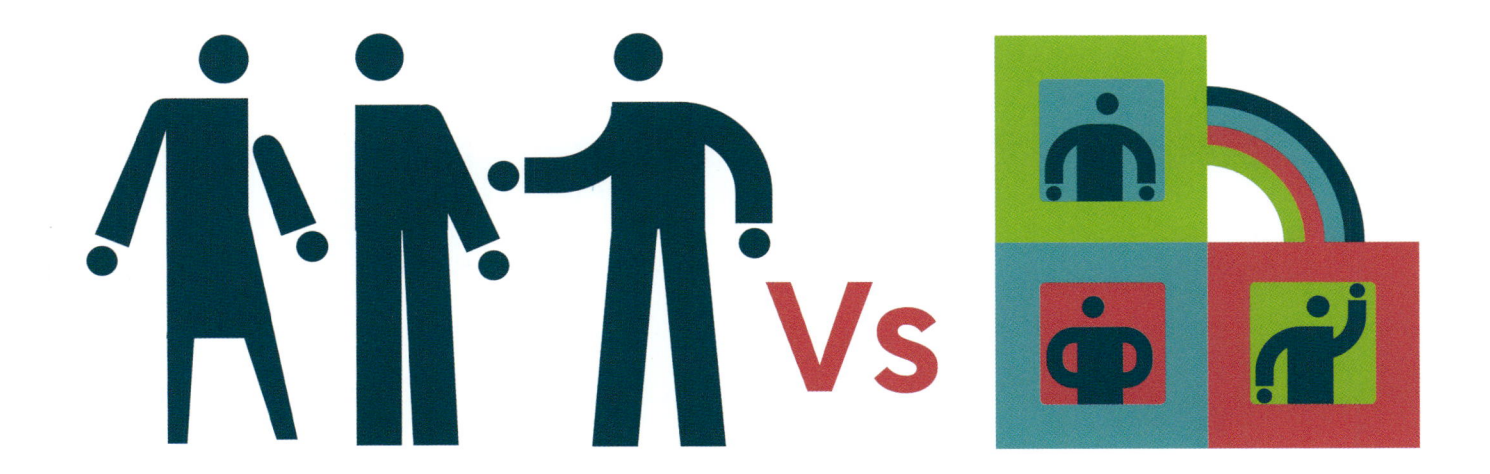

Face-to-Face vs Online

It doesn't seem that long ago when a meeting that wasn't face-to-face was either very rare or only for international companies and remotely located teams. Even then, there was lots of global travel, and meetings were frequently face-to-face. We'd spend ages setting up a room with the conference phone, making sure it was plugged in properly and rehearsing the call so the CEO wasn't wasting his time. Or we'd sparingly use Skype, so infrequent that every time you logged in, you'd need to reset your password and install software upgrades. Then, shortly before 2020 it was becoming more and more popular with platforms trying to establish themselves, such as Zoom and Teams, and then all hell broke loose and to keep going during the global pandemic, we became permanently logged onto these platforms. We had never heard of 'Zoom fatigue', but now it's a thing. Zoom is also now synonymous for the myriad of ways in which we can meet online. Add your own to the list but I've been inducted into Zoom (my preferred), Teams, BlueJeans, Ring Central, Adobe Connect and have supported use of these with various apps and programmes such as Mural (one of my preferred) and Concept Board.

Part of the dictionary definition of virtual is 'almost or nearly as described'. Because of this, the pedant in me likes to make sure that we refer to a meeting that is not face-to-face, i.e. in the same room physically, is either online or remote and never virtual. A virtual meeting, like virtual reality, is not real, and therefore, almost or nearly a meeting – that's not good enough. Meetings should be real and add value – even if it's just a great conversation to check in with team members or colleagues. So, let's look at the considerations of face-to-face and online meetings:

Online – There will be pros and cons when planning an online meeting. From my experience, some of these are:

Pros
- It saves time travelling and allows people geographically spread, to engage with each other.
- It is an appropriate medium for some personality types who may struggle to interact when physically in the room. I have seen the more introverted, logical and task-focussed engage well in online meetings.
- It can be extremely cost-effective and cost-saving from a resource point of view. Such as, no room hire, their own refreshments, and no travel expenses.
- Can still break out into smaller groups for discussions and idea generation with an appropriate platform.
- Great to get people together quickly by sending a diary invite and session link if people are free.

Cons
- You can't always gauge the energy or do much to control the energy in the meeting.
- Some people can challenge the use of having cameras on and affect the levels of interaction. I noted a lack of visual engagement in organisations with a younger staff profile.
- It can be energy zapping if on screen for long periods.
- Restricted understanding of body language – limited view, often just head and shoulders or even less.
- It can encourage poor behaviours such, as keyboard warriors, due to lack of physical boundaries. This can have huge negative effects on the psychological safety of members of the meetings.

Face-to-Face – being in the same room when collaborating is quite traditional, but now there are options. Let's look at the pros and cons:

Pros
- Can manage the energy by encouraging people to stand or take part in activities.
- Often feel a much better connection with those in the room.
- We can see much more body language and tune into each other.
- Provides opportunities for hands-on collaboration, showing and sharing ideas with each other is easier than it can be online.
- It allows for other non-planned conversations during break times and meeting set up.

Cons
- Attendees can better use travel time.
- Costs of travel and other expenses can build and be better used elsewhere.
- It can cause some personality types to behave less effectively and appropriately than if they were online.
- More difficult to find a suitable time to get people together.

Trust The Process – basic facilitation

If meetings are about getting work done, it's important to use the right tools for the job. Later in this book, I'll go into the detail and processes of a range of specific tools. Before then I want to explore some basic facilitation tips to help you get the best out of the process. It is key to keep the following points in mind when facilitating:

- The facilitator does not have the answers. Taking on this role is about enabling the audience to provide insights, ideas, possible solutions and experiences. You must be willing to challenge the audience and ask lots of questions.
- Choose the most effective tool for the desired outcome. Understand the tool, prepare its use and follow the process - like riding a bicycle. If you don't fit it to the rider, ensure the tyres are pumped up and oil the chain, it won't get you to the required destination as effectively as it should.
- If the process is applied well to the right problem, it will undoubtedly feel uncomfortable at times. You may feel as a facilitator that it isn't going in the direction needed. Be agile enough to adapt your plan, slow down and review before proceeding further down an unnecessary path. But also, sometimes it may feel like it's not doing what you want it to, but the group are getting exactly what is needed.

Call in the professionals

Or simply someone who's not emotionally attached to the meeting, its people and expected outcomes! If you work in a large organisation, surely there is someone who can give you some time to help you to facilitate a chunky meeting or workshop. I know many learning and development managers who spend lots of their time planning and delivering training to support the organisation, but equally as much time facilitating for colleagues around the business. If you can't find one there are lots and lots and lots and lots of consultants who you can call on. Many specialise in a specific area of business, a sector, or a topic. Many also specialise in using really powerful methodologies such as generating business models, building a strategy with graphic facilitation, or solving problems with LEGO® Serious Play® (LSP). I am one such consultant.

Why should you ask someone else in the business to give up their time and help you or even pay someone external to help? There are many reasons why you might choose to do this. If you haven't done either before, here's why you should consider it:

- If you are usually the meeting chair and, at the same time, the group's leader, your inputs may be biased or even the language you use loaded. Depending on levels of trust within your team or how you delegate, team members may contribute less when you facilitate your own meetings.

- As a leader, by facilitating your own workshop-style meetings, you are less likely to be in the right mindset to contribute fully or truly listen to what's happening. You might be thinking about the next agenda item or keeping half an eye out for the sandwich trolley to be delivered to the door for lunch.
- A strong external facilitator is trained to challenge and provoke everyone in the session. This will include you as the leader making it a fair and inclusive process. They will ensure that everyone gets the best possible airtime. They will also be likely to have had experience in other areas and may be able to offer insights to give ideas or break the insanity loop of doing the same thing repeatedly.
- Using a process such as LSP or Business Model Generation provides a tried and tested framework to help you to achieve your desired aims. These experts have spent time training and practicing the methods that many different organisations often use, and the benefits are in the process. You can read more about this in my OCD section [Page 64].

I would add that if meetings are short or very frequent, you may want only to get someone to support you for the first one or two occurrences with a view to helping create the best process and culture, but to then make it sustainable for you by helping you lead these yourself. It might also be useful to ask someone to join an existing meeting to act as a 'fly on the wall' to give a different perspective of how they see things running. But be careful about how you introduce this person to your audience and who they are – I've found it is very effective but give meeting attendees time to get used to it, don't just turn up with someone they don't know.

This could also be an opportunity to bring someone in to help with your team development, whether onsite, offsite or online. It could be additional to your meeting or workshop schedule and could be a fun team-building-type session of activities such as a chocolatier, archery, ropes courses, treasure hunts, command tasks, and many more. I believe these should have a clearly defined purpose, often called fun with a serious intent. It could be building trust, increasing verbal communication effectiveness, developing ways of working or learning about team strengths. It may be part of your day's agenda, or something added afterwards.

Be aware of the irony and miscommunication of taking part in activities like paintballing to help build the team. I have often seen this after a period of change or stress or even when a new leader comes along. You are given a short training session, face shields and body armour and put in teams, but regardless of who's in your team, you spend the time giving people feedback in the form of pelting them with paintballs and giving them little bruises as a reminder.

Is there an IT Wizard in the room?

How many times have you gone into the room where your meeting is being held, or maybe just innocently walking past on your way back from another meeting, when you hear, "Does anyone know how this projector works?" or "Can you help me? I don't seem to be able to get the sound working on this video clip." Having spent many years with the words Venue Support in my job title, I'd be a rich man if I had a pound for every time I'd heard this and even richer if I was able to charge a consultant's fee every time I pressed the 'source' button on a projector or for 'Function F8' on a laptop. Not everything can be prevented, as cables become damaged, or the internet has a wobble at a critical time. However, I feel that there can be fewer 'awkward' moments when you're waiting to see the slides or see a video clip. What's the well know phrase here? 'Prior Preparation and Planning Prevents a Poor Performance'.

It's important to have a contingency plan in case there's an issue that cannot be resolved. This might be simply having printed notes and using them to present (I still revert to packs of little index cards as a backup sometimes or a printed set of slides with lots of scribbles on), it might be transferring key aspects to a flipchart or whiteboard or re-arranging the agenda to use the slides or play the video after an activity or break. These types of contingency plans help reduce stress and make a challenging few minutes look more professional and calmer. It's also key to have a rehearsal and, ideally, use your own equipment. I'm a bit of a control freak in situations like this! If I'm running a session, I want to use my laptop or check the formatting of the slides if added to the main slide deck and have a run-through of how I will transition from one laptop to another or speaker to speaker. If it's my session, I get other people's resources for sharing and put them onto my desktop, or better still, merge them into one slide deck for the whole session. Likewise, I will get there early enough to do a trial run if I'm using someone else's computer.

If face-to-face, you need to ensure you have the right adapters for the myriad of devices available now (the well-known piece of fruit with a bite missing from its logo can be the worst offender for this – every device seemed to have a different adapter for some time). It's a good idea also to have your resources on a USB memory stick or easily accessible in the cloud somewhere. If online or remote, log on before your scheduled start time and run through the transitions of everything you'll be sharing even if it's just you and your virtual background.

Finally, in the words of a well-known TV Meerkat 'Simples!' Don't overcomplicate things. If you can use one platform for everything you plan to do, keep it that way. Try not to have slides, videos, spreadsheets, add-ins and more. As you'll read in the book, they all add value to meetings, but the more you use them, the higher the risk is of you having to eat into valuable meeting time by having to ask, "Is there an IT Wizard in the room?" During the Covid-19 pandemic, I spent time getting used to and trying different tools for online collaboration and found some fantastic things out there. My most stressful sessions where those that tried to use too many different mediums to engage the group.

Donuts, bacon butties and sweets, why not all?

I used to quote the title of David Pearl's book, 'Will there be donuts?' when talking about effective meetings and sharing content from this book. But then I experienced it first-hand in my own events and when acting as event support for a client.

A - For several years I ran a particular training course for a client. The course was about the delegates and, with personal outcomes/insights, had a kind of rinse and repeat formula, and we did our best to ensure it was standardised wherever we ran it. I ran the course at around ten different venues around the UK and was able to keep the same format (this was a big challenge). Coffee and bacon butties on arrival, morning session followed by a hot lunch, afternoon session, lots of fun, and washed down with good coffee throughout the day. The biggest variable I found was the amount of bacon on a butty at each venue. I remember one venue having around eight rashers of bacon per sandwich. When we had captured most of the business the first time round and were planning to run a level 2 version of the course, we gathered a working group together to review the journey to date and design the next steps. This was undertaken at a different venue, and as it wasn't part of the rinse-and-repeat programme, I neglected to order bacon butties. But because they had attended the other courses with me, I was repeatedly verbally abused (in a fun wind-up kind of way) and it did cause a bit of a distraction for a short while, but also, as some attendees were used to the provision of a breakfast item, they skipped the golden arches on route to the venue and were flagging by late morning.

B – At our venue in Cheshire, Successfactory™, we were really proud of the approach to supporting clients with energy management throughout the day. Our lunches were brain-friendly. Coffee, tea and other refreshments were fresh and flowed freely. We provided small bowls of popular childhood favourite sweets such as Swizzles, Refreshers, Drumsticks and Maoam. One of our regular clients was a well known manufacturer of paint products and created a paint tin and label for us as a cute little gift. Most paint colour has a name like Revival, Bamboo, Happy Daze, and Sunrise and so our paint tin was called Success. A nice gesture. The paint tin became very popular, or shall I say the contents did. Much to our surprise our sweets were one of many quoted reasons why clients came back to the venue time and time again, but we didn't quite realise it is until the day I was clearing the room during the break. On this day, a colleague took the paint tin offsite for a large event, and the CEO of the client in the venue collared me and asked where the sweets were. We had a good relationship, so all the jibes I got were taken in good humour, but he seemed genuinely disappointed about the lack of sugar. I remember him saying, "How are they going to get through all the agenda points this afternoon without that sugar boost?"

As David says in his book, "If people attend your meeting only because they heard there'll be donuts, you've got a problem." But there are benefits to these types of provisions. You can't please all the people all of the time, but the more you try, the more likely you are to please most people most of the time. By providing morale-boosting type foods and provisions here's what you get:

- You get a group of attendees who feel valued and appreciate the small things. I remember a gentleman from the USA attending a whole week of training sessions held by a client. At first view, this guy was grumpy and irritable, and just saw my team as chaiwallahs. At lunchtime on day one, I noticed the group helping themselves to a cola-type drink and heard this guy say he only drinks Dr Pepper. The following morning, he opened the fridge and we'd put a pack of Dr Pepper in there, he was quite obviously delighted. Later in the week, the meeting organiser approached me and said that by getting the cans for one of her group members it had relaxed him, and he was a much more positive and active member of the group afterwards.
- Not everyone wants or needs a sugar boost, but if your meetings or workshops are full of productivity, you might find that there are times when a little sugar (It could also be natural sugars in fruits by the way – I'm not biased) boosts the group's energy and helps them push through a tough conversation or solve a complex problem.
- Packs of plain white mint imperials are unlikely to have the impact I'm about to describe. There are many things out there that do though. They build trust! What, you don't believe me? As a simple rule of thumb, I have found over the years that the more I know someone, the more I am likely to trust them. In some team development models they call it vulnerability-based trust. Learning that a Black Jack or Fruit Salad (well-known UK confectionery) was a favourite sweet for a colleague as a child and all the other retro sweets to be found in our Success paint bucket, have reminded them of visits to their gran as a child, who not only was a fun gran, but lived right next to a brilliant little sweet shop builds trust. Learning things about people, opening up to colleagues and having shared experiences helps build relationships and trust.
- Unwrapping a sweet packet or picking from a bunch of grapes is also a very simple way of keeping physically engaged and engaging the right brain.

Even though we do not operate our own venue anymore, I still ensure these sorts of things are considered in the planning for events, meetings, and workshops. Knowing when to introduce them to a group is key too, don't peak too soon. It works with teams, exec groups, open training courses and more. Remember to manage expectations too and don't start something you can't finish.

Critical Incidentals

"Small things make perfection, but perfection is no small thing"

I remember using this quote to explain my experiences of running workshops and conferences to the owner of an outdoor activities centre in the Southwest of England. As we talked and I shared examples, he looked at me and smiled. "Critical Incidentals" he said. Now I love a good snappy phrase and decided there and then I was going to borrow this one (Thanks Mark). Our discussion continued and our experiences of providing a personable, subtle, and remarkable customer experience aligned fully. But what are critical incidentals, I hear you ask? I would define them as the things that you do to be nice and help clients; without realising it, they become an important part of your set-up or offering. I would also use an analogy of a savings account here. We often give our savings accounts names like 'rainy day fund' or my favourite 'fire extinguisher'. A bank account where we hide away a few pounds for the times when it might feel like the shit could hit the financial fan, the washing machine may break, the car fails its MOT or payment to you is delayed, and you need to cover some bills to avoid paying excessive fees. Well, the critical incidentals here are a little like this. The things you put in the bank build trust, favour, and good will with the meeting attendees. The things that they will balance the mood in a not so favourable situation to offset their loss or discomfort.

Let me give you an example. Unexpectedly, there's a drop out of the internet by the service provider whilst streaming a key presenter at your conference. I know it's not your fault, but that's not how it could come across. It lasts around 20 minutes, and you need to hear the remainder of the presentation before the group undertakes some activity. Earlier in the day you have put sweets and other gifts or gizzits in each of the delegates' places, they have all had a fantastic lunch and the coffee is constantly topped up (as opposed to only having three servings throughout your meeting and at certain times of day). The group are excited to hear from the presenter, but as a result of all the goodwill and small things that you have treated them to and the fact they're having a good day, they take a leg stretch, grab a coffee and continue to catch up with friends whilst they wait for the connection to come back on line and whilst you phone the speaker to make a plan. The incidentals have become critical to keeping morale up in a tough few minutes. If however, coffee had been rationed, the sandwiches were bland, the tables were bare, the pens on the tables had been chewed by previous attendees and didn't write (yes, this has happened to me) and you hadn't splashed out on Danish pastries for when they arrived, the savings bank would be empty, and the group may not have been as understanding.

Many of the individual items in the section here of The Meeting Environment could be considered as critical incidentals, and it's your choice as to which you focus on and add to your meetings and workshops. Things that maybe you see as more incidental than critical.

I learned a well-known fable from the outdoor industry when undertaking leader training many years ago.

A life with lemons

It is a summer evening in Northern British Columbia. The water is clear and glassy as the paddle stroke hums through the water. The Douglas firs reflected in the lake's mirror-like surface. The canoe is edging toward the end of a nine-day trip and the taste of our first cold beer is on the tips of our tongues. Not far now, the cedar deck is fast approaching with the promise of hot showers and a comfortable mattress.

Our party of four sit with post-trip smiles studying the cold beers in front of us while the lodge owner joins us: "You have an amazing place here. The lake is so beautiful and peaceful." Richard chirps up looking out over the picture-book view.

His weathered face turns slowly, and he considers, "It's not always like this, last year two people had their lemons come up".

We make eye contact around the group, perplexed expressions from all, and Richard continues, "How do you mean 'their lemons came up'?"

He turns, "Well, life's like a one-armed bandit slot machine, and if four lemons come up, you're out."
Still confused, we press for more, "Sorry to be slow on this, but we're from the other side of the pond. Could you explain about the lemons?"

"Life's about looking out for lemons, and each lemon is a hazard which unless it gets sorted could prove a problem. If you get four of these, it is not looking good. The paddlers last year had their lemons lining up:

They were novices and not confident swimmers - Lemon 1

They were not wearing buoyancy aids – Lemon 2

They ignored advice and were paddling in the middle of the lake - Lemon 3

It was 4.30 in the afternoon, and starting to get dark, the wind picked up, and they capsized - Lemon 4.

Four lemons, and sadly they didn't make it."

"So, it is like a risk assessment looking at hazards and what can go wrong."

"You can call it what you like, but it's common sense. We just talk about looking out for lemons."

A life with lemons is another way of looking at the critical incidentals. I agree with the saying, "Don't sweat the small stuff." But on the hand, I would also say, "Don't ignore the small stuff." Your meeting lemons could be tech, presenters, catering, the room, the service, etc. The more these lemons come up, the less likely people will want to return to your meetings and bring good energy with them. Don't gamble with the critical incidentals for your meetings and workshops.

Have you got a notepad with you?

Is note-taking a lost skill, or are peoples' memories better?

I'm amazed at how many meetings I attend and observe where people aren't taking any form of personal notes. As a young army cadet it was drilled into me from a learning and briefing point of view. I always have some way to take notes and, it's generally on paper. Sometimes, I write down names, times, locations, prompt words to create anchors; other times, the notes are more comprehensive. If someone is taking the time to share information we should take notes in order to best play out necessary actions. It also limits the need for me to go back and ask 'stupid' questions such as, "Who's doing this?" and "When is that happening?" and other simple things that could have been noted down.

Am I right to hold on to this old world behaviour of note-taking? (I'm not judging those that prefer other methods, but I prefer a notepad.)

Often when working with new teams I will provide materials for meeting attendees to take notes. When running projects, the provision is often something that I can give each member of the team that will last the whole project, such as a branded note pad. When working with teams regularly, I work hard to model note-taking behaviour and encourage others to do so. Note-taking can take many forms, and they've generally got to be suitable for the note-taker. If the subject is right, I like to use mind mapping to capture lots of detail and organise it in my head as well as on paper. I will write lists or tables if it's something to do with an event or project. It's just got to work. Some of the benefits of effective note taking include:

- Keeping you alert and actively involved.
- Engaging your mind.
- If necessary, create a record for you and other meeting attendees.
- Helps to organise information in your mind.
- Assists in prioritising actions.

Props or No Props

I like to have boxes of fidget toys, tangle toys, juggling balls and slinkies, and I like to take them to venues. It doesn't have to be costly. You can build up a selection over time. For me, they help in a couple of areas:

1. Something on the table or around the room generates interest. People pick them up and naturally use them to fidget. Whilst they have many proven benefits for people concerning stress and anxiety, they also help with attention.
2. The toys that I take, also have possible secondary uses, such as juggling balls, LEGO® Ducks or Six bricks®, dice and bendy snakes. Each of these of these can be used for short activities that make a point, re-energise the room, or create ideas.

You can overuse these things and should be careful of too much style over substance. I'm sure we've all experienced meetings where there have been many fun things, but not much value has been added. If you're facilitating a meeting and having to travel by train or plane, maybe a small selection in your bag will add some value. If using your own transport or working at a regular location, maybe some bigger props and equipment in the room could help. They don't have to be used all the time but having them available gives you some flexibility.

Pens, Sticky Notes and Blu Tack®

I was travelling by train for a one-day programme, facilitating a team development session for a client. I had to go the night before, so, along with my overnight bag, I had limited space and ability to carry the kit. I like to feel in control when running events, so I called the venue several times to make sure they had what I needed and that it wasn't going to be added to the invoice at an excessive rate. How many flipcharts do you have? Will there be pens and sticky notes available? What other stationery is in the room and included in the day delegate rate? There would be 15 clients attending so I wanted four flipcharts and lots of pens and sticky notes. I was assured that there would be everything available that I needed, and there was no limit on what was included in the cost. Due to my travel times and bookings at the venue, I could only access the room an hour before my planned start time. The room was set up as I had asked, and everything looked fine. I had a few things to draw up on a flipchart at the front of the room and needed to set up a couple of experiential activities before the group arrived. As the day started, we quickly went into group work around the flipcharts to explore hopes and fears for the session.

Strike 1. The group started to write down their hopes and fears for the day. I ask them individually to think about what they do and don't want to happen during the day, then they should share them with their group, and each take a pen to write their own on the flipchart. The first pen was ok, not great, but it wrote, the second, third and fourth pens were as useful as a chocolate tea pot. I scrabbled around to get pens off the other flipcharts, so each group had more than one working pen. There were 16 pens in the room and only five were useable. I had to ask the venue staff for more pens and what they brought me were poor quality.

Strike 2. Later in the session, I was using the sticky notes for an idea-generating activity. I asked the group to add one idea per sticky note before we added them to boards to cluster for the next stage. Within a minute or two of applying them to flipcharts, they started to fall off on the floor. We all scrabbled to pick them up and push them harder to the paper. When this failed, I remembered I had a roll of masking tape, so we started to tear pieces up to use for attaching the sticky notes to the flipcharts. At this stage, I could feel a little frustration in the room about the poor resources.

Strike 3. After lunch, we planned an exercise where each team member used a piece of flipchart paper to chart the things that make them Mad, Sad and Glad at work. So, once I'd grabbed a sandwich and a sausage roll (classy joint I know), I took enough sheets of paper off the flip chart so that each person could have one each, well I tried to, but on inspection over half of the flipcharts had used paper from other meetings. I scrabbled together what I needed and asked for more paper, it took them over an hour to find some and bring them into our room.

The worst thing is that from previous experiences, I was already a little obsessive about pads and pens and post it notes, amongst other things, and I should have known better. I'm sure I'm not the only one who's had these experiences, and on finding a duff pen, throws it straight into the bin. I do have a kit that I take with me, and I do have quality criteria when buying this kit, however, there are (in my humble opinion) very good reasons for them. Let me explain:

Pens – I take a selection of pens with me, depending on what I'm delivering. Ballpoint-type pens for personal use and note-taking. Chisel tip whiteboard pens (these will usually work on both flip charts and whiteboards) – chisel tip to allow me to get creative with their use on thick and thin lines. A selection of Sharpie® pens makes a huge difference when working on sticky notes, as dark colours can be seen more clearly. If asking the client to draw or to mindmap, I will take lots of fibre tips or fine-tip multi-colour pens. Importantly, I periodically check that the pens are still useable and, if not, throw them away or relegate to non-client use.

Sticky Notes – There are lots of brands out there that sell 'super sticky' or 'extra sticky' meeting notes. These are the ones you should get. They're, naturally, a little more expensive, but that saves the embarrassment as they float frustratingly to the floor during use. They are also available in different sizes. I have a selection ranging from around 7 centimetres squared to 20 x 15 centimetres. A selection of different sizes and vibrant neon colours make sorting and clustering more fun and allow the process to be used.

Additional Stationery – It's always handy to have a selection of the following with you. Consideration should be given to its flexibility of use and its impact in use (e.g. Blu Tack® on walls).
- Scissors
- Masking Tape
- Blu Tack® or White Tack

YOU CAN LEARN MORE ABOUT A PERSON IN AN HOUR OF PLAY THAN A LIFETIME OF CONVERSATION

Plato

My OCD (obsessive compulsive disorder) is so bad I've alphabetised it to CDO

I've been known to embody the phrase, 'the devil is in the detail.' But. I've also come to realise it's a combination of having the detail and understanding why. There are dozens of models, tools, and methodologies (which I'll now refer to collectively as tools) that I love to use in meetings and workshops. Many of which I've either referred to or shared in this book. But I write this section out of a combination of respect for the creators of the tools and for you to appreciate the differences and possible benefits.

My early working career was spent in retail. In particular, I bought and sold clothing and equipment for expeditions and mountaineering. This is where I discovered for the first time how brand names became synonymous for a style of product, but I also realised the brand name had features and benefits different to some of its similar competitors. I'll share more examples shortly, but the prominent item for me was a windproof, and insulating smock called a Buffalo. I'd known of these for a long time as I owned one, but the shop I worked in didn't sell them. They were superb quality, lasted a very long time (I still have one that's over 20 years old, and they still sell the same version) but the price tag matched its reputation. Not many customers in our shop would spend so highly on these prized items. I got so fed up with being asked for them and having nothing to compare that we went to a trade show to explore options. The item was a windproof, water repellent outer with a fibre pile liner and at first glance there were over a dozen suppliers of similar items, but there was a huge difference in recommended retail price. So, I set about discovering why. It turned out that there were different levels of measured windproof quality, water repellence (Pertex). The fibre pile varied in quality and had different tog ratings, a bit like the duvet on your bed. In its true form a buffalo used the highest quality of these fabrics and was used by the armed forces around the world in Arctic-type environments. That's how durable and effective it was. Other brands made their competitive price points through a combination of graded materials and construction methods.

Whilst they were often very good, they didn't quite make the same grade. Once we chose a version to sell, we trained our sales team and our mindset. If we were asked if we sold Buffalo, we had to reply that we have a great Pile and Pertex smock that's very similar to Buffalo, and that's all most customers wanted. Some wanted the real deal, and we helped them find somewhere local that stocked it. During our quest to find a product that we could sell to our customers when they asked for a Buffalo, we also learnt about some of its nuances, for example, that it should be worn next to the skin for the best effect. I found this a bit weird at first. We were told that direct body heat trapped in the pile fibres was more efficient at maintaining warmth than if worn on top of base layers. On a winter climbing trip I decided to try it out. Standing still in snowy mountain conditions, I realised I had been given good advice on how to get the best from this awesome garment. To this day, if I want the best from my Buffalo shirt, I wear it next to the skin.

I've drawn similarities to this with tools in this book and methodologies I've been trained to use. Here are some other well-known synonymous items:

Hoover® vs Vacuum Cleaner

Barolo vs Full bodied red wine

Jeep® vs four-wheel drive off road SUV

Champagne vs sparkling wine

Sellotape® vs any sticky tape

Coke vs other cola drinks

Stanley Knife vs retractable utility knife

And many more...

But why am I sharing this with you, and what's it all got to do with meetings? Well, these names, such as Buffalo, Hoover, Jeep, etc., are all very proud of what they have and who they are. They sell themselves based on their features, advantages, and benefits. Likewise, there are many tools that can be used to help in meetings if done to the letter of their intended use. You can often get far better results than just doing a version of it. I will tell you a little about some of the differences that I see in a moment, but here are some that I believe have benefits when used as intended:

World Café
Open Space
LEGO® Serious Play®
Masterminding
Radiant Problem Solving

Let's discuss two of these in more detail.

Example One - Open Space Technology

Without the features described below, something you may call Open Space would be very different. It would be a round-robin, a free-for-all, a marketplace or just a mess. It's a great and flexible approach that can work for group sizes from 10 to 1000 (or even more). It works very well in large venues, face-to-face, but I have taken part in some online Open Space sessions, where, with the right guru, it has worked very well. I have found it has a great impact in latter parts of conferences or programmes and can be a fantastic way of engaging people in taking ownership, solving problems, and creating ideas. But what is it? Open Space is a tool for running meetings or aspects where participants create and manage the agenda themselves. As mentioned here, it can be used as a medium for a whole meeting, but equally, if you allocate sufficient time for the group to get benefits from it, it could be used to answer one agenda question.

An Open Space session has Four Rules, One Law, Two Insects, and a coffee/tea station.

The four rules of Open Space are:

a   Whoever joins the session are the right people.
b   Whatever happens, is the only thing that could have happened.
c   Whenever it starts is the right time.
d   When it's over, it's over.

The **law of Two Feet** states that, 'If, during the course of the gathering, any person finds themselves in a situation where they are neither learning nor contributing, they can go to some more productive place.'

The Insects are:

- Butterflies. These people hang out, maybe with a coffee in hand and don't appear to do much. However, they may just be involved in the most important discussion of the day.
- Bees. They flit from conversation to conversation bringing new ideas and fresh ideas to the table. They can also encourage mingling for those for whom the law of Two Feet feels a bit rude.

A topic or questions should frame the whole session. This will then be used to help participants post their own questions which will be used to form the meat of the session. The venue chosen will need to accommodate everyone together. It must have walls or space to stick the programme and questions to and have enough space for several discussions to take place.

You will need paper or sticky notes for people to write their questions on and a template/timetable with the different sessions and locations, like the one below:

	1 – Breakout room A	2 – Blue chair corner	3 – Dining area	4 – Breakout room B	5 – Table with flowers on
Opening	All together to set the scene and gather ideas				
10am to 11am					
11am to 12pm					
Lunch					
1pm to 2pm					
Closing session	All together to harvest ideas/summary				

Running Open Space

Explain to people the four rules, the Law of Two Feet, the insects and how to record discussions. You also might include a bit about how to facilitate at the tables. For instance, making sure one or two voices don't always dominate discussions or the art of making people feel safe and welcome so they have the confidence to take part.

Then offer people the opportunity to propose a question. If they do this, then they must:

- Host that discussion
- Record the conversation themselves or arrange someone else to do it for the benefit of anyone unable to participate
- Write their name on the sheet

Then they post the question on the timetable.

Then say, "Go!". This is the nerve-racking bit. You may worry that no one will come forward, but eventually, one person does, and more will follow. Then the following needs to happen:

- Ten minutes of people proposing questions and sticking them up on the timetable
- You may well end up with more questions than you have slots available, in which case, place similar topics together.
- Once your timetable is full, allow people a few minutes to look at it and work out where they want to go to, and then ring a bell, or something similar, to announce the start of the first session
- People then go to the space where their question is being hosted, and the discussions begin

In theory, the rest of the day will organise itself if you do the following:

- Ensure each break-out space has plenty of flip-chart paper and pens
- Tell people when each session starts, and remind them about the Law of Two Feet
- At the end of each session, ring a bell to let people know it is finished
- Go around and collect the note-filled sheets
- Put them up on the wall in the area you have pre-designated as the 'Market Place'
- You may also choose to have someone typing up the sheets if you are posting the proceedings live on the web or if you want it typed up to send out quickly
- Leave 30-40 minutes or so at the end to allow one person to feedback from each discussion and for everyone to give feedback on the process
- The notes generated can be typed up and circulated to everyone who attended

Harvesting and Completion - You may decide that this day is about harvesting ideas, and no specific decisions are reached. Future activities might emerge from the session, but you might want actions to be agreed upon and taken forward. This will determine what shape the closing session takes. It could be a brief thank you and hope you had a good time, to more specific planning, setting up working groups or anything else that needs to happen. In which case, more time is needed to come to agreements.

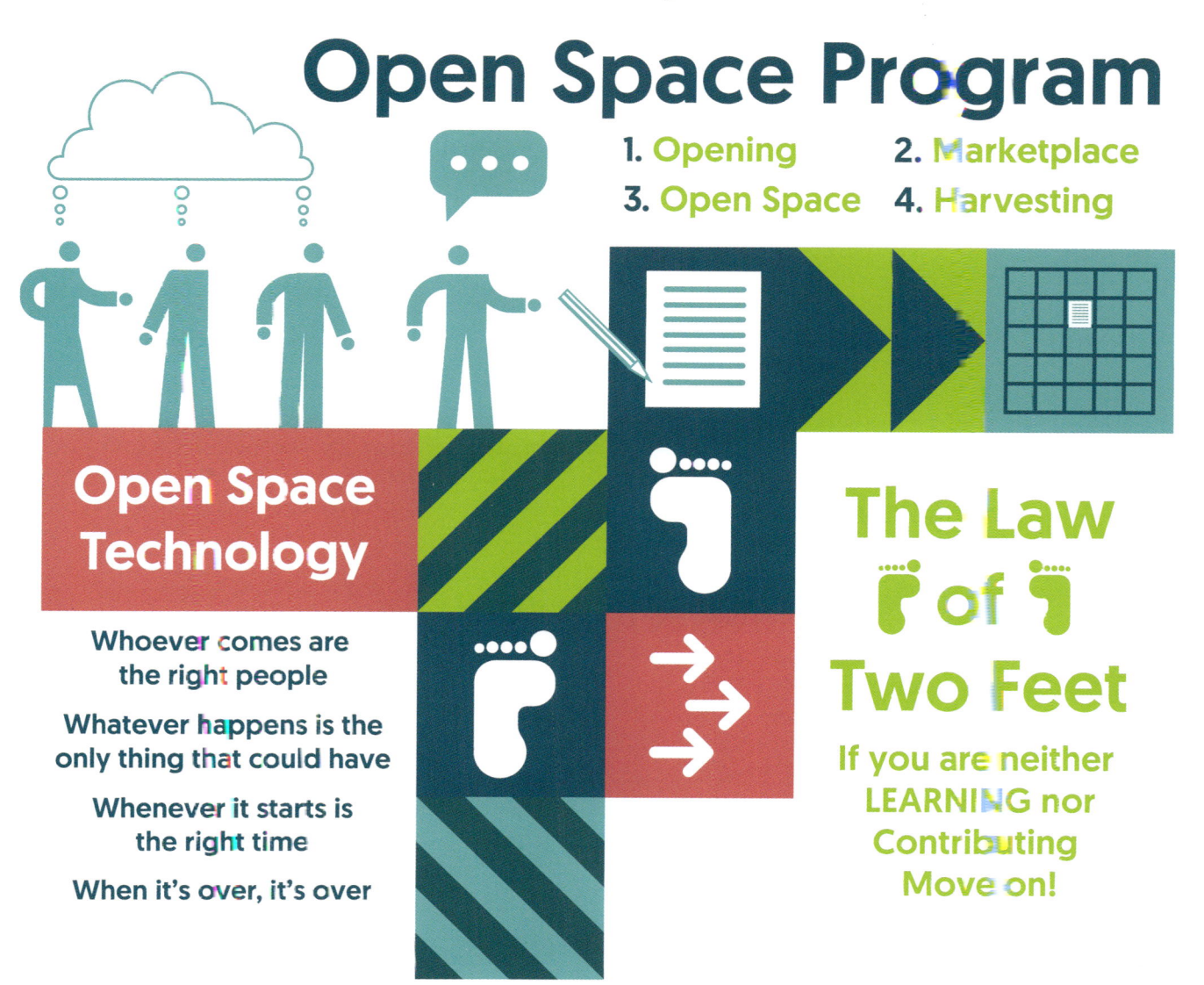

Open Space Program

1. Opening
2. Marketplace
3. Open Space
4. Harvesting

Open Space Technology

- Whoever comes are the right people
- Whatever happens is the only thing that could have
- Whenever it starts is the right time
- When it's over, it's over

The Law of Two Feet

If you are neither LEARNING nor Contributing Move on!

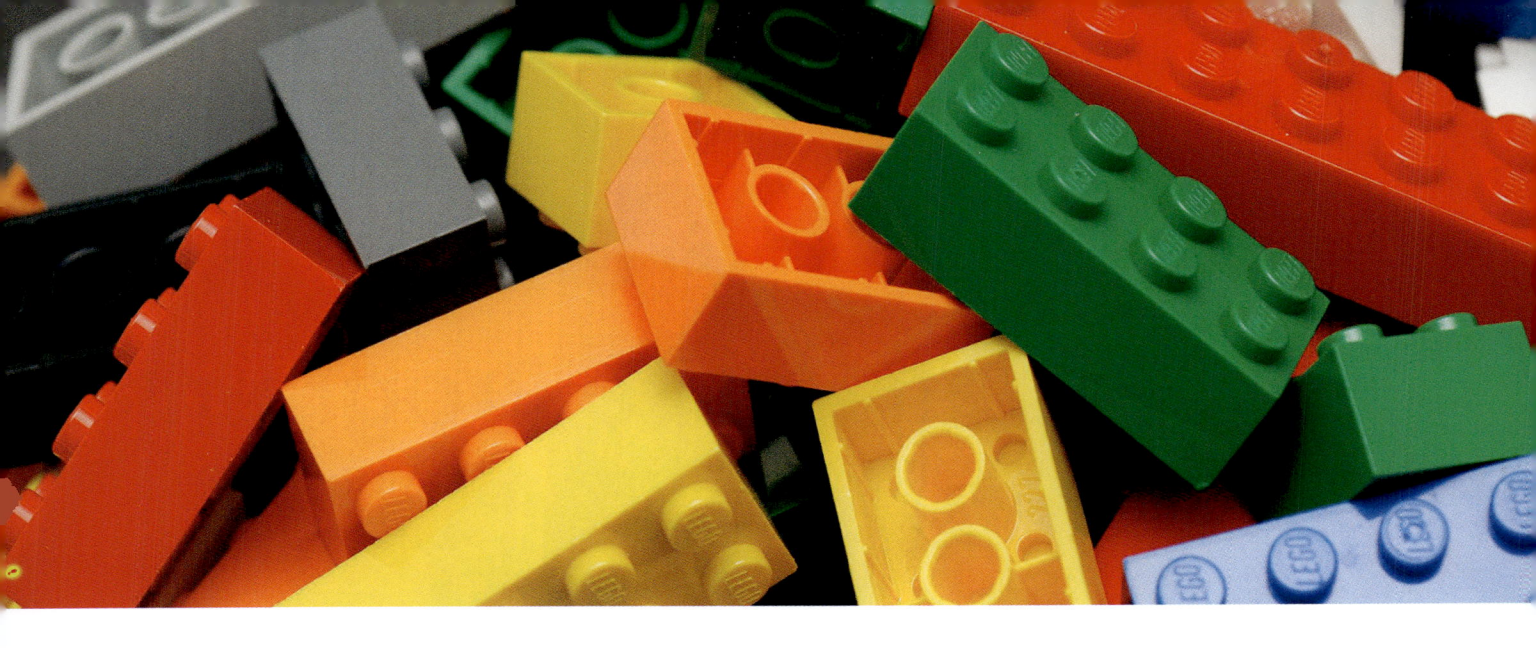

Example Two - LEGO® Serious Play®

In 2017, I trained as a facilitator of the LEGO® Serious Play® (LSP) method with Rasmussen Consulting a founding member of the Association of Master Trainers. There are other providers out there who deliver facilitator training and of course the method is open source (not Open Space Technology), so you can use the methodology without any formal training, something that I wouldn't recommend. It is something I am extremely passionate about so I must be careful here not to over egg it. I chose to train in this methodology for different reasons:

- I am a keen adult fan of LEGO® (AFOL) and saw a link with my hobby and my career. Something to be careful of, as last time I tried to turn a hobby into a career, I noticed boundaries got blurred, and it wasn't as fun as I imagined. In this case, my journey with LSP so far remains fun and exciting. So, all good there.
- In my earlier days as a facilitator and trainer, I had heard that the methodology was powerful, unique and had been described as serious fun. This fitted well with my roles within Successfactory™, where we described much of what we deliver as fun with a serious intent. LSP has been used effectively worldwide in companies such as IKEA, Samsung, Siemens, Arup and many more. Some of these I have since used it with.
- There was a point in my development where I felt at a crossroads. I knew some of the checkpoints on my journey but had to start considering the route to take. It had become obvious that trainers and facilitators had areas of specialism and maybe their approach. Such as project management or leadership and delivered using graphic facilitation and appreciative enquiry approaches. So, I decided I would go down the route of using LSP as part of my own brand.

I took part in a very comprehensive and immersive four-day training programme. Over the years, I have been on many, wide-ranging training courses to qualify in areas such as Rock-Climbing Instructor, Rope Rescue Training, Archery Coaching and Rifle Range Management. Many were intense, safety critical and had key assessment elements under pressure. My LSP facilitator training was by no means as critical or pressured, but on return from the course, I was so connected to the process, methodology, principles, and nuances that I felt like I had some strange kind of Post Traumatic Stress Disorder (PTSD). For weeks every gap in my mind was taken up by thoughts of the process, the resources, and memories from the days. Some said the course was overly academic, and that might be the reason why it felt so intense, my opinion is that is not the case, but it was that the course delivery, content and approach were of such good quality that it made such strong and memorable connections in my brain. There are also very few courses I have been on over the years where I have remained in contact with all group members since, but this was the one. We have professional and personal links that keep us connected and have met multiple times since, despite being spread across Europe.

I will explain a little more about what it is and how it is done, but I want to be clear that there are other things out there using modular brick-type products for learning and development, some exclusively for grown-ups, some for children and others can be used for both. These include LEGO® Education®, PlayMobilPro® and simple team or learning activities that use bricks and blocks. I have added some of these to the toolkit section of the book, but they are NOT LSP. They are meeting tools using LEGO® Bricks. When I use LSP, I am very respectful of its processes and applications and as often discussed in my networks around the world on this, if it's not applied with its designed intention it is just training with LEGO®. Very much like my earlier references to synonymous products such as Hoovers and Champagne.

What is LEGO® Serious Play®?

It is a facilitated thinking, communication and problem-solving technique that encourages groups (organisations, teams, and individuals) to build their answers to questions in 3D using LEGO® bricks with metaphors and stories. Its core process builds confidence, insights, and commitment to the topic at the heart of the session. It is based on beliefs that leaders don't have all the answers, people naturally want to contribute to things that they are passionate about, the best decisions are made when each member contributes, and we live in a world that is ever increasingly being described as volatile, uncertain, complex, and ambiguous (VUCA).

Successful facilitation of a LEGO® Serious Play® session changes traditional meetings from those where 80% of the input is provided by 20% of the people to meetings where attendees lean in and everyone contributes to all aspects of the discussion. It will not provide a clear set of documented actions and to-do lists for all attendees. It will also go deeper and generate more possibilities than traditional approaches. Imagine, if it is possible to combine six eight-stud LEGO® bricks in 102,981,500 different ways. What could the possibilities be of combining many different bricks, shapes and colours when answering focussed questions in a simple, effective, and inclusive process?! It can be used in areas of team development, organisation strategy, problem solving to name but a few.

What makes LSP so powerful?

Extensive research and application took place, and the methodology hasn't changed much. It rests upon a core 4-step process and seven application techniques.

The core process:

Step 1 – Posing the question. It should have no obvious or correct solution and be framed in such a way so the participant can connect it to the context.
Step 2 – Construct. In an allocated time frame, participants should construct a model using the LEGO® materials, developing a story to convey the meaning of their model in answer to the question.
Step 3 – Share. Each model and story are shared between participants.
Step 4 – Reflect. To allow everyone to digest the insights and information, reflection should be encouraged.

The design of an LSP session will be progressive and enable participants to become more comfortable with the core process as they progress through application techniques in their sessions.

1. Pose the Question
2. Build + Give Meaning
3. Tell + Share the Story
4. Learn + Reflect

The application techniques:

Each of the seven application techniques are designed to tackle progressively more complex problems. Experience and mastery of the previous application technique will aid use of the next one. This is the facilitator's responsibility as part of the design and delivery of the session. The application techniques are:

- Building individual models and stories
- Building shared models and stories
- Creating a landscape
- Making connections
- Building a system
- Playing emergence and decisions
- Extracting simple guiding principles

It's worth considering at this stage that this type of thing has been happening in organisations worldwide for many years. For example, The Army Orders Group (O' Gp)

I remember my first set of ambush orders as an army cadet in the early 1990s. A model of the operational area was constructed, and moving parts with toy soldiers, blocks of wood, rocks and coloured ribbons were used to tell the story or plan. I saw the benefits of the orders process early on and recognised how a simple, memorable, detailed and, more importantly, tried and tested approach got us all involved, bought in and committed to the mission. There was a process of remembering, much like the LSP core process of all that needed to be covered – Greedy Sergeant Major Eats Small Cadets (or more accurately Ground, Situation, Mission, Execution, Service Support, Command and Signal). Since my first O Gp, I've seen them done at many levels, I've seen them done brilliantly and poorly. They are done well when the process is followed. The team will 'Lean In' and get it, much like LEGO® Serious Play®. A big downside for me with this comparison is that until the firefight, this is very often someone else's plan, unlike LSP, where the plan can be created together, simple guiding principles are developed and decisions can then be made at all levels right from the start.

Let's now reflect on this section a little and remind ourselves why I have written it. Any products you buy for a particular use or service will have guidelines for use. Be it a car, a kettle, a tent, etc. They may provide some functionality if used outside of the recommended process, but this functionality may be limited. They will probably also come with some health warnings advising of the risks associated with not following the manufacturer's recommendations. This could be in relation to its effectiveness or to the general health and safety of the user. Likewise with the tools I have explored and referenced here, there are reasons behind the process and principles. Explore what they are and be clear if what you are doing is an interpretation of, or the real thing and have clear expectations of outcomes.

Tech Top Tips – online and F2F, platforms, projectors, computers, and interactive whiteboards

As the host of a meeting, you will be looked upon by attendees to ensure it runs seamlessly. I remember about 10 years ago going to the cinema to see a movie that had been on the big screen for a while. We went then in the hope that the viewing would be quiet in the last few weeks before it went to DVD. It was a local cinema, so we arrived just in time, got our popcorn and drinks, and took a seat. My partner and I made up 25% of the people wanting to watch the film that evening. When we sat down, the adverts were showing. You know the ones, those cheesy ads that tell you about the latest mobile phones or a big sports brand who've sponsored the cinema company. These were on loop for 10 to 15 minutes as usual, and then they faded, we sat and waited for the trailers for upcoming movies, and we waited, and we waited. The screen stayed black, the room quiet, with just enough side lighting to see around us and very little conversation. I like to think I'm a patient man, but on this occasion, I was too patient. We sat silently, waiting for someone to hit the play button for around 30 minutes. It eventually started, unprompted by any of the eight of us in the cinema that evening, and it also went without an explanation or apology. It's a good job that we went to a restaurant before the film and not afterwards, as we would have either missed our booking or the end of the film. For those who are wondering what the film was, it was Daniel Craig as James Bond in Skyfall, it was worth the ticket money and the wait and as a family favourite, we've watched it many times since.

The film had a running time of 2 hours and 24 minutes, which is 24 minutes longer than most team meetings, as far as I'm aware. Many teams schedule their regular meetings as 2 hours - time that could be spent working on your to-do list and getting real work done. Unless your meetings are awesome and you get real work done in them. If I asked people to attend a meeting and then forgot to press play, or couldn't link the projector to my laptop, or key 'cast' members for the meeting were late, I'd expect the rest of the meeting to be a thriller and well worth the wait. Our roles in meetings vary. Whether we're the host, the chair, the secretary, or an active participant, we often choose to use technology to help support our objectives. This technology can range from a laptop and projector, interactive whiteboard, zoom type platform, video recording and in-room speakers, voting technology such as Mentimeter, or it may even be the software programme such as PowerPoint (more on this later in the book), excel or adobe. The transitions between using these various technology items can be the difference between keeping the attendees in flow or loosing flow.

Here are my tips for using such a wide array of tech in your meetings:

1. Keep it simple. There are benefits to be gained from using technology to engage meeting participants or to portray your message, but the more you use in one meeting, the higher the risk of things going wrong. This is equally so of the number of items you expect your audience to use – try to avoid multiple voting platforms or different collaboration techniques – limit your use to one or two methods per meeting.

2. Rehearse, rehearse, rehearse. Try the functionality of your chosen medium when there isn't a live audience. Get a volunteer or two to experience it in advance from the point of view that's not yours. Get to the meeting room or log in early and try all the transitions you plan to use to ensure your use is smooth.

3. Delegate or die. If you can give the responsibility of the smooth running of the tech to someone else, it will not only enable you to engage more fully in the session's content and share the responsibility for its success. But remember here, I say share not abdicate.

4. Have a backup or plan. If in face-to-face settings, plan an alternative. For example, if you're using PowerPoint put the presentation on a USB drive to use on another device if possible and ensure you have all the correct cables and chargers for the devices in use too. Print the slides to take key information onto a flipchart if necessary. If online, holding your session remotely, provide a plan of what to do if the connection is lost, i.e., message the Whatsapp group boil the kettle and wait 10 minutes before re-trying the link. Check your links and QR codes on things like Slido before the session starts but have a backup idea, such as using the chat function or in meeting polls.

PowerPoint

In the interest of fairness, I must point out that there are different software programmes out there to develop a slide show. Some of the popular ones I've seen are Prezi, Keynote and PDFs in full-screen view, but I'm going to refer to the synonymous Microsoft PowerPoint here. I don't intend this to be an argument, but I hope you will feel comfortable enough to challenge your thinking through my thoughts here. Over many years now (probably starting with the use of overhead projectors and acetates or Fablon), I've heard many so-called experts tell me the BEST way to use PowerPoint. Classics such as all content must be in size 24 font; the fewer slides you use the better. I've made my current judgements based on how the use of PowerPoint has made me feel, how it engaged with me and how much I can remember from the presentation. I have taken inspiration for some of my summative thoughts from the work of David J Phillips, How to Avoid Death by PowerPoint. I am also drawing from memories of some of the best presentations I remember experiencing.

Before delving into the detail of how I believe this medium can be used to best effect, I'll remind you of one of my many meeting mantras – start with the end in mind! Slide shows can be used to present an idea, generate ideas, tell a story, share data, teach a method or present findings, amongst others. You must be clear when putting a presentation together about what you are trying to achieve. This may vary as you progress through sections of your presentation, but always know what you are trying to achieve with your use of slides. I would say, however, that if a large part of your presentation is to share information, why don't you send it in advance and share the headlines in the meeting? Also, consider your approach and ask yourself if using flipcharts, printed posters, or online whiteboards would be a better alternative. If not, and you still plan on producing and using a presentation, please use the following tips and try your best not to be a contender for the worst slides ever like these images.

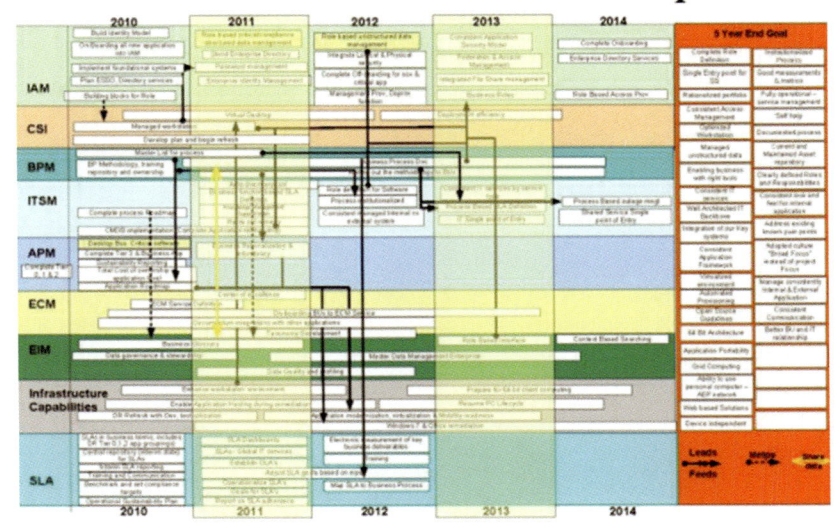

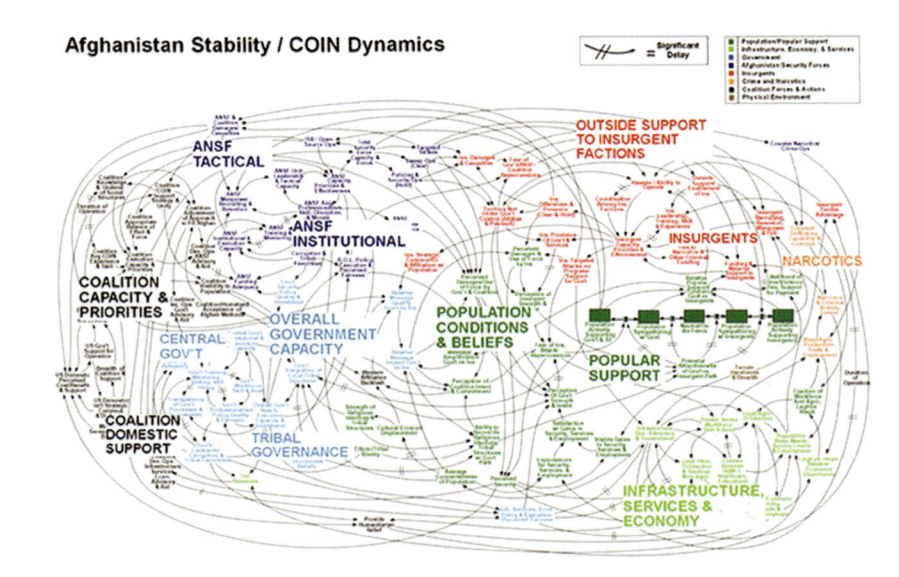

Why do I use PowerPoint? Well, when I'm using a slide deck that I've designed, it is often to provide visual links and reminders of what I'm talking about. For example, suppose I'm sharing the traits of high performing teams in one of my training programmes. I may use big pictures of teams that I consider high performing, such as the England Rugby Team, The Red Arrows, a poster showing the cast and crew of a West End stage show or a Formula 1 racing crew. Or if I were introducing a model showing an approach to leadership, I would use an image showing the simplest version of the model I can and talk around it. Whether you're looking at a slide from the back of a conference room or directly on your laptop, it will only ever be so big, and people need to see and understand its content comfortably.

So here are my golden nuggets for the use of PowerPoint (in the style of a BBC TV presenter 'other presentation software programmes are available'):

1 **The more the merrier.** I believe that if you have a presentation to give and it requires the use of slides that there should be lots of slides. "Whaaattttt????!!!!!" I hear you scream. Well, some of the best presentations I have ever seen, and the best feedback I've had from my presentations has been when there was a quote, an image or a statement on a slide and the narrative told its story. The small amounts of visual data shared connect better with the audience; they don't just spend their time reading the words or trying to decipher the flow chart whilst you're wasting your time talking to a load of empty seats. I have worked out that for a presentation with very little audience participation, I need approximately 1 slide per 60 seconds and ideally this slide will have very little on it.

2 **Step-by-step.** I have been taught many different teaching and training techniques over the years and each has its place. One technique I was taught on a military course was E – R – T. Explain, Reveal, Teach, and I have tried my best to apply this to my presentations. Either a blank slide or just a title as I explain what is about to be shared, its context and its reason. Using the software's animation features I have then revealed one item at a time and allowed appropriate time for them to read it before I moved on to teach or talk through in more detail with stories and examples. Animate your limited content and take them through step by step using the E – R - T approach.

3 **Size Matters. No really, it does.** There are so many opportunities here to lower the bookstone, so I'll try to resist. For the last twenty-plus years, every time I've been (loosely speaking) taught how to use PowerPoint, they have always told me the optimum size for the text of a slide, and strangely enough, yes you've guessed it, they've all said something different. None of which I'm going to share here. The most important thing on your slide should be the biggest and that is not going to be the slide title. If you have a picture to share, it should be the main thing they see and your supporting notes help you with what to say, if it's some data or a quote, this should be the biggest thing on the slide.

4   **Cocktail Party Effect.** Imagine yourself at a party, the music is playing loud and you're in deep (or seemingly deep) conversation with a friend, the base of the music is drowning out most other noise whilst you're talking, but then somewhere in the room you hear your name, your mind wanders away from the existing conversation to try and tune into where your name was heard and simultaneously your friends carry on talking. Moments later, you tune back in just as your friend says, "And don't you agree?" You have no idea what you're about to agree with, but to save face you nod and say yes. This is what we call the Cocktail Party Effect. It's the same with presentations using slides. If you have more than one message on a slide at any time, the chances are that whilst you're explaining one of them, your audience will be reading the other(s) and not listening to your great content.

5   **Hook up, humour or heighten.** To engage the audience with your presentation, you should do your best (in an authentic way) to hook them, provide humour or heighten their emotions.
   a   A hook is something brief, catchy, well-rehearsed and relevant to the topic that catches their attention. It could be a series of rhetorical questions, a story or a scenario starting with 'What if?' or quoting a foreign proverb like, "You'll never plough a field by turning it over in your mind." It could be creating a vision using the word 'imagine', like 'imagine a life without ...'
   b   Using humour starts to get them to like you. If you can make them laugh early on, you'll keep their attention for some time - pictures of irony, cartoon metaphors and cynicism or even a funny story. A little appropriate humour spread throughout can have a great impact. However, I would add a word of warning - know your audience!
   c   Telling stories that heighten emotions keeps the attention of your audience. The number of times I found myself looking at a photograph on a slide whilst listening to the emotional story of a great presenter, hanging on their every word. The emotions could be positive or negative, but I'd suggest leaving them on a high.

In his work, David J. P. Phillips asks, "Why spending forty minutes in a meeting with dull slides, do we go back to our desks and prepare a presentation which will have the same impact on your intended audience? Is this some sort of vengeance?"

Next time you're preparing a presentation, ask yourself, what would you think if you were in the audience looking at this?

73% Of Statistics Are Made Up

With each meeting type, there is a different need for data to be shared. Sometimes none at all, and sometimes you need the information to help build context. Then for others, you need to share a report showing your success. I have been told often that a good accountant can make most accounts look good, but only for a short time. This is also the case for managers sharing updates in meetings. We should be clear, open, and honest when sharing data. Data gives an impression, let's take a few statements with different viewpoints:

Six of one and half a dozen of the other.

In God we trust. All others bring data.

Torture the data, and it will confess to anything.

Is a glass half full or half empty?

Lots of meetings will review KPIs (Key performance Indicators), KRAs (Key Result Areas), OKRs (Objective and Key Results), Metrics, etc. I've frustratingly been to many meetings in the same organisations where they constantly show data in different formats. This often causes me to spend time re-aligning my thinking with what's being shared. I believe it should be consistent if you use data to help guide plans, share results, and make decisions. It should also be simple to view, top level and allow discussions to open up. It's also something you can get creative with. Several years ago at Successfactory™, we introduced a visual dashboard. It contained the numbers of training days delivered, venue bookings, income for the quarter broken into months, total income year to date and comparison with the same period last year. It also had some space for text to add some simple context. The use of this in monthly meetings created far more dialogue than spreadsheets with detailed breakdowns and if we felt we needed to delve deeper into an area, we could then pull up the information on that one area to build on the conversation.

Unfortunately, in other parts of my life, I've attended quarterly meetings where we've reviewed the same information every time we got together, such as participation figures, successful completions, levels achieved, number of people trained etc. Still, the information was presented in a different format every time we met. The focus changed due to a lack of clarity about what we were actually measuring. This may have been down to whoever was banging the drum the loudest at the time, but it doesn't create consistent action to follow up on.

People will always look at data differently. Some may look at numbers, and it will blow their mind. Another may be like Dustin Hoffman's character Raymond in the 1988 film Rain Man, because of that, here are my tips on sharing data in meetings:

1 Know your audience and share the data they can relate to.

2 Share no more than five headline statistics or figures that relate to your metrics.

3 Have further detail available to offer and use for context building if asked. This helps with decision making and trust-building.

4 Keep the format consistent. Maybe if you're starting a project team and are just getting started, make the data an item to discuss in your earlier meetings and let everyone agree which format works best.

5 Question the data. Ask questions to understand why it is as it is. Numbers mean nothing without meaning.

SMALL THINGS MAKE PERFECTION, BUT PERFECTION IS NO SMALL THING

Henry Royce

The things you can't see...

Exploring how things feel in your meeting environment

The things you can't see

I've called these the things you can't see, mainly because you can't grasp them with your hands. They often appear intangible. You certainly will see the results of these things, but I would say the attitudes, behaviours, mindsets, thinking and processes that takes place in a meeting get the results. The image to the right of Betaris Box is a really simple and effective way of demonstrating how important these things are, how they are constant, unavoidable and as much what you do, as what others do too.

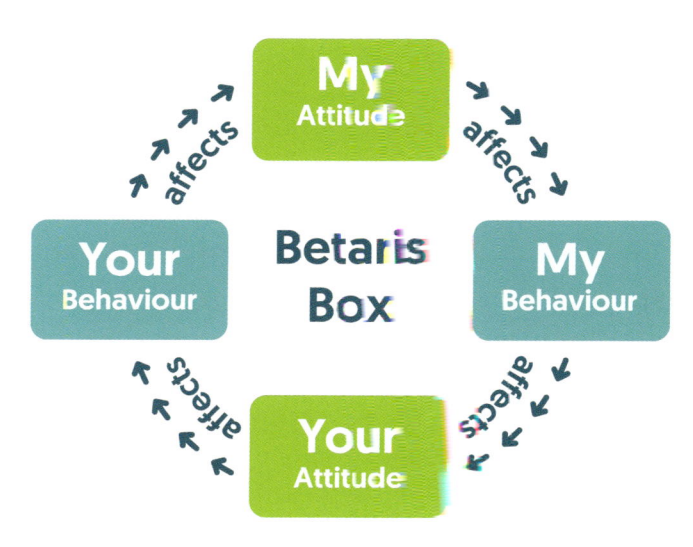

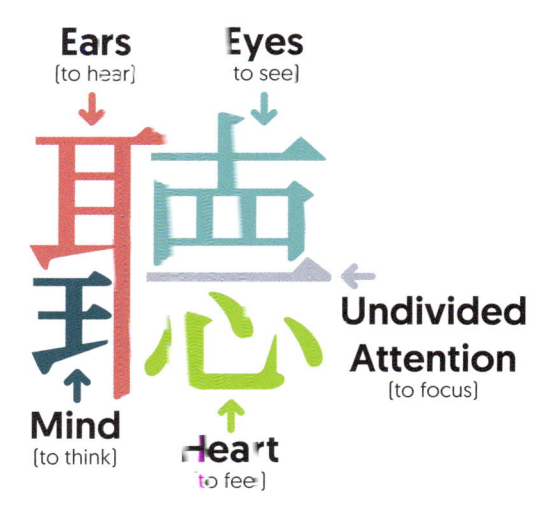

To get the best out of everything in this section, I want to draw your attention to something which was shared with me many years ago - the Chinese symbol for Listening. Chinese characters are one of the oldest systems of writing in the world. Each character has its own specific meaning, and by slowing down to consider this one we can learn a lot about how we can best make use of the things we can't see in meetings.

Not just the five areas that this symbol is broken down into, but the structure of it too. Across the top are the Ears (to hear) and the Eyes (to see). It's not just the words but the expression and body language too. Across the bottom are the Mind (to think) and the Heart (to feel). We often try to fill the gaps between people's words, but to truly hear, we need to slow down and understand — to think and feel. In the middle of the symbol, the single stroke that represents the need to give our undivided attention (to focus) and to me, the true focus is the ability to really listen to what's being said and taking it all in, not just listening for the opportunity to make your next statement or question.

There's much more behind the scenes and more to think about when it comes to what can't be seen in meetings, so let's take a look at a few.

Psychological Safety

Psychological Safety should exist everywhere! In life, at home, at work and in meetings we should have the skills and confidence to say what we're thinking, share ideas, and accept feedback and criticism. This helps individuals, organisations and ideas grow. Unfortunately it has become 'a thing', where, I believe:

- People have become scared or embarrassed to receive negative feedback. They don't take it well and very often think their ideas are great and can't be improved on.
- What could in the past have been described as 'banter', has become bullying (and rightly so), but has stopped some people from giving feedback at the risk of being accused of bullying or crossing the banter line.
- Poor leader and follower behaviours, have stopped people talking at all. A lack of trust, that they will be treated fairly has caused people to not contribute to some discussions and meetings.

Lots of the ideas and tools in this book, by way of their process and guidelines naturally create psychological safety. Many of them will prove even more effective for you if there are high levels of psychological safety. Here are ways that it can be developed in meetings and conversations:

a Build a culture where self-awareness is promoted people are aware of the impact that their behaviours have on others.
b Include people in decision making. Even if that is just explaining why something has or is changing. Help them understand why.
c Take ownership of mistakes, as both a participant and leader.
d Ask great questions and encourage/develop others to do the same. Questions create curiosity and increase awareness.
e Provide different ways for people to engage throughout the meeting and discussions.
f Thank people for their engagement and especially when they challenge ideas and thinking.
g Encourage people to call out poor behaviour and deal with it in the moment.

The Left and Right Brain

There is a lot of information out there that says people are either left or right-brained. Firstly, what does that mean, and secondly, is it true? Well, if you are described as left-brained you are likely to show traits such as being logical, analytical, and orderly. If you are described as right brained you often tend to be creative, emotional, and intuitive. This is called Hemispheric lateralisation. We often hear that people use both sides of their brain but have a preference. This preference could be down to their chosen career or their chosen career, or could be down to their brain preference.

Generally, I would say that from my own experience and the brief reading of research by different neuroscientists, we do have a preference. However, I believe that my own experiences have shown that we can perform much better when both sides of the brain work together. In meetings, we need people to perform at their best. We need to get the best out of their whole brain, by not forcing them into fight or flight mode and creating an environment where they can think openly. Outside of the meeting people can do things to help connect their two sides of the brain. They could include:

- Brain games/puzzles
- Learning a new skill, such as juggling
- Take the Stroop test
- Practice mind mapping

In meetings we can do this with a combination of the tools we use and how we set up our space – creating opportunities for people to physically engage in the meeting by building things, writing on flipcharts, throwing dice etc. Creating opportunities for the group to stand up can make a huge difference. Tools that have pace and help with flow such as Radiant Problem Solving, World Café and use of LEGO®, can help with this. You can also chunk things up and use bigger whiteboards or graphic facilitation boards and large sticky notes.

Left Hemisphere

Responsible for logical thinking

Focused on analytics

Responsible for language skills

Controls speech

Responsible for memorising facts and names

Controls science and mathematical capabilities

Specialises in sequential processing of information

Controls right part of the body

Right Hemisphere

Focused in intuition

Conceives non verbal information

Responsible for spatial orientation

Focused in synthetics

Responsible for ability to draw

Responsible for imagination

Responsible for musicality

Creates emotions

Produces dreams

Specialises in multitasking and parallel processing of information

Controls left part of the body

Pen Clickers or Misophonia

Do you suffer from Misophonia? Quite possibly, but do you even know what it is? Misophonia is a condition in which individuals experience intense anger and disgust when confronted by sounds made by others. Ok, it's called this when it becomes quite extreme, but I'm sure lots of us have a little of it. Sounds like lip smacking, loud breathing, yawning, chewing, pen clicking and tapping on the desk can also be included. I don't want to trivialise it, as it does cause some severe issues for people. But from a meeting point of view, there are some things that I've considered over the years. One particular instance was whilst in a meeting where someone had been staring into space, clicking their pen and visually appearing not to be engaged. When reviewing the topic, I asked some summative questions to different group members. I didn't get the responses I expected. Those who appeared to be engaged, who had been looking at the screen or the presenter during the meeting struggled to answer some questions, whereas the 'annoying pen clicker', rather irritatingly could answer the questions well. I was intrigued by this and realised that clicking the pen was a way of keeping the brain active and connecting both sides of the brain for them.

Since realising this, I've had to work hard to ignore the sound of the click as now I accept it to be adding more value for that person than a distraction for me. I've also found other things for them to fidget with (See Props or No Props) that are quieter yet still help them. Things such as tangle toys or spinners. Another situation that helped me understand this was when I'd looked at a colleague's notepad during a break (I only glanced at it on my way past the desk, I wasn't reading it 🙂 and noticed lots of doodles, pictures, scribbles and what appeared to be very few words. I watched them during the next part of the meeting and spotted that they were still doodling lots, which showed no resemblance to the meeting content. After watching a little longer, I saw them turning the page too. It turned out the front of their notepad was for their useable notes and record of the meeting and later in the pad, they just doodled. They told me that this helped keep them engaged and it was a strategy they had learnt at university from another student.

So don't assume people aren't engaged, don't get too annoyed by clicking of pens and doodling and if you want to help the situation, provide support for those who need to keep their brain engaged like this.

Flow

There is a lot of material available on the topic of flow, including many books too. Most have started with defining being in the zone, extasis or even challenge and support. For me, in this context, flow is literally being 'in flow' where your body and mind are working at their best. Some very concise work has been written on Flow by Hungarian American psychologist Mihaly Csikzentmihalyi and, in particular, his 'Finding Flow.'

Have you ever been in meetings or workshops, looked across the room and saw someone falling asleep? Have you been the person falling asleep? Maybe just staring at your notepad or the wall with nothing going on 'upstairs' due to boredom and disengagement? This is often because the level of challenge is too low for the audience or what they're trying to achieve.

How about the other end of the spectrum where you're invited to a team building day and the activity leader takes you straight out in the woods, gets the team fitted into a harness and invites you to be the first to climb a 12-metre pole and take the leap of faith? This could also be when you're asked to present feedback to a conference audience with no warning or preparation. Generally, a situation that has pushed you very quickly to your limits and out of your comfort zone. I'm sure we've all been there. Some of these situations are healthy and good for our development; sometimes, the situation, timing and the challenges are just too much and can cause anxiety, stress, worry and more.

When I talk about flow it's about getting the balance right between your skills, the group and the level of challenge. I've had situations with different clients that demonstrate the extremes here:

1. Clients in the construction industry who work on the electricity supply and often spend their working day at height in a high physical risk environments have been very happy to climb towers and jump for the trapeze bar but were completely freaked out when asked to stand up and speak about their strengths in front of 15 peers.

2. A small team of computer technicians who spend their days in quiet corners of a room coding parts of new programmes and then, in the evenings, enjoy playing guitar in local bands. Even though they were more than happy to play to large audiences in a crowded bar, it took huge amounts of coaching to get them to work together and climb a 10-metre Jacob's ladder.

The image below shows how important it is to have progression in meetings and workshops to keep people in flow and building on the skills and challenges as appropriate so as not to create levels of anxiety that are too high or give challenges that are well below their level of skill. I have found that there is also group flow, where the energy outputs of others help keep the whole group in flow. This works as long as the group have good levels of psychological safety and appreciates that not everyone will be challenged all of the time and that this is ok.

Physical indicators of being in flow are when everyone is leaning into the table, talking or even standing up. There's intuitive chat, where multiple conversations might happen simultaneously, and everyone is ok with that. The proper use of tools, techniques and appropriate behaviours in meetings achieves flow, as you'll see when I cover the Inspired Meetings Framework later in this book.

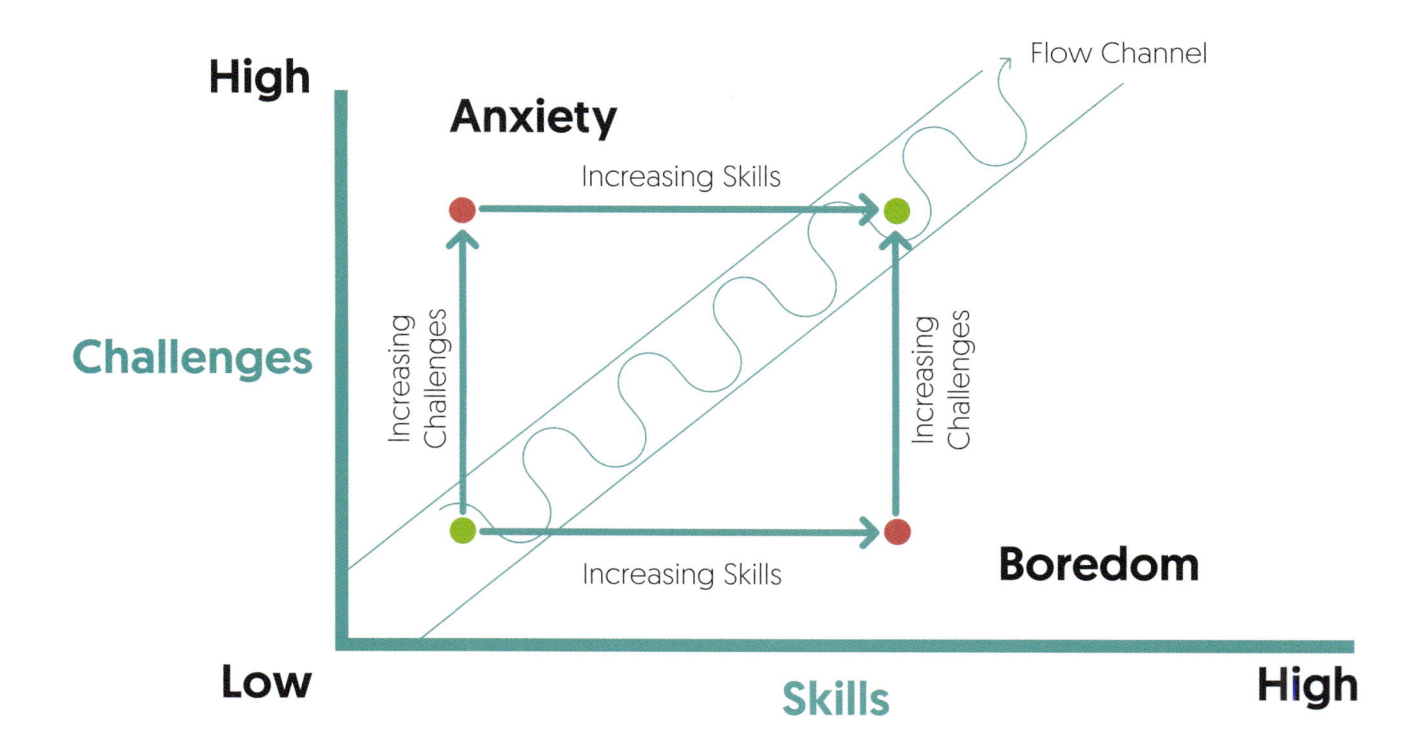

Adapted from Mihaly Csikszentmihalyi's flow state diagram

Pilot, Holiday Maker, Prisoner and Passenger

No matter how much preparation and hard work goes into getting ready for meetings, I find people who attend fall into one of these four character roles. I'm sure that just by looking at the words Pilot, Prisoner, Passenger and Holiday Maker, you can work out which role you want people to play. As leaders through a combination of preparation and remedial actions at the beginning of a meeting or engagement throughout, we should aim to create as many holiday makers and pilots as possible. There are many reasons why people take on these roles, some within your control and many outside of your control. As I describe each character role, consider each of the roles you have played (or still play) and which you see in the meetings you attend. It will be obvious in a combination of actions, body language and words.

Pilot – You can have pilots in meetings even when they're not the person intended to lead. These people can lead certain aspects of a meeting or the whole thing. They may even get involved before the meeting starts. A pilot will often do some or all of the following:

- Lead a discussion or agenda item by sharing ideas, insights, and experiences.
- Ask lots of questions in a positive and appropriate way.
- Keep attendees on track if the conversation starts to wander.

Holiday Maker – These people want to be there. They have bought into the team, purpose and approach and want to make the most of their time there. Holiday makers will prepare for the meeting, be present throughout and contribute fully to all aspects. They'll usually be there early and spend time at the end of the meeting chatting to other holiday makers who aren't in a rush to get to 'something more important.'

Prisoner – You might often find prisoners, but hopefully, the better your meetings get, the fewer there will be. You can turn them into passengers or even holiday makers. When someone attends with the prisoner mindset, you'll see it on their face. They will check their watch regularly – even before the meeting starts (if they turn up on time, that is), and they will only contribute with negative statements like 'that'll never work' and 'last time we had to do that it didn't end well.' The prisoners will have such a busy schedule they'll leave at the first opportunity.

Passenger – Passengers aren't good or bad. They are often there willingly because they have nothing else pressing and want something to do with their time (maybe they attend in the hope there'll be donuts). They won't contribute much unless they absolutely have to because, really, they're just there for the ride. They may even be there because they have a little FOMO (Fear of Missing Out) and want to be able to take 'gossip' back to their team.

100/100

I'm sure you've been in meetings where 80 per cent of the talking is done by 20% of the attendees! This is a real problem, especially if it occurs in a meeting of five people – I call this a thorough de-brief. If you attend a meeting and the person holding the meeting spends all the time on send mode, before saying something ineffective such as 'right, you all know what you need to do, go and do it', you're almost guaranteed to get the following:

- No buy-in to any actions – being told what to do doesn't result in any level of commitment.
- Additional meetings happening at the coffee machine – people are found saying in a low volume, 'what was he saying?', 'I don't agree with any of that!', 'that'll never work', and 'who does he think he is?'.
- Misinterpretation of tasks – getting no verbal affirmation of what is required often results in people not having the right understanding of what is required.
- Bad decisions – a 'briefing' that is one way assumes that the giver of such briefing has the right answers when more often than not, the real knowledge is with those who will carry out the work, and they should be involved in its creation.

For this reason, we should strive for 100/100 meetings. I've proudly borrowed this phrase from my training and involvement in LEGO® Serious Play® over the years but realised it's something I've always strived for. In short meetings, the solution is quite simple, you can involve people by asking them questions and creating a culture that enables them to answer, or you can use one or two of the simple tools explained later in this book, such as the Duck, Blob Journey, or NICE to talk. It is a little more difficult for longer meetings, workshops, and conferences, but please believe me when I say 'only' a little more difficult. For bigger activities – choose a process and trust the process! Bringing the session to life using activities, flipcharts, collaboration, and problem-solving tools to help engage people and respond to the challenges will be a big step to getting 100 per cent of the attendees involved 100 per cent of the time.

But how do you manage that with the sceptics, the old and bold, those who have been there, seen it and done it? My experience shows that progression is the answer to this. It even helps to ensure you don't frighten off those keen and engaged by being too much too early. Here's an example of how I gained empathy in this respect:

A short musical interlude - Not long after I'd started working at Successfactory™, we were preparing for some big events, some of which included drumming and boom whacker workshops. It was arranged for our team to have a boom whacker session with one of the providers to help us understand and get ready for the bigger events, but also as a team development opportunity for our team. We were told that the provider was awesome at his job and at the time, was famed for being a head percussionist in the West End stage show of the Lion King, so there was no pressure there for him or us! To top it off I had achieved an 'F' in my music exams years earlier and wasn't exactly excited by the opportunity to fail at something else musical. My mindset at the start of our team session was a combination of nervousness and interest in the session but not wanting it to be too 'happy clappy' and high energy high five, theatrical type. Not a great mindset, I know, but I was younger and a little more naive back then.

When we entered the room, there was a load of colourful plastic tubes (these were the Boomwhackers) under the seats, I noted some of our team looked quite excited by this, and others looked equally, if not more, nervous and sceptical as I felt. The session started with an introduction from the facilitator who very quickly asked us to grab what was under our chairs, and he led us like a conductor of an orchestra for a very simple set of notes. As he pointed to each small group of us, each group having a different colour/note of Boomwhacker, we hit them with our hands – red, yellow, green, orange, purple or to the musically minded, it was d, e, c (C, G). It sounded familiar to me, but one of our team got it straight away as the well-known notes from Spielberg's Close Encounters of the Third Kind. Wow, just by hitting these things, we could create recognisable music. Next, we worked in smaller groups to play around with themes from nursery rhymes. Not quite as easy as we imagined, but it started to feel like fun. The final activity that we did was as a whole group. There where groups on notes, and rhythms that each colour had to play and Mark, the facilitator, again led us like an orchestra but with a more complex sequence. One at a time and consecutively at different paces, he stopped one of the colours playing their rhythm – this kept some great music going but sounded weird every time something stopped. We were really having fun, our bodies moving (almost dancing), everyone smiling and doing something outside our comfort zones. If we'd had started with that, he'd have lost half the group. As well as fun, shared memories and learning a new skill, there were some amazing lessons to learn here about teamwork too.

I use this progression principle in my outdoor experiential learning – when using ropes courses for team and personal development, I start with low rope activities or high rope activities with lots of teamwork before progressing to things like the Leap of Faith which is a very individual activity but with lots of support. Similarly, with my LEGO® Serious Play® sessions, I start with the Skills Building and the well-known tower, simple storytelling and metaphor use before progressing to challenge the builders more and eventually, making shared models and connections. In a meeting scenario, when collaborating, solving problems, and generating ideas, the session should be progressive in every sense too.

There are no difficult people in meetings

Ok, maybe there are difficult people, but hear me out on this one. In my earlier days of attending formal meetings, I remember looking around the table thinking things like:

- I WISH HE'D JUST SHUT UP AND TAKE A BREATH.
- SHE'S REALLY GOOD AT THIS STUFF. WHY ISN'T MICHELLE SAYING ANYTHING?
- I'VE GOT A GOOD IDEA. WHY WON'T HE LET ME SHARE IT?
- IF HE SPOKE TO ME LIKE THAT, I'D GIVE HIM SOME FEEDBACK.
- HERE WE GO, MAKE YOURSELF COMFORTABLE; IT'S PETER'S TURN.
- WAS THERE ANY NEED FOR CHARLOTTE TO SHOUT LIKE THAT?

> **THAT'S NOT WHAT MIKE TOLD ME WHEN WE WERE GETTING A COFFEE THIS MORNING.**

> **WHAT PLANET IS JOHN ON IF HE THINKS THAT'S IMPORTANT RIGHT NOW?**

On reflection, I'm sure there were times when people were thinking similar things when I spoke. On the above occasions, I saw these people as difficult people because I didn't have the knowledge, skill, or experience to decode their message or intent. Some people can be very self-aware and know that their actions and behaviours provoke and probe a response that suits only their cause. On these occasions, they can be playing on it and overcompensating. But often, what we see as difficult is differing priorities or personalities that we just aren't aware of. For example, when Mike told me something different at the coffee machine than he said in the meeting, I hadn't realised that he was thinking aloud, and by the time Mike spoke to everyone he had refined (and in one case changed) his plan. Neither did I know that when John was raising an issue that I didn't think was important, it was vital to his project's success, and he was struggling to find a solution by himself. Or when people seemed aggressive, it was actually that they weren't feeling listened to.

Sometimes we need to be inquisitive and ask questions to understand the situation. Asking questions doesn't just help us choose how we respond to a situation; it can often be just the interruption someone needs to make them stop and think about their own behaviour. Some behaviours may also be a part of the individuals' personality that brings strengths to a team, so we may need to understand this and develop team approaches and coping mechanisms to accommodate and make the best use of their strengths. The next section on Playing to strengths will provide more in-depth information on this.

There may be times when you are in a meeting with people you're not familiar with or when you still see un-useful and unproductive behaviours despite knowing people quite well. Here are some possible solutions to commonly experienced challenging behaviours:

AGGRESSIVENESS – Blaming, criticism, hostility

Possible solutions:
- Allow them to make their point and let off a bit of steam – if nothing else, they'll feel better afterwards
- Listen and show empathy
- Gather facts, NOT opinions. Don't take sides or match their behaviour
- Ask the person what is wrong
- Question them on the facts – how do we know that?
- Locate the source of the problem – are they stressed, insecure, nervous, etc
- Ask the opinions of other neutral members of the group
- Don't put potential cynics side by side at the meeting
- Add an appropriate touch of humour – not aimed at anyone, but something everyone will relate to
- Re-focus the group by reminding them of the common purpose or goal
- Focus on what's in the attendees' control

COMPETING/SEEKING RECOGNITION – People trying to talk the most and loudest, people who ramble and those trying to draw attention to themselves.

Possible solutions:
- Ask closed questions, i.e., those requiring only a yes or no answer
- Question them on the facts – focus on the objective
- Ask specific questions to the whole group
- Don't compete with dominant members
- Use group collaboration techniques and tools – there's a great selection later in this book
- Ask them to explain the relevance of their comments if they have drifted off
- Restate the objective of the meeting
- Bring in the opinions of others. For example, "Hang on Paul, I think Leanne may have a point to make."
- Stay alert. Ensure you spot when the conversation is drifting and when other people signal they want to wade in
- Hold a short review of feelings and behaviours and agree on improvement actions for the team/meeting
- Don't interrupt people mid-sentence, it will make them want to continue further or, worse, start again

SYMPATHY SEEKING – telling long stories, getting off the point, and making a drama out of their situation.

Possible solutions:
- Use nonverbal signals to indicate that the conversation has drifted, such as leaning forward, standing up or fixing eyes on the speaker to get their attention
- Make a polite comment to agree or park and move on
- Summarise the main point the person is trying to make
- Suggest a conversation outside the meeting one to one to sort out their specific problem or issue

BLOCKING – Rejecting ideas without listening, consistently contradicting suggestions of certain members due to long-standing differences or priorities.

Possible solutions:
- Encourage active listening of all members
- Give off positive body language
- Paraphrase visually using flipcharts or online platforms
- Separate the person from the problem – flipcharts and LEGO® bricks de-personalise extremely well
- Focus on solutions
- Check-in to see what others think
- Use probing questions like, "How can we?"
- Use anonymous electronic voting systems (or sticky dots work well too)
- Set ground rules
- Use creative problem-solving tools and approaches

NEGATIVE HUMOUR – Sniping, negative jokes

Possible solutions:
- Question their facts
- Challenge them to elaborate on their comments
- Change the course of the conversation
- Set ground rules at the start and challenge them if they don't follow those rules during the meeting

WITHDRAWING – daydreaming, whispering, doodling, not contributing

Possible solutions:
- Ensure the right people are at the meeting and they can gain or add value
- Ask questions to bring them into the process
- Use group exercises and process tools
- Ask questions to the whole group and get responses from everyone
- Use smaller group work to engage everyone
- Have a break
- Change state or energy with an energiser or learning point activity

Many different things that can be done to overcome and remove challenging behaviours. Prevention is better than cure. If you can spend time with the people in the meeting, building relationships, trust and understanding, there will be less chance of experiencing negative group dynamics. As you'll see in the Inspired Meeting Framework later in the book, a correctly crafted meeting will create the environment, energy, and process to stealthily prevent behaviours from being an issue.

Playing to strengths

I've lost count of how many different profiling tools I have completed over the years. Some of these have been used with negative intent (Psychometrics for recruitment mainly), some have been over-complicated. I felt like I needed to have studied the topic at university to understand it. Still, in the main, they have added huge value to me, the teams I have been part of, and how we work together. They have often been instrumental in building high levels of vulnerability-based trust making conversations and interactions in meetings rich, productive and fun. Whatever approach you take to discovering people's strengths and approaches, you must apply some simple principles:

1. Do not overcomplicate it with jargon and label people.

2. Always apply it to context, i.e. when we do this it's due to this.

3. Remember, it's a way of demonstrating people are different and the difference should be valued.

4. Make it a part of what you do and consider it when designing processes.

Before we go into a little more detail, it is very important to bear one thing in mind when understanding these tools. In the words of a great friend of mine (you know who you are) "These things are just conversation starters." Each tool has its benefits and features that can be applied to your situation, but the most important thing is that whatever you choose to use adds value.

Some of my favourites include:

- **Life Orientations (LIFO®)**
- **Facet5**
- **TetraMap**
- **Belbin Team Roles**

Other popular tools include Myers Briggs Type Indicator® (MBTI®), Everything DiSC®, Insights Discovery™, NEO PI-R and 16 Personality Factors (16PF).

Later in the **Tools for Meeting** section of this book, I have included two very simple, costless tools you can use to help understand strengths, build a team, align people to meetings, and having fun. These are called MAD SAD GLAD and Shapes.

I have chosen to share a little more detail about Life Orientations® (LIFO®) here in this book, mainly because I have used it for over 15 years and applied it in many sectors and organisations. It has many applications but I'm going to put my spin on its use in the context of a meeting.

Life Orientations® or LIFO® as it is often referred to is used in over 30 countries around the world and has specific applications in areas such as Leadership, Team Development, Learning and Teaching, Stress, Time Management, Culture, Sales and Negotiation. It was created by Dr Stuart Atkins and Dr Allan Katcher and is based on the work of Erich Fromm and Carl Rogers. LIFO® goes back to the late 1960s and continues to be extremely powerful and impactful today. The method identifies four distinct styles with different drives and motivations that generate behaviour patterns. Personality forms a part of someone's behaviours, but LIFO® isn't a personality profiling tool. Originally a paper-based questionnaire of 18 questions and, at the time of writing is currently available on paper and electronically in different countries and has been translated into many different languages. Completion of the survey will provide scores in the four styles or orientations indicating your behavioural strengths in favourable and unfavourable circumstances (under stress and pressure).

The four styles or orientations are:

SUPPORTING GIVING
CONTROLLING TAKING
CONSERVING HOLDING
ADAPTING DEALING

Though we'll explore what each of the orientations means in relation to meetings, I thought it might be useful to describe each at a fairly top level to help tune in with the model. Beforehand, though, let me share a little insight from my initial training in the method that has stuck with me since I first discovered it.

Windows to the world

On the training course, we were shown a picture of a building and told it was called La Rotonda. A beautifully built stone building on top of a hill in Italy – I'm sure there are many like this around the world. The sides of the pictured building were open and held up by huge stone pillars. From inside the building, you could look out from all four sides and had stunning views across Italy. You could see for many, many miles on a good day. Because of its position you had a different view out of each side. If you stood and looked directly out of each side, you had a choice of looking at the distant mountains, the rolling farmlands, the beautiful forests, or the distant ocean. We were asked to imagine ourselves standing in the building and to stand in a place in the room that we would be most comfortable looking out. There were 8 of us on the course, and we all stood in different places to simulate our preferred view. When asked, I explained that I love the outdoors and being active, so I imagined myself standing in a place where I could see the mountains and the forests to think about

97

adventures I've had or want to have. Each person, in turn, gave their reason for where they stood and as well as learning something interesting about the others, the penny dropped about what was to come – we can often be in the same place as others, but we will all have our preference and perspective on what we see and experience.

The facilitator continued with this analogy and chose to use my example. She said there were four windows from which I could look out, but I, as did a couple of others, chose to find a place where I could see out of two of them, whilst others stood firmly looking out of one window. This was interpreted as them having a strong preference for one view and that I liked a blend of two. No one at this stage said they like all four, but that is possible. But here's another thing, if I have one or two strong preferences and stand near to that window it is visible and predictable. If I had no strong preference and were happy to see all four views, I would find it difficult to find one place where I could see them and would therefore have to move around quite a lot, and others may be confused a little by that.

My biggest takeaway during this was that there is no best fit or right answer. Each person has their own view of the world, which affects what they see and how they behave. It also shows that things can change. Although I'm not a fan of the seaside, I could look out of that window if I needed to. Or I may experience something that changes my mind about going on a cruise ship, so I would then develop a preference to that particular window. This is the same for our behaviours and is how we often describe our use of LIFO®. I may have a strong preference for the Conserving orientation, but a change in job role or way of working may cause my preference to move more towards the Supporting or Adapting orientation. Or it may also be that in certain (possibly stressful) situations, I display behavioural strengths of a different orientation and then revert to another preferred style when not under any stress.

Let's take a brief look at the four orientations or styles within the LIFO® method:

SUPPORTING GIVING	
Philosophy – "If I prove my worth by working hard and pursuing excellence, the good things in life will come to me." "I value excellence."	
Goals – Prove worth. Be helpful.	Values Excellence
Language (pronoun) – We	Emphasis – People/Reflective
Strengths – Principled, cooperative, dedicated, pursues excellence, considerate, idealistic, trusting, responsive, and helpful.	

CONTROLLING TAKING	
Philosophy – "If I can get results by being competent and seizing opportunities, the good things in life will be there for the taking." "I value action."	
Goals – Be competent. Get Results.	Values Action
Language (pronoun) – Me	Emphasis – Task/Active
Strengths – Persistent, initiating, urgent, directing, forceful, competitive, persuasive, quick to act, confident and seeks change.	

CONSERVING HOLDING	
Philosophy – "If I think before I act and make the most of what I've got, I can build up my supply of the good things in life." "I value reason."	
Goals – Be careful. Get it right.	Values Reason
Language (pronoun) – It	Emphasis – Task/Reflective
Strengths – Systematic, analytical, maintaining, tenacious, practical, thorough, methodical, detail orientated, factual, reserved, and steadfast.	

ADAPTING DEALING	
Philosophy – "If I please other people and fill their needs first, then I can get the good things in life that I've wanted all along." "I value harmony."	
Goals – Know people. Get along.	Values Harmony
Language (pronoun) – You	Emphasis – People/Active
Strengths – Empathetic, tactful, flexible, enthusiastic, sociable, adaptable, experimental, animated, inspiring, and negotiating.	

When it comes to strengths and behaviours, there are risks. In my view, there are two main risks:

1   Overplaying or overusing strengths. When this happens, people tend to become rigid in their approach, and a lack of flexibility can use strengths to excess. For example, the strength of liking a quick pace, variety, and new opportunities can in excess, turn into not paying enough attention to maintain existing projects.

2 Strong or dominant strengths which are opposite to those you are working with. For example, a people-focussed strength of being flexible and adaptable can be seen by others as inconsistent and lacking conviction.

There are simple ways to self assess yours and others preferred LIFO® orientation, by looking at their strengths or the language they use. Or if you want to complete a full survey or get your team to complete the survey, you'll be able to search on the internet for a provider in your country.

Each of the four orientations has preferred ways of working and conditions in which they operate best. Here's how I believe they translate into a meeting environment.

SUPPORTING GIVING	CONTROLLING TAKING
Needs to know the purpose, looking to understand who benefits. Wants to help others. Will look to do things in the best possible way.	Will be driven for results. Wants to know the advantage of doing anything. Will play to a hierarchy.
Will be keen to collaborate and work as a team. Conversations will be Warm, friendly, questioning and listens before talking.	They will be direct with you and challenge you. Everything appears urgent. They will get straight to the point with little small talk. Often direct and to the point. Volume will increase with urgency and can interrupt others.

CONSERVING HOLDING	ADAPTING DEALING
Wants to know why it's required. Will look to find out if and how something has been done before.	Is interested in knowing what others think. Wants to know that the outcomes are good for reputation of them or people in the team.
Will behave in a cautious manner. Comments and contributions will be methodical, analytical, and based on data. Will be serious and precise when communicating. Direct but calm. Can often be silent. Seeks clarity with questions.	Will be uncomfortable with too much formality. Wants to make friends and get to know people. Is flexible and open to ideas. Will talk lots, lively, enthusiastic and use stories and humour (sometimes when not necessary), enthusiastic but may not listen well.

Simplicity

I often talk about the benefits of simplifying the complex. There are great resources out there that aid in demonstrating the power of simplifying things, one particular resource that I love to use is a TEDx Talk by Graham Shaw, called, "Why people believe they can't draw - and how to prove they can." In the video Graham introduces a process that can be followed to drawn cartoon-type characters using some easy steps. Each step has options, for example there are many types of mouths that can be added to each character, or hair and hats. Regardless of the options, each character is created with some simple steps – nose – eyes – the mouth – ear – hair – neck. Very often, if we think something is difficult, we over complicate it, create too many options in our heads, delay action or worry and don't event try, a bit like being asked to draw a picture of a person.

When it comes to meetings, I think the same can be true. We may know that something needs to change to improve our meetings, but we think it is too big a job or that people won't like it. I believe it's important to break it down. Think about what you want to change or what you want to happen in a meeting or workshop and then break it into simple steps. Take these steps and do them one at a time. Once that change has embedded and you can see the difference it makes, try the next one.

If it's a new meeting or you're starting fresh with changing an existing meeting, keep it simple. Consider different aspects of this book and instead of being overwhelmed by so many pages of great thoughts, ideas, and tools, choose a small selection and give them a go.

Don't add too much to a meeting with bells and whistles; don't create too much work for yourself or overwhelm the attendees. Sometimes less is more, particularly when the 'less' is done well.

Thunks – it's all in the questions

I was introduced to a book by Ian Gilbert, called 'The Little Book of Thunks' some years ago, and since then have tried to think very hard about the questions I pose in meetings (I don't always get them right). The front cover of his book describes a Thunk as 'a beguiling question about everyday things that stops you in your tracks and helps you to start to look at the works in a whole new light.' Here's a few examples (there are more later in the books toolkit)

What colour is Tuesday?

Is a broken-down car parked?

What colour is a Zebra when you remove its stripes?

Is there more past or future?

Are you man made or natural?

Is a leaf on the tree or part of the tree?

The use of great questions in meetings has many benefits. Questions can be used in the planning phase, as part of an agenda, specifically within the process of a tool such as World Café, LEGO® Serious Play® (LSP) or Team Manifesto. They instantly get people thinking. If you know what you want the question to do, you can get very creative. They could be to;

- **Gather ideas**
- **Get feedback**
- **Explore data**
- **Give feedback**
- **Create options**
- **Make people think**

Questions don't always need to be such that answers received are definite or correct. You can create hugely impactful questions that generate information yet are still vague enough not to restrict thinking.

The poem, 'Six Honest Serving Men' by Rudyard Kipling also reminds me of the importance of the language used in questions when he starts by writing:

"I keep six honest serving men: (they taught me all I knew) Their names are **What** and **Where** and **When** and **How** and **Why** and **Who**."

A though the poem does say more, I want to just focus on this. Use of these six honest serving men will each get different types of answers within questions, so use them as a variety. Depending on their values and drivers, people will also respond differently. For example, constantly being asked, "Why?" could make some people feel under pressure or lots of questions, with '"Who?" could look like a lack of accountability.

For some of the tools later in this book, you'll see examples of questions and how they fit into different scenarios. All I ask is that you consider developing questions as part of your meetings. You'll be surprised at the impact they can have!

Repetition, Repetition, Repetition

As I write this short section, I am reminded of a quote that stuck with me from a conversation some years ago. We were discussing safety-critical skills such as knot tying in rock climbing, rifle maintenance in the forces and operating machinery on a construction site. One member of the conversation threw in the well-known phrase that, "Practice makes perfect." Whilst another person quickly jumped in and said that he believes the truth of the matter is, "Practice makes permanent." This still resonates with me, as I recall the conversation moving on and we agreed that practice will only ever make perfect if learning reviews happen and we are constantly adapting to changing needs and technology. Practice will also only be perfect if what you are doing is right in the first place.

But what has this got to do with meetings and repetition? If you like the sound of anything in this book and think you'll give it a go in your team meetings, please have the courage to do just that. But I want to warn you that, there is a high likelihood that you will either get negative feedback from the group because they didn't like it, or it was too childlike, or you may not get the desired output the first time around. This is not an opportunity to throw 'the baby out with the bathwater', but an opportunity to reflect, learn, adapt, and go again.

The first time I ran the Radiant Problem Solving (RPS) process with a team, it took nearly an hour, the sheets looked a bit messy, and conversations drifted. I was tempted to discard the process and try something else, but I decided to reflect on what happened and tweak it for the next time. Working with a different group a couple of weeks later, I led another RPS session with the changes I decided to make. The session was smoother and faster, with more outputs and more positive energy. I realised that it was certain elements of the process that would make it perfect, and it was the repetition that would make that perfection more permanent. Groups have since left those sessions and gone onto use them themselves, getting great results when solving problems.

So, call it what you want, 'repetition, repetition, repetition', or 'if at first, you don't succeed, try, try again'. But whatever you do, try something new, give it a go and build it into your meeting routine or drumbeat, and I can assure you it will make a difference to your meetings and workshops.

IT'S NOT UNTIL YOU HAVE SAID WHAT YOU ARE THINKING, CAN YOU TRULY THINK ABOUT WHAT YOU HAVE SAID.

— Bateson

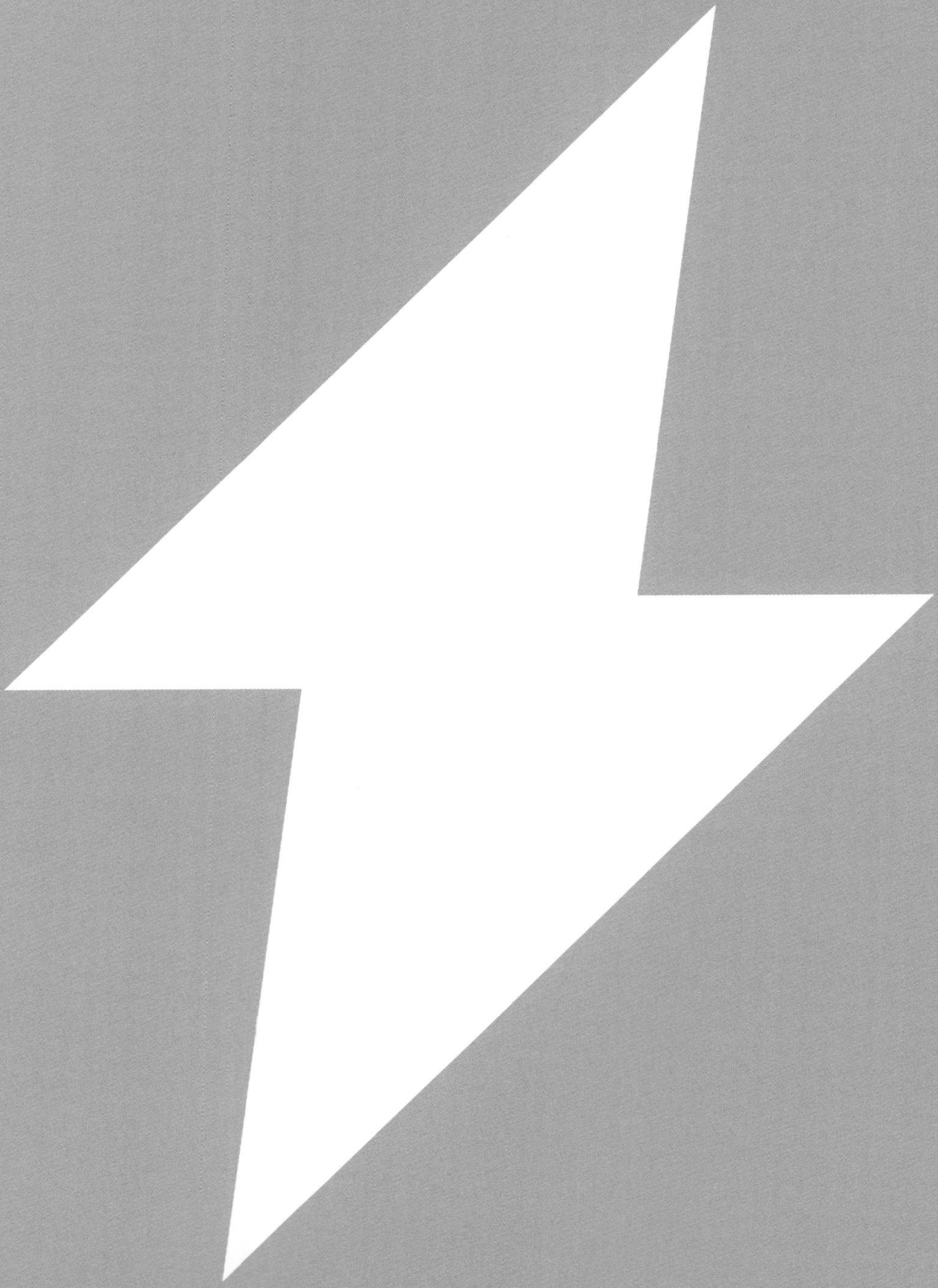

Section 2

The Inspired Meetings Framework

The key steps to successfully planning and executing your meetings

- The Inspired Meetings Framework ... 110
- CADAI – Crafting Aligning, Doing, Agreeing, and Implementing ... 111
- Craft your meeting ... 115
- Agendas ... 118
- Classic Meeting Agenda ... 119
- Tactical Meeting Agenda ... 120
- Visual Meeting Agenda (OARRs) ... 122
- Align everyone to the meeting ... 124
- Doing some stuff ... 126
- Agreeing actions and way forward ... 128
- Implementing agreed actions and way forward ... 132
- Inspired Meetings Health Checker ... 134
- Meetings Reality Check ... 140
- Inspired Meetings Framework overview ... 146

The Inspired Meetings Framework

Here's the game changing section. The bit you've been waiting for. We've had a deep dive into The Meeting Environment and given you lots of food for thought. Now, I will share with you the five steps to great meetings.

You may associate the abbreviation IMF with Tom Cruise films, where he solves global problems, saves people from high-risk situations and prevents devastation from occurring across the globe. Here the abbreviation will also help solve problems, support people and plan global strategies, but it will not be the impossible Mission Force; it will be the Inspired Meetings Framework. This chapter will explore the effective process that every meeting should go through in order to be successful. Created and modelled by myself and the team at Successfactory™ over many years, the Inspired Meetings Framework takes you logically and sequentially from the initial idea of a meeting right through to ensuring what happens afterwards is completed timely and makes a positive difference.

CADAI – Crafting, Aligning, Doing, Agreeing, and Implementing

There are five stages to the Inspired Meetings Framework, which can be remembered using the acronym CADAI. They are:

Crafting
Aligning
Doing
Agreeing
Implementing

Later in this section, I will go into detail on each of these, clarify what we mean by each of the words, what you should be doing, how and what you will gain by doing it.

Earlier in the book we delved into The Meeting Environment and compared it to the natural environment. Let's use this theme to explore how we can enjoy the environment. I've been lucky over the years to enjoy many different aspects of the natural environment in many different ways. I am proud to be able to call myself a competitive runner, a fell runner, a rock climber, a mountain biker, a mountaineer, and expedition leader. There are many more ways people enjoy the environment, but I have reflected on my experiences and how they link to the Inspired Meetings Framework.

Before we delve into the framework, we must consider the life of a meeting. All of my successful outdoor adventures (and some of the less successful) have started with what people often call a crazy idea, or a need, or maybe a desire, but importantly they have started before the actual activity. I'll delve into this more later in this section. For now, it links well to the image on the next page. When meetings are successful, it is because they fall into the green line. All good meetings start as soon as someone thinks, 'let's have a meeting to discuss that', if this is shared with potential attendees, it starts the green line, and we're off. Giving attendees opportunities to prepare and then checking in with them at the beginning is key to a meetings success. If you're in a good place, dealing with any negatives, such as poor sales, performance, or detrimental announcements, will cause feelings to drop but not create a deficit.

But why should we create negative emotions and deal with the 'bad' stuff early on? Well, one of the models I teach when running sessions on leading change is called Drivers Cap. Put simply the model starts by creating Dissatisfaction with the current Reality (DR), sharing, and building an Inspirational Vision (IV), establishing Easily Recognisable Steps (ERS) and planning for the Capability to change (CAP). We could look at most meetings as an aspect of managing and leading change, be it implementing new programmes and projects, increasing sales, or developing new products. This would mean that the lifespan of a meeting could be broken down into DR IV ERS CAP. Specifically though, if we want people to leave a meeting inspired to act on what has been agreed and make a real difference, we need to build a dissatisfaction with reality by sharing reasons why what is currently being done isn't the most effective (DR) and building an inspiring vision of what good can look like (IV) it may create discomfort, but it will encourage meeting attendees to buy in and engage in the items throughout the meeting. This is often called conflict, but essentially you are provoking meeting attendees and encouraging full participation. If you create the right environment with the best possible structure and use the most appropriate tools for the job, you will be well on track to creating instant results in the meeting and a real desire to leave the meeting and make a difference.

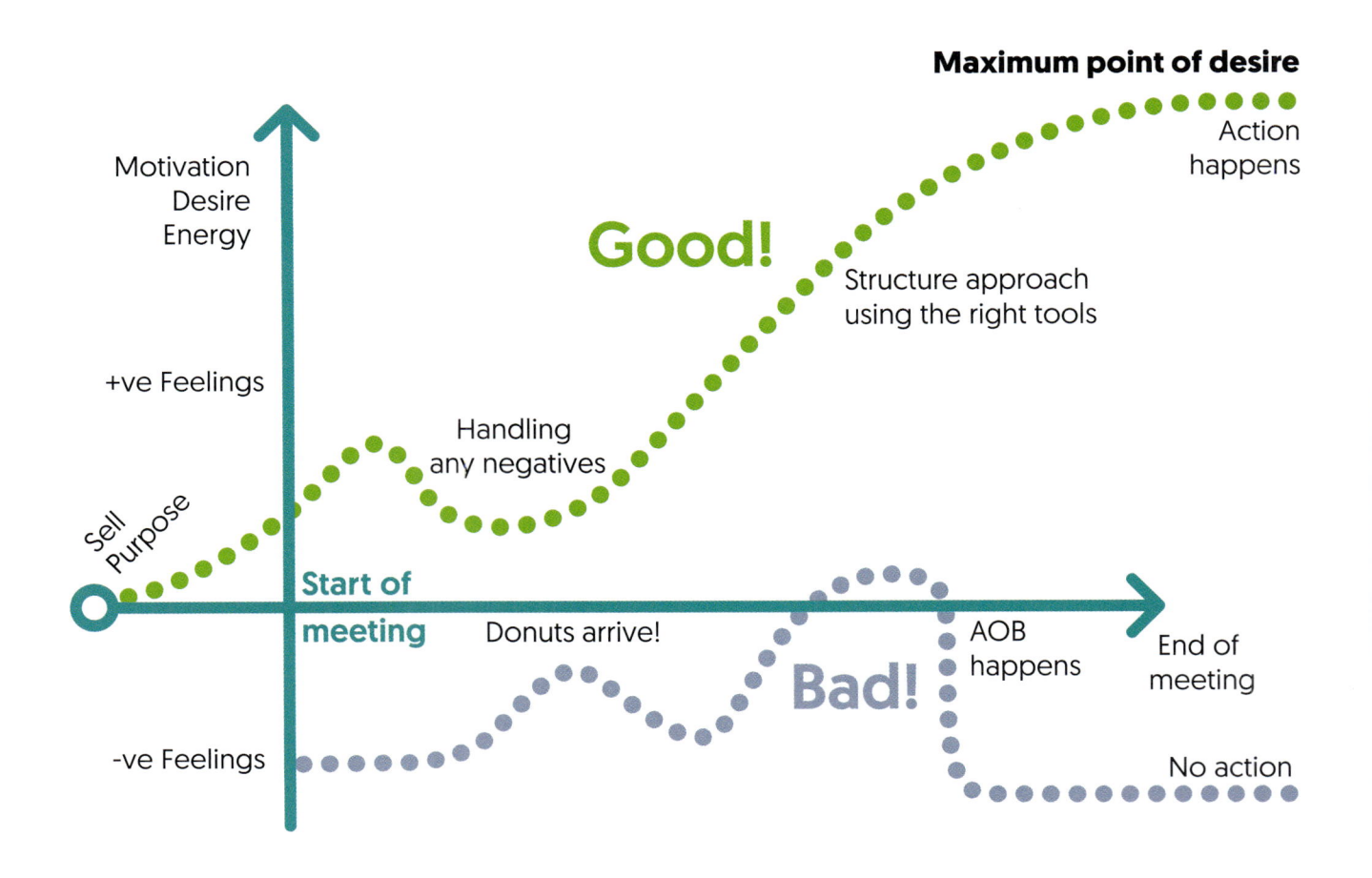

If there is no communication about the meeting, its purpose or objectives before the start time, there's a high chance that it will result in no or even negative impact. There will still be two highs in these poor meetings. Firstly, when there is a break and the body is topped up with not-so-helpful chemicals induced by caffeine and sugar, and secondly, when the penultimate agenda item is raised, known to many as 'any other business'. This is where people get their own back. Attendees think, "Right; I've had to put up with this crap meeting. Now I'm going to get something off my chest." Usually very tenuously linked to the meeting's purpose (if the purpose was ever known at all) and relevant only to one or two attendees. Someone will then state the date and time of the next meeting, which no one hears because it's already in their outlook calendar and their head is already in their next meeting which started five minutes ago. Everyone leaves and nothing happens.

Imagine if the bottom dotted line on this graph was how I approached my climbing trip. Just before I left the house, I might throw a rope and harness into my rucksack, a few other bits of kit and a guidebook. As I filled my car with fuel, I'd grab a stodgy end-of-life sandwich and a chocolate bar and an extortionately priced bottle of water, arrive at a busy car park, stuff the last half of the sandwich in the bag with the bottle of water, greet my climbing buddies and walk into the crag. We'd each share how bad our week had been at the office (probably because of 'piss poor back-to-back meetings') and then announce that we each need to leave at a completely different time during the day, limiting how many routes we can climb and leaving at least one of us high and dry on his own for about 90 minutes before they were planning to finish. Once we got that off our chest, we'd start to get going. Harnesses on, one would browse the guidebook to choose which route to start on and who would lead. The leader would then look at the crag and announce that they haven't got the right gear to do the route and ask if anyone could lend it to them. We scrabbled enough kit together and set off. A bit lacklustre, but half an hour later, all party members had climbed that route, and it was time to choose the next one. I open my chocolate bar and it starts to rain, reminding me I hadn't packed my waterproof jacket. After my soggy chocolate bar and sandwich we start again, successfully lead a nice route and swapped over. As my buddy climbed, he dislodged some loose rock which I just managed to dodge as it fell to the ground, reminding me that my climbing helmet was in the doorway at home, not on my head. I climbed after my buddy and spotted his gear was well placed. I reached for my nut key (a little metal problem solving tool) but I didn't have it. I have to unclip his gear, climb past it, and leave it for someone else to remove later on (if they could). We did a couple more routes, probably five in total, as our climbing buddies started to slowly depart one at a time to their other commitments. We got some stuff done, not as much as I hoped on the drive there, and the risks were high with kit left at home and poor time management. To top it off, I got home to read a text of one of the lads who had got to his car to find a parking ticket, something that would have been avoided if we had read the guidebook to the crag.

Truth be told, whilst I've had one or two 'epics' on climbing trips and one memorable accident, I've never had a day as badly planned and executed as the one described here. Partly because I've always planned in advance and partly due to having climbed with good people too. But I've seen many people on the hill or crag in this state. As we explore the Inspired Meetings Framework, its keys to success and links with different ways to use our meeting environment we will examine some more examples.

CADAI – Crafting, Aligning, Doing, Agreeing, and Implementing

There are five stages to the Inspired meetings framework, which can be remembered using the acronym CADAI. They are:

Crafting
Aligning
Doing
Agreeing
Implementing

In this section, I will go into detail on each of these, provide clarity on what we mean by each of the words, what you should be doing, how and what you will gain by doing it.

Craft your meeting

Purpose — To ensure we have designed the right approach for the right meeting.

Activity — During this phase, we confirm the meeting's purpose, generate ideas, develop an agenda and select the tools to be used.

Outcomes — If your meeting is effectively crafted, you will have created an appropriate agenda, gained buy-in from meeting stakeholders and chosen the right environment for the meeting.

Tools, Techniques and Templates
There are many tools that crossover, but the following specifically add value at this stage:
- Agenda templates, including:
  - Tactical Meeting Guide
  - Classic Agenda
  - OARRs Template
- Stick to the Plan
- Group dynamics and ground rules

Imagine saying to some friends let's go and climb a mountain, giving them a date, location, and time to meet. Then for weeks you don't speak. You plan a route that involves a little bit of scrambling, some quite steep hills, a section of open moorland and a large area of forest. But you don't share the route with the group because you didn't think it will add any value, it would take too much of your time, and they all know what they're doing anyway. As the date approaches, you and the group watch the weather forecasts and start to plan clothing, equipment, and food for the day. You hear from a friend that there's a nice coffee shop at the end, so the day before you send them all a message saying, "See you tomorrow for a great but challenging day. It'll all be worth it, and I'll buy you all a coffee at the end from the lovely café I've been told about."

When you meet your friends at the agreed car park, there are some very mixed responses, especially when you share the planned route with them. Here's what happens:

- One member of the group had been there before, so they arrived early, had plenty of change for the pay and display car park and saw that the weather was looking mixed, so he had warm drinks with him, the most appropriate kit for a mixed day and you had a chat whilst waiting for the others.
- As one or two more arrived, they were a little flustered by the directions that the sat nav had taken them down a tricky single lane, and they had stopped carrying cash and couldn't pay for parking. Thankfully you and your first friend to arrive had a little pot of loose change and could pay for their parking.
- One group member arrived with a wrist brace following an accident she had a few weeks earlier. You'd heard about it, but weren't aware of her injuries and realise she might be unable to do the scrambling section.
- Eventually, you have all but one friend (seven turn up), who has sent a message saying they can't attend due to childcare and had assumed it would be a long day and wouldn't be able to get back in time for picking his son up from the childminder. The message was late and you don't start the walk until nearly 45 minutes later than planned.
- As you set off, you pass the lovely-looking café and tell the group that's where you'll all finish the day. All but two of them reveal that that would have been lovely with more notice, but they have to get back to their families, so they won't be able to stay. This annoys you a little, and you think they're not really committed friends, but you don't say anything, instead behave in a frosty manner for the start of the walk, which definitely doesn't help the mood as the rain has also started.
- Finally, as the rest of the group is engaging in a bit of small talk at the start of the day, you're trying to think of alternatives to keep your friend with the injured hand involved in the route, keep everyone else safe, yet still have a challenge as that's why you wanted the scramble part of the route.

This isn't the best start for what you hoped would be a really good day with friends, sharing an experience together, having some fun and learning together.

Have you done this to your friends?

Has this been done to you?

Does this feel like any meetings that you've attended?

I'm going to hazard a guess that you've answered yes at least one of these scenarios? My best trips to the outdoors have been when I've shared the full intent and plan with friends and, better still when we've CRAFTED the plan together. We poured over maps, shared ideas, and agreed what we were going to do. We've then shared responsibilities such as finding out what facilities like parking and cafés are nearby, plotting the route on a map and route card, emailing the group well ahead of the date and even planning to share the driving. Everyone was excited about it and messaged each other before the trip with things they'd found out about the area and if they were missing some kit, they also asked each other. No one was surprised about anything in the plan, and decisions were made together. On occasions when friends have been busy and said to one member of the group, "Why don't you plan a route or pick the location?" That worked well, too, because the person who suggested the location would share with the group and group members who maybe wanted something different or had any thoughts on this would openly share and feel comfortable doing so.

My first example here reminds me also of so many meetings that I've been invited to with no agenda, no idea of the purpose and therefore, no opportunity for me to plan effectively, both physically and mentally. I'm a big believer in the phrase 'inclusion equals commitment'. This isn't just in relation to meetings; it's in many of aspects of work and life. If you engage key stakeholders early in planning, they buy in, feel accountable and commit. It could be simply asking them what they want to get out of a meeting? If they would like to commit to helping run part of the meeting or take on a specific role?

Remember, meetings start from the moment some has the idea, 'let's have a meeting'.

Agendas

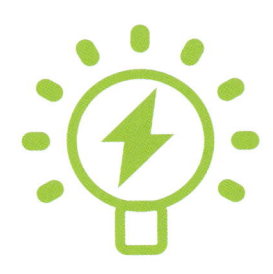

Classic Meeting Agenda

But with two twists. The example agenda template here is a great and simple format. It can be used for most types of meetings, but the key to its success is the effective use of the 'Topic' and 'How' columns.

1. Topic – The topic should be written as a question. Not the old, outdated statements or abbreviations such as Health and Safety or Project Update. We should be sending agendas in advance with questions that will get attendees in the best mindset possible and allow them to prepare. Questions could be, "How is each department working to keep our staff safe?" Or, "Where are our projects up to, and what's working well with them?"
2. How – attendees will get a good idea of what the meeting will look and feel like when they see what's in the 'How' column. This might be PowerPoint, verbal briefing or one of the many tools described later in this book, such as Radiant Problem Solving, World Café, Ease Impact Grid, etc.

Meeting Name/Title:				
Purpose:				
Date:				
Location:				
Start and Finish Times:				
Attendees:				
Meeting Roles:				
Timing	Topic (written as a question)	Who leads	How (tools, techniques, process)	Expected Outcomes

Tactical Meeting Agenda

The following template can be used or adapted to work well on any meeting that is short, sharp, and regular. Tactical items can be covered at pace in this format. It isn't very useful, if at all, for strategic items that require discussion, problem-solving and idea generation. With this approach, it is key to have a clear process and format, but the actual content will not be known until the meeting occurs. It can be supported with some of the tools from the toolkit to add variety and get below the surface. I would recommend you consider its use for Daily Stand-Up type meetings, Weekly Tactical meetings and other short remote/online meetings. It is important that pace is maintained, and attendees are encouraged to follow the rules and timekeeping. This helps with flow, content and generally keeping on track. The following example works for up to 60 minutes but can be adjusted by shortening items or removing them depending on the need and team size. It should never take longer than the agreed format time, but if it takes less time, accept it then move on. A template can be created and used on a big board to provide a stand-up focus point, each member may have a template to write on personally, or it could be annotated online in programmes such as Concept Board or Mural.

1. Lightening Round and Check-in	2. Key Metrics Review Goal / Metrics R A G	3. Tactical Agenda Items Order topics • • • •
4. Cascading Messages	5. Decisions, Actions & Check-out	6. Potential Strategic Topics

Adapted from Patrick Lencioni's Death by Meeting

1. **Lightening Round and Check-In.** (5 – 10 minutes) – each team member is to list and share their top three things on their plate for the coming day/week, depending on meeting frequency. This should take no longer than one minute per person, even with a couple of follow-up questions. The meeting lead or relevant other team members should note anything that needs further discussion.
2. **Key Metrics Review.** (5 – 10 minutes) – Review the key metrics of the business, department or team and note the current status of each. These metrics should be those which the team have previously identified as critical for your success.
3. **Tactical Agenda Items.** (30 minutes) – Discuss the potential tactical issues to be covered, assign an order for the discussion and dive in. These issues may have come up in the lightning round or the key metrics review. Using problem solving tools such as Radiant Problem Solving or the '5 Whys' may be appropriate to help answer a question or provide focus.
4. **Cascading Messages.** (5 minutes) – Discuss what, if anything, each team member should communicate to their direct reports following the meeting and agree on a time frame for that to occur.
5. **Decisions, Actions and Check-out.** (5 minutes) – Ask one team member to chart the decisions and actions that were committed to during the meeting. Team leaders should note these as well. Check-out by confirming everyone knows the actions and that everyone is onboard.
6. **Potential Strategic Topics** – As you progress through your meeting, use this area to note topics that you need to cover during a strategic meeting. Be sure to resist the temptation to resolve these issues right away.

Visual Meeting Agenda (OARRs)

A fantastic structure from The Grove Consultants and is often referred to as a Meeting Start-up. This template works equally for small group meetings and large conference-type events. I truly believe that inclusion equals commitment and by spending time agreeing on the desired Outcomes, Agenda, Roles, and Rules (OARRs) as part of your meeting process increases trust and buy-in to the event and increases the likelihood of greater results.

YOUR COMPANY'S MEETING

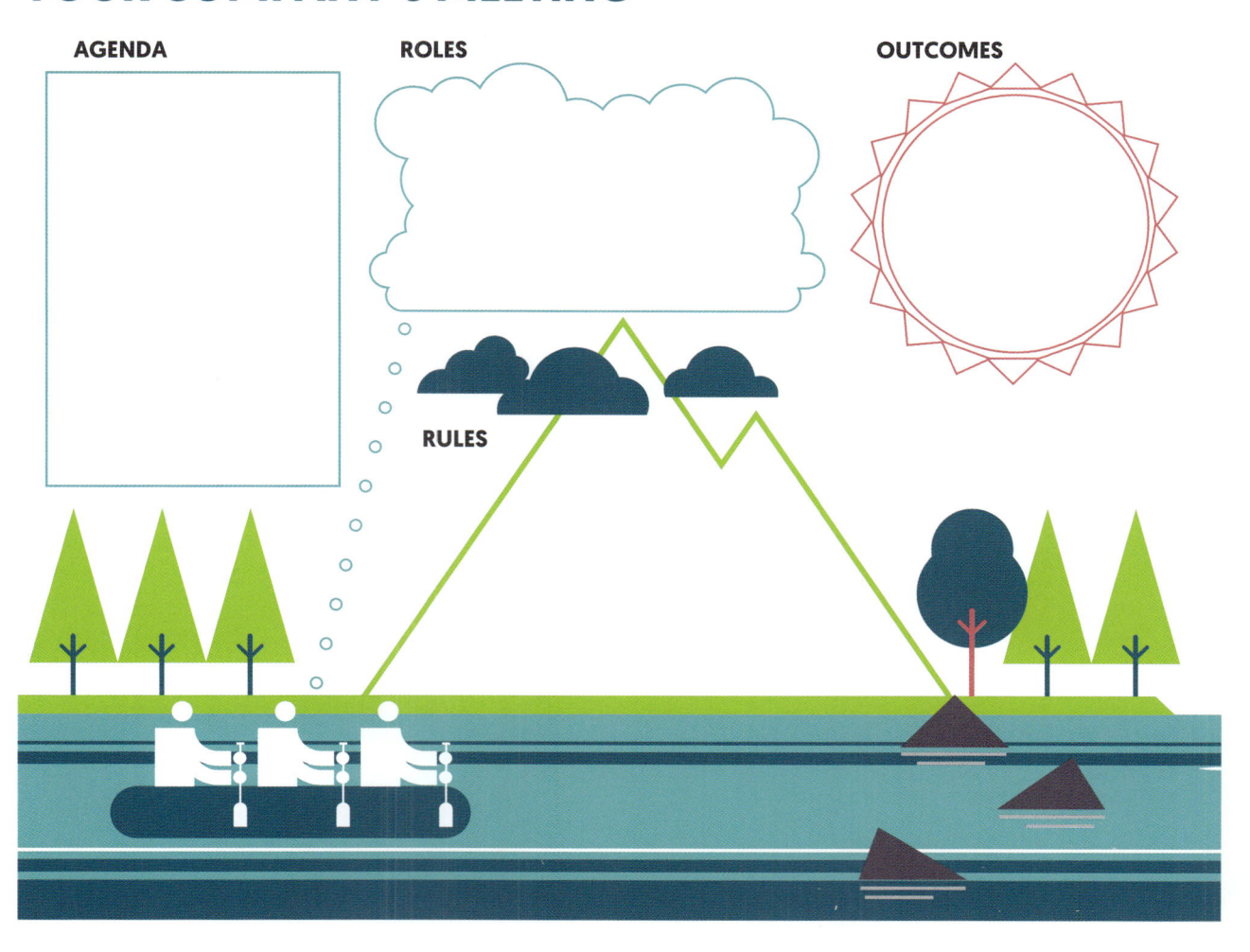

AGENDA

ROLES

OUTCOMES

RULES

PRIOR PREPARATION AND PLANNING PREVENTS A PISS POOR PERFORMANCE

Anon

Align everyone to the meeting

Purpose – To ensure everyone knows why they are here and can contribute fully.

Activity – Whilst aligning attendees to your meetings, you will clarify its purpose, confirm or create the agenda, ensure buy-in and undertake activities to enable them all to 'be in the room'.

Outcomes – Successful alignment will ensure the meeting has the right energy at the right times, everyone will have clarity around the meeting, be committed and have de-risked the meeting.

Tools, Techniques & Templates –
- Hopes and Fears
- OAARs agenda
- Questions
- Check-ins
- Fluctuating feelings
- Blobs
- 5 Whys
- Experiential exercises and icebreakers

I've led many events in the outdoors, from multi-activity trips where attendees take part in rafting, rock climbing, hiking, cultural visits, kayaking, mountain biking and more to multiday expeditions where participants have been on a self-sufficient journey, across wild country terrain, in unfamiliar environments and often with team members that they either don't know at all or have very little knowledge of. Our aims have always been met, but with varying degrees of success. The more we've included them in CRAFTING the venture, the easier ALIGNMENT has been. If collaborative crafting has been minimal, alignment has had to be more formal, structured, and purposeful. As you can imagine, these trips can be extremely challenging, need lots of co-ordination and involve many of different people dynamics. There was one particular event that I led on an annual basis for several years. The way we shared the event programme each year was the same. A small team developed it, had it approved by the organisation's HQ, and then shared it with successful applicants by email with some follow-up questions from those who wanted to engage. However, that was about it. Up to 40 young people would attend to take part in a 7-day event which had a main aim of planning, preparing for and undertaking a 4-day, 3-night expedition in wild country (known widely as a Duke of Edinburgh's Award Gold Expedition). The first day would include a series of briefings, icebreaker type activities and route planning. The second day would be an acclimatisation walk, it should be in similar terrain to their main 4-day expedition to check knowledge and skills and to allow the group to tune in to each other, and the day would finish with adjustments to their main route as a result of the findings from the acclimatisation day, kit checks and often a hearty final freshly cooked big meal before an early night. Day three would then be the start of their Gold Expedition, and off they would go with safety support, remote supervision, and little interaction from their leaders unless necessary for their safety or the aims of the venture.

The degree to which each team would succeed has always, for me, linked directly to how their first two days of alignment and acclimatisation went. Some of the keys to their success were:

- They often lived in different parts of the country and came together for the event for the first time, they were different ages (often between 17 and 24), and it was important to understand what had got them to where they are now and what they wanted to achieve on their expedition.
- The location of the event would often have an influence on their aim/purpose for the main expedition, but overall, they had to decide an aim and agree upon it. It could be as simple as 'to explore the changing flora and fauna in the area they were in' or maybe 'to assess, examine and study a particular part of the area such as previous industrial uses.' Sometimes it was less about the area and more about how the team operated together during a challenging venture.
- Each young person had different levels of skills in areas such as campcraft, cooking, navigation, first aid equipment selection and exploration techniques. This was fine as long as they each had a base knowledge in each area to help them through the event. But they could each settle into roles and responsibilities based on their skill – navigator, chef, etc. A real opportunity to put aces in places.
- Their acclimatisation walk had to strike a balance. Between demonstrating they had the skill to complete their plan and not pushing too hard that it stretched them too far too early. Essentially, we had to establish what 'flow' would be for them. I don't recall a time when my team set too hard a challenge for the group on the acclimatisation day, but there have been a few occasions when they haven't matched it to their route, and the group hadn't been tested for the appropriate level of the challenge ahead of them.

Doing some stuff

Purpose — To ensure we are using the right collaboration tools and techniques.

Activity — Meetings should be about doing stuff, not just sharing information that could be on a bulletin or email. The right activity will facilitate the agenda appropriately and ensure ongoing review and full participation.

Outcomes — Using well-selected processes and tools will get the insights that you need, ideas created, suitable actions identified and ensure accountability.

Tools, Techniques & Templates —
- Radiant Problem solving
- Cross that Bridge
- World café
- Disney technique
- Masterminding
- Nice to Speak
- History map
- SPOT Matrix/SWOT Analysis
- Story Dice
- Global CV
- Open Space
- LEGO® Serious Play® (LSP)
- Tough Discussion Dies
- Experiential learning activities

I once arrived early for an outdoor activity session. Whilst in the car park waiting for others to arrive, I saw other groups kitting up by their cars and vans. I decided to do the same. Wet suit on, floatation device, sticky shoes, and my old kayaking helmet. I was ready to spend the day gorge scrambling and jumping into rock pools. It was raining, but there was some shelter under the trees. I remember being told by the instructor it was going to be wet, we'd need good footwear for the slippery rocks, and to bring a helmet because he didn't have enough for everyone. It turns out I'd prepared for the wrong thing, and we were going rock climbing for the day and when he said it was going to be wet was more about the weather forecast than the activity. I guess I should have asked more questions and paid less attention to the others in the car park.

There have also been times when I had seen the weather forecast and thought it might cause us to change our planned activity. On one occasion, we were actually due to go rock climbing, but it was a popular area and the weather looked very heavy with rain. I packed my climbing kit, but also took walking boots, a different rucksack, some maps, and my other walking gear. When we arrived at the agreed start point, we had a chat, looked at the weather and decided a short drive to a different start point, and a walk in a slightly dryer (still rainy) and generally safer area was the way forward. So sometimes, over planning, having spare kit and having options is a good idea.

In a meeting context, this reminds me a little of the phrase, 'If the only tool you have is a hammer, you will start treating all your problems like a nail'. Good crafting and sharing of the purpose and plan will allow you and other meeting attendees to prepare. It will provide opportunities for the right tools to be selected for the aims you are hoping to achieve. Once you've agreed on the agenda and selected the tools to use (ideally from the awesome toolkit in this book) you can plan, prepare and, if necessary, rehearse. If the tool selected for a particular agenda item is unfamiliar to you or the group, I'd definitely recommend a practice run and when it comes to using it for real, be prepared to be uncomfortable being uncomfortable. The more you use something, the easier it will be and the better it will flow.

As well as selecting the right tools, they should also be used to the best effect and with the best equipment available. There are lots on this in the 'things you can see' section of this book.

The worst thing you can do in the DOING section of any meeting is not to engage with the audience. Problem-solving and idea generation should be collaborative, as should data sharing and briefings. Asking questions to specific parts of the group confirms they're 'getting it' and gives you the confidence to move on. In planning routes for hiking and expeditions, these are called check points and are opportunities to review, reflect and check learning, a time to take on fluids and check no one has lost any vital equipment. Don't always ask the same people. If it's a briefing or data sharing, using a tool such as NICE to Speak can be a very effective way of keeping people engaged.

Agreeing actions and way forward

Purpose — To ensure we make effective decisions and aligned action plans.

Activity — During the last phase of the meeting, you will ensure effective decisions are made, create a plan and agree on the plan and way forward. You should always take the opportunity to review the meeting.

Outcomes — A clear and agreed-upon action plan that everyone in attendance can live with, is committed and bought into.

Tools, Techniques & Templates –
- Gantt Charts
- Route Mapping
- Stick to the Plan
- OGSM – Plan on a Page
- Action Plan
- Ease Impact Grid
- Game Plan
- Desirable Viable Feasible
- Dr Iv Ers Cap
- Agile Board
- Cover Story
- Red Teaming
- Playing Emergence
- Gaining Consensus

There have been many times when on expeditions and mountain walking trips where other party members and I have been 'geographically misplaced' or, as others have mistakenly called it – lost. Only on one or two occasions has it caused enough stress and concern to really be a problem, even though there have been many times it has cost lots in respect of time and the occasional bus ride we weren't planning. Getting misplaced on a journey, side tracked by the weather or even an opportunity that arises isn't a bad thing. The important this is to know how to get back on track and limit any negative impact on the overall aim.

I remember on one occasion, planning routes and itineraries in detail for a multi-team trip. Each team had a purpose for their venture. It may have been to explore the local slate mines and their impact on the environment. For some it was to observe and record moorland access methods for different recreational modes of travel, and one team were to look at the impact of the route and the weather on the team dynamics. With this in mind, they planned suitable routes to help them achieve that aim and allocate time at different locations to explore. They decided what food, equipment, and additional support they may need. One team decided they needed some additional training to help them best achieve their aim. Another team discovered that one team member had a recurring injury and that it would be beneficial to have some equipment re-positioned so they didn't have to carry everything. Each team member took on a role such as navigator, first aider, camp chef and photographer. Whilst they were all able to undertake each role one individual was responsible for that area. They all went through their plan in detail, asked what if and developed contingencies. They had a thorough and workable plan.

The day came for them to set off and undertake their journey. My role as a leader was to ensure a team of supervisors and support staff facilitated the success of these teams, monitor their progress but keep a distance and ensure they were meeting the agreed quality criteria. The teams all completed their ventures and achieved their aim. One team without a glitch, one team took a wrong turn that took them hours out of their way and they had to find an alternative wild camp before getting back on track the following day. The third team (not with the guy with the recurring injury) were delayed on one day by an injury in the team and the time taken to recover her, then when back on track the following day, saw an opportunity to delve a little deeper into the purpose of their venture which gave them greater learning than anticipated and a little less journeying time due to the amended route. They were all successful because they operated with their purpose in mind, followed the plan as best they could, used the training and contingencies to solve problems and all played their part.

If the teams hadn't planned to the right level of detail, agreed roles and rules, and truly bought into them, it would have likely been a different outcome and less successful. In the Agreeing Actions and Way Forward stage of the Inspired Meetings Framework, the same appropriate level of detail is planned and agreed, in a format that works for the team, with clarity and accountability. This will drive an urge for action, mean that the agreed outputs are driven for, and the team(s) are able to get back on track if de-railed at all. A plan is simply the best guess at what you want to happen and whilst teams will often succeed it won't be without some deviation or changes to the plan. For me, success with 85% accuracy is better than no success due to being too rigid.

Using some of the tools above to harvest, collate and prioritise the findings from your meeting will ensure that everyone leaves knowing what needs to be done, by who and when. Accountability and commitment are key, and you need to use methods and approaches that get more than a nod from the group members, and that means when they leave the meeting, they are all on the same page. I remember hearing someone say, "You don't have to agree with everything, but you must be able to live with it." I think this is a great way to end a meeting, ensuring that you've used the best processes possible to gain clarity and consensus, but then (as is often the case in life) when you don't fully agree with something you show a united front and work with the team to pull in the same direction.

Take a moment to think about your meetings and ask yourself if attendees are always clear about what needs to happen next. Are they clear about their own actions and have enough knowledge of each other's takeaways to be able to support them and give what I call a gentle nudge as things progress?

THE MOST IMPORTANT PART OF A MEETING IS WHAT HAPPENS AFTERWARDS.

Graham Wilson

Implementing agreed actions and way forward

Purpose — To ensure everyone is committed to making the actions happen.

Activity — Attendees will follow through on activity and actions, support each other and hold each other accountable. Progress will be reviewed, and success celebrated. Learning will be implemented.

Outcomes — The benefits of the meeting will be realised; action will be sustained, and attendees will look forward to the next meetings.

Tools, Techniques and Templates
- Action Learning tools
- Stop Start Continue
- S-WOT's your story
- Quick Coaching
- Ease Impact Grid

Most events that are a success are often repeated. Sometimes a repeat of the project or process is happening concurrently whilst a similar item is underway. This has been the same in my time in the outdoors as in my work life. There are always similarities and, at the same time, major differences. I like to think about well-known phrases and challenge them, so here's one that embodies the importance on Implementing agreed actions and way forward. You have heard the phrase, 'if you always do what you've always done, you'll always get what you've always got.' For some time, that was true, but now with the pace of change and the complexity in our world, I believe that 'if you always do what you've always done, you'll get less than you always got'. The reason for this is that things are changing around us constantly, and we need to learn, adapt, and evolve. We need to get more efficient, effective and, at the same time pay close attention to the ever-changing needs of our people.

Reviewing our activity and learning is not a nice to have. It's imperative if we are going to achieve our desired successes and improve our performance. Let's consider this in the outdoors before we jump back to the meeting environment.

For several years I ran a progressive programme of outdoor activities for some groups. They would start their training at the end of the winter, learning skills and techniques and building their fitness for each stage. They would then undertake a series of events, each giving them a greater challenge both physically and by way of skill. They would span the spring and summer culminating in late summer or early autumn. I had a fairly steady team of around 8 – 12 staff, where most would attend each event, but some due to availability and skill set, would only join for two or three events. At the end of each activity my team and I would undertake a review. We would start the season with a detailed review to get us used to the process and gather as much feedback as possible for the season ahead.

The following events reviews were rich but simpler and shorter as we got into the flow of things, and at the end of the season, we would undertake a full review to allow us to plan ahead and implement any lessons learnt. The reviews took place in different settings and formats, but the information was always gathered – sometimes by email, sometimes in a 'hot debrief' style before leaving the event and occasionally round a table in the local pub.

The information gathered not only made everyone's lives easier, i.e. how to use a piece of equipment better or that an access point to a rock-climbing venue had been closed and there's a new way around. But it also had the potential to prevent serious harm by identifying damaged kit and improving ways of working or finding route issues where small streams had all of a sudden become very fast rivers. We were able to get to rich enough levels of conversation to learn about our behaviours and their impact on each other – what was working well and what had the potential to ruffle feathers. Our team members would go on other events with other teams and bring back learning from them or share our learning with them.

Some of our learning reviews were really simple, where we just asked a series of questions and took note of the answers:

- What's working/worked well?
- What would make it even better?
- What are we doing that works and that we need to continue?
- What do we do that adds no value or is a risk, and we need to stop?
- What things could we start to do that make us better?

Other times we spent longer and took a more structured approach to our reviews using the tools above. Regardless we knew that we needed to explore a combination of things – the task itself, the outputs, outcomes, methods used, behaviours displayed and feelings of team members at various stages – see the action learning tool for more.

We need to do this in our meetings. If we have a daily scrum/team check-in, it might be that the only thing we review daily are the agreed actions, but periodically we stop and ask if the meeting format is working and review more in detail. For larger meetings, I believe it's important to canvas feedback from participants as part of the review, and the leadership team use that feedback to evaluate the meetings. In meetings, the review might help make the meeting more efficient and effective, or even just shake things up with new ideas and approaches. It may also help identify any particular team members who are not completing their agreed actions or are struggling with them. That's where the coaching tools become hugely effective.

Inspired Meetings Health Checker

Take some time to read the statements in each of the five sections below and score your meetings out of 4. You could think about a range of meetings or a particular repeating meeting that you wish to review, it's up to you, but I would keep that choice through the whole review. Maybe you want to do it multiple times or get colleagues to do it too.

If you answer the questions in this health checker honestly, you're more likely to get results you can do something with that makes a difference and are less deceiving. Consider the Watermelon and Kiwi Fruit as you complete this. A watermelon is a big, juicy fruit, with plenty of water content and pips inside, but it is only green on the outside. The Kiwi Fruit is much smaller, but with green skin and green flesh has a much more solid centre too. If you use the colours of the health check to give yourself a rating, ask if you have been honest with your answers. If your answers aren't honest, you might get a green outside for everyone to see, but when you slice into it, it is bright red, has irritating pips and can be sticky to handle.

| 1 | Never | 2 | Hardly Ever | 3 | Sometimes | 4 | Always |

CRAFTING

		1	2	3	4
a	Meetings that I lead or attend have a clearly defined purpose.				
b	People are invited to meetings because they can add or gain value from being there.				
c	Desired outcomes from my meetings are clear.				
d	When planning for meetings, it is done with the end in mind.				
e	My meetings are necessary and cannot be done by email or 1 to 1 phone call.				
f	The structure and tools used to conduct the meeting are planned to give the best structure.				
g	Meetings that I lead or attend have agendas.				
h	Agendas are created and sent out in advance to allow people to prepare.				
i	People other than the meeting owner are involved in the planning process to gain buy-in.				
j	Meetings are planned to have time in between for planning, reflection and 'real work'.				
	Total:				

| 1 | Never | 2 | Hardly Ever | 3 | Sometimes | 4 | Always |

ALIGNING

		1	2	3	4
a	I check in with everyone at the beginning of the meeting to see 'what sort of head space' they're in.				
b	The meeting doesn't progress unless the purpose has been confirmed and the agenda agreed.				
c	Rules and guidelines are 'bought into' in order to ensure there are no distractions.				
d	Bring the right 'me' to the meeting and contribute with the meeting purpose in mind, not their own local benefits.				
e	We have a culture in our meetings that allows people to participate fully.				
f	The meeting environment (physical or online) is set up to enable meeting success.				
g	People arrive on time and are prepared for the meeting.				
h	Names are used to connect people during the meeting.				
i	The plan ensures there is no need for any other business (AOB) at the end.				
j	Attendees feel 'safe' and can therefore contribute fully to discussions.				
	Total:				

| 1 | Never | 2 | Hardly Ever | 3 | Sometimes | 4 | Always |

DOING

		1	2	3	4
a	The meeting agenda is facilitated in line with the plan and purpose.				
b	Actions and learning are reviewed regularly throughout the meeting.				
c	Any negatives are aired and handled early in the meeting.				
d	When running or participating in meetings, I actively include everyone in the conversation.				
e	Agenda items are facilitated using a selection of collaboration tools as appropriate.				
f	Collaboration tools used allow all attendees opportunities to use 'the pen' and capture their ideas and thoughts.				
g	Attendees are given feedback and praise throughout the meeting to manage energy and contributions.				
h	When getting people together we spend time checking in on their feelings and emotions, not just tasks.				
i	If preparation or check-in is required, people turn up/log in early to do this.				
j	Longer meetings have breaks and space to reflect, digest and re-energise.				
	Total:				

| 1 | Never | 2 | Hardly Ever | 3 | Sometimes | 4 | Always |

AGREEING

		1	2	3	4
a	We give opportunities for people to challenge and disagree with the actions to ensure they can 'live with' the plan.				
b	Actions and key outcomes are summarised and agreed at the end of a meeting.				
c	Effective decisions are made using agreed processes and tools.				
d	A plan of action is created and recorded.				
e	Meetings are reviewed for impact, effectiveness, and format before the end or soon afterwards.				
f	We check how people are feeling at the end of a meeting, not just the outputs and outcomes.				
g	The next meeting or check-in is agreed before departure.				
h	Actions and insights are captured to enable follow up and implementation.				
i	Attendees feel they can support all actions and don't just say yes to speed the meeting up.				
j	A review of meetings is conducted to help improve future collaboration opportunities.				
	Total:				

| 1 | Never | 2 | Hardly Ever | 3 | Sometimes | 4 | Always |

IMPLEMENTING

		1	2	3	4
a	I believe that people leaving the meeting are committed to making the actions happen.				
b	Attendees feel they have support available to complete the actions as needed.				
c	Actions are prioritised and attendees start working on them at their first opportunity.				
d	We see the benefits of having the meeting by sustained action.				
e	Changes are made if the meeting review shows improvements can be gained.				
f	There is no need for attendees to re-convene in private at the coffee machine.				
g	Outcomes and actions are communicated to stakeholders as required.				
h	Notes, minutes, and resources are sent out as soon as possible afterwards.				
i	Follow up is done by team and individuals as necessary and actions not left to go stale.				
j	Attendees look forward to the next opportunity to get together and make a difference.				
	Total:				

Health Check Totals and Diagnosis

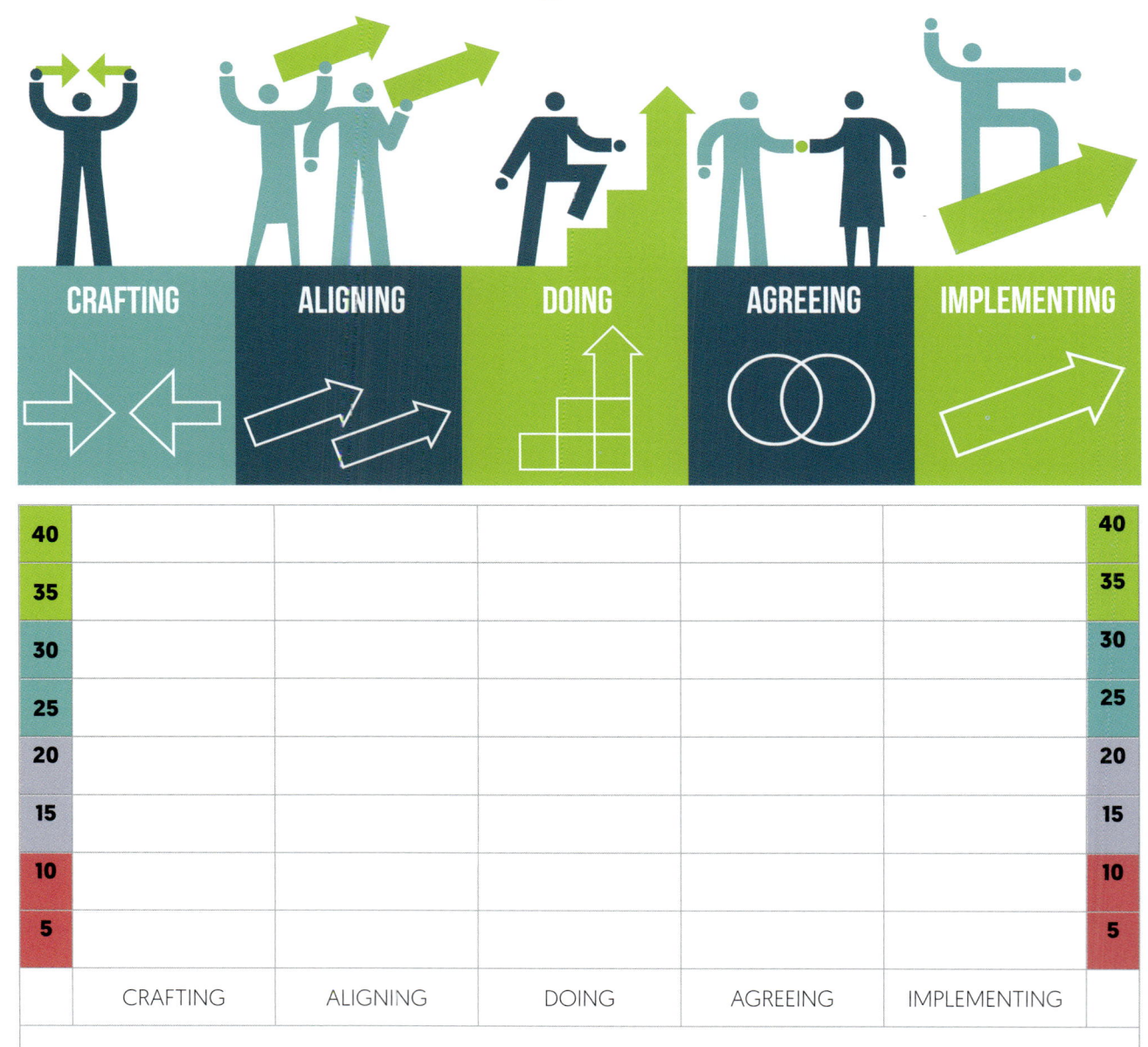

	CRAFTING	ALIGNING	DOING	AGREEING	IMPLEMENTING	
40						40
35						35
30						30
25						25
20						20
15						15
10						10
5						5
	CRAFTING	ALIGNING	DOING	AGREEING	IMPLEMENTING	

Plot your health check scores above to provide a visual representation of the condition of your meetings.

What are your initial thoughts and observations of your results?

Based on your observations of the questionnaire, what do you think you should:

STOP doing that adds no value to your meetings:	**START** doing, that you've have identified as missing:	**CONTINUE** doing that is working well and would be missed if you didn't keep:

Inspired Meetings Speedy Recovery Plan

Now you have taken some time to assess the health of your meetings. There might be things you need to look at to improve meeting experiences for your attendees. As with your personal health, you must create new habits to make changes and improvements. This means that some of the actions may initially feel a little uncomfortable until they have been repeated a few times. Here are some steps that you can take in each of the areas of our Inspired Meetings Framework (IMF). Let's make meetings a pleasure to be part of and drive action and results in your organisations. Good Luck!

CRAFTING
- Involve others in planning your meeting. This gives accountability, buy-in and great decisions right from the start.
- Consider the addition of collaboration tools within your agenda – Radiant Problem Solving, 6 Thinking Hats, Journey Mapping, World Café, etc.
- Tell attendees the purpose and agenda as far in advance of the meeting as you can.
- Consider the space and its set-up. Arrive early to make the space right for the meeting – don't just accept the boardroom layout.

ALIGNING
- Conduct a 'check-in' before the agenda starts to see what sort of head space people are in.
- Enable attendees to be 'in the room' by dealing with distractions, putting them at ease, and creating the right environment.
- Clarify the purpose of the meeting – why is everyone there?!
- Confirm and agree the agenda meets the meeting's purpose.
- Ensure a culture is created to allow people to feel safe contributing.

DOING
- Allocate clear roles such as Chair, Note Taker, Gatekeeper and Tech Support.
- Use collaboration tools such as Blob Bridge, Action Replay, IDQB and Graphic Game Plan.
- When collaborating, make it inclusive and get everyone's input.
- Change positions – stand around the board/flip chart.
- Review actions regularly throughout the meeting.
- Check-in with attendees during the meeting.

AGREEING
- Know and agree on how decisions will be made – votes, feasibility, etc.
- Ask attendees to verbalise their actions to ensure understanding and buy-in.
- Coach to kill risks and build commitment before closing meeting.
- Check-in on how people feel about the content and actions. Even if they don't agree with everything, they must be able to live with it and leave supporting the actions.
- Document actions as you go and if possible, have them for all to see – flipchart, on screen, etc.

IMPLEMENTING
- Share actions as soon as possible after meetings.
- Don't plan back-to-back meetings – give yourself and attendees a chance to 'do work' and refresh between meetings.
- Plan forward and agree on the next check point/meeting.
- Create a supportive culture where it's ok to be nudged about the actions and projects.
- Tell others what has been achieved/agreed upon in the meeting – don't surprise your stakeholders.

Meetings Reality Check

Let us take a look at the number and types of meeting you have. This health check can be done on your own, in teams or with project groups. Its aim is to take an honest look at how many meetings you have and to consider their quality/impact at a top level. You can then decide what to do with them. Often just creating the visual representation of your meetings paints a powerful image for you.

If doing this on your own, you'll need to set up a template to work on. If it's with a remote team or face-to-face you will need this template in a suitable format to work with i.e., large board, flipchart, or template on your chosen platform. It's good to have pens and sticky notes, and coloured stickers for voting.

Create a table like the one below, with timescales along one axis with increasing time intervals (i.e., daily, weekly, bi-weekly, monthly, quarterly, etc.) Then label the other axis with 'full team', 'part team' and 'individual contributor'.

	Daily	Weekly	Bi-weekly	Monthly	Quarterly	Annually
Individual Contributor						
Whole Team						
Part Team						

As part of your preparation, you will also need to set up a table with the titles BIN, BANK and BUILD. We'll explain more about this one shortly.

BIN	BANK	BUILD

Set a purpose so that everyone is clear on the aim of the activity. It could be 'to review our ways of working' or 'to streamline our meetings to be more effective' or another of your choice. Define what will be added to the first table as a repeated activity that involves collaboration with others in support of the team, a service or organisation. You can also specify if this is strictly work only or personal/social commitments too.

Agree a time (or even ask them to do this beforehand) while the group writes one activity/meeting per sticky note to add to the table; they should then add them, stand back and review – remove duplicates, identify gaps, and agree that this now reflects a true picture of the team's meeting rituals. It's a good idea to ask contributors to look at the calendar for the past few months to remind themselves.

Give each member of the group a selection of coloured stickers/dots:
Green to keep (BANK) – to continue moving forward, you must keep doing these.
Orange to improve (BUILD) – to deliver your vision, you need to make better, create or implement.
Red to remove (BIN) – to achieve success, you need to leave this behind.

And ask them to vote on every meeting that has been added. Once voting has been completed, you can move them, based on votes to the BIN – BANK – BUILD template and begin to discuss what you're going to do about them. Because they may involve other stakeholders, some may need a little more work than others to BIN or BUILD. Other tools in this book can be used to work through your actions here. Be sure to record actions and follow up on them as appropriate.

Other tools that could be useful are:
- Gaining Consensus
- Ease Impact Grid
- Tough Discussion DIES

IF ALL YOU HAVE IS A HAMMER, EVERYTHING LOOKS LIKE A NAIL.

Bernard Baruch

INSPIRED MEETINGS FRAMEWORK

	CRAFTING	**ALIGNING**
Purpose (To ensure...)	I have designed the right approach	Everyone knows why they are here and can contribute fully
Activity	- Confirm purpose - Generate ideas - Develop agenda - Select tools	- Clarify purpose - Confirm agenda - Ensure buy-in - Enable attendees to be 'in the room'
Outcomes	- Created agenda - Gained buy-in - Chosen right environment	- Energy - Clarity - Commitment - De-risked meeting
Tools/Techniques & Templates	Agenda Templates Route Mapping Group Dynamics Ground Rules	Hopes and Fears OARRs Questions Check-ins Fluctuating feelings Blobs

DOING	AGREEING	IMPLEMENTING
We are using the right collaboration tools	We make effective and aligned decisions and action plans	Everyone is committed to making the actions happen
<ul><li>Facilitate the agenda</li><li>Ongoing review</li><li>Ensure full participation</li></ul>	<ul><li>Effective decision-making</li><li>Creating a plan</li><li>Agreeing way forward</li><li>Reviewing meeting</li></ul>	<ul><li>Follow through on actions</li><li>Review progress</li><li>Plan forward</li><li>Develop learning</li></ul>
<ul><li>Insights</li><li>Ideas</li><li>Actions</li><li>Accountability</li></ul>	<ul><li>Clear and agreed action plan</li><li>Commitment and buy-in</li></ul>	<ul><li>Sustained action</li><li>Benefits realised</li><li>Learning implemented</li></ul>
Radiant Problem Solving World Café Cross that Bridge Creativity Bag of Tricks NICE to Speak Gaining Consensus Disney Technique Six Thinking Hats Brain Gym Context Map SPOT Matrix History Map	Gantt Chart Route Mapping OGSM Blobs Cross that Bridge Ease Impact Grid Game Plan Desirable Feasible Viable Dr Iv Ers Cap Agile Board Cover Story Decision Making Tools	Action Learning Tool Stop Start Continue Leader Manager Coach Coaching Toolkit S-WOT's your story Changepro

Section 3

Tools for meetings

Tools for Meetings	152
Radiant Problem Solving	154
Thunks	156
Stick to the Plan	158
Cross That Bridge	160
Tough Discussion DIES	162
Disney Imagineering	164
Fluctuating Feelings	166
S-WOT's Your Story?	168
NICE to Speak	170
Masterminding	172
Action learning - iceberg	174
Ease Impact Grid	176
DFV (Desirability, Feasibility, Viability) Analysis	178
Harvesting Ideas	180
Blob journey	182
Global CV	184
Shapes	186
Gaining consensus	188
Team Manifesto	190
World Café	192
Open Space	194
Mad Sad Glad	196
BIRDS Review	198
Story Dice	200
Hopes and fears	202
Magic Cane	204
Team Juggle	206
Marshmallow tower	208
The Lego Duck	210
Brick Tower and Their Best Self	212
OARRs	214
Tactical Meeting Agenda	216
Power of Synergy	218
Parking Lot	220
Recipe for Success	222
Quick Coaching	224

Tools for meetings

In this chapter there is a selection of my favourite tools, the most versatile approaches, activities, and processes for use in meetings. Some are my own creation, and others are borrowed from established ways of working. Where they are not mine, I have tried by best to reference the creators and would recommend searching out further information on them to add depth and meaning if you are planning to use them. As I mentioned earlier in the book, it's not OCD. It's how to get the best from the model and be respectful of its creator.

Many of them require some resource, and I have made clear if they are mandatory or optional. The most important resource for you to consider with these is your time. Time to learn, prepare and rehearse the use of the tool and the appropriate time allocated to do them justice with your group to get the best possible outcomes.

When choosing which tool to use, always start with the end in mind and consider what's important for you. Don't be afraid to say that the reason you chose a tool is to change the energy in a room rather than to respond directly to an agenda item. The energy you create will greatly impact on how people deal with the agenda items.

Try also not to be overwhelmed by the choice. Just pick one or two to start with and give them a go. Allocate more time than you might think you need for them and make the most of that particular tool rather than give yourself too much work to do or overwhelm your group with style over substance.

Most importantly give them a go!

Following on from the life of a meeting earlier in the book, the image on page 153 shows how the tools can be used throughout a meeting.

Motivation Desire Energy

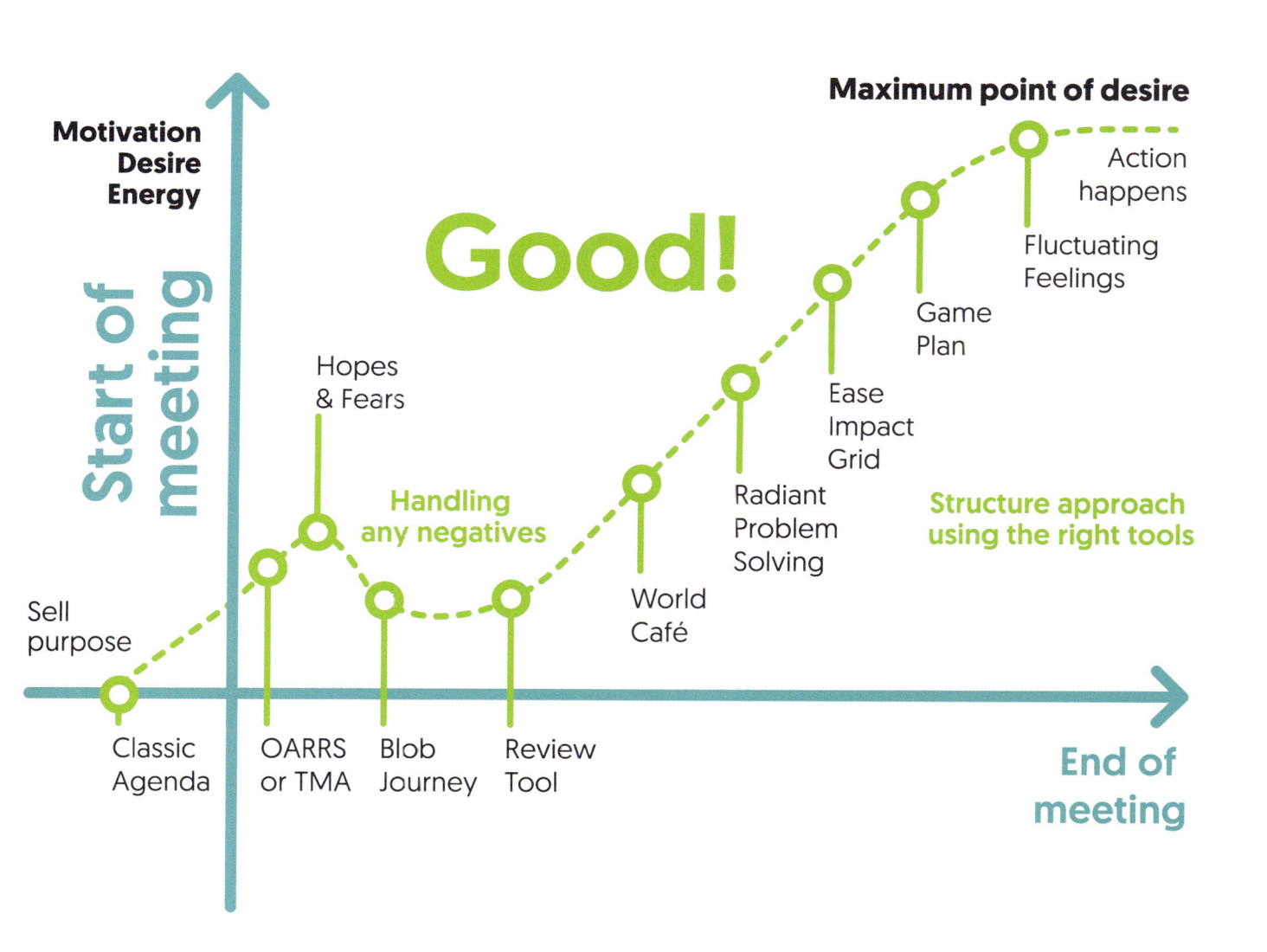

Start of meeting

Maximum point of desire

Good!

- Sell purpose — Classic Agenda
- Hopes & Fears — OARRS or TMA
- Blob Journey
- Review Tool
- World Café
- Radiant Problem Solving
- Ease Impact Grid
- Game Plan
- Fluctuating Feelings
- Action happens

Handling any negatives

Structure approach using the right tools

End of meeting

Radiant Problem Solving

What is it?
Radiant Problem Solving (RPS) is, as it says on the tin, a process tool for generating ideas to solve a problem. It is a fast-paced, high-energy method to quickly and effectively explore what blockers exist to solving a problem and generating ideas to remove them. Used effectively, it not only helps generate specific solutions to your problems, but also creates a visual representation of how many options are available for you and will generate ideas that can be used as contingencies.

What's the process?
There are four main steps to RPS. The successful application of each is relied upon for the next steps to be as effective.
1. Define the problem, state its solution as a goal and write it in a bubble in the centre of your paper/chart/template. Do this as a group to get best clarity on the real issue but apply a time pressure of between five and ten minutes maximum. There are many ways in which a goal can be articulated, SMART is one, but whatever you choose, it must be clear and agreeable.
2. Brainstorm all the blockers/barriers to achieving the goal and add these as further bubbles, satellites around your goal. Use the same colour pen for each of your blockers, and ideally, a different colour to your goal. Spend no more than three minutes on this. Time should be monitored and adhered to.
3. Change the pen colour and then take each of your blockers one at a time, using two or three members of your group as scribes. Discuss and write down as many ideas as you can as possible solutions to the blocker. Your ideas should be written and not discussed at this stage. Stick to one minute per blocker and work logically (clockwise or anti-clockwise) through the blockers.
4. Review and reflect on the ideas generated. Feel positive at the number of ideas generated (i.e. the mass of the outer colour). Ask yourself, is there a theme? Are there any quick wins or ideas that can be turned into strategies? If there are many great ideas, what additional tools can be used to prioritise and delegate actions?

Possible uses
RPS can be used for individual thinking and brainstorming. It can be done in groups using the same problem or where each group has a different problem. Steps can be rotated, or the harvest of ideas done by other team members.

Suggested resources
Paper such as flipchart or bigger is ideal. The bigger the better to capture the ideas and allow people to stand around. Good quality pens, chisel tip markers with a selection of colours are recommended. If using a whiteboard, try to have a simple means of collecting the raw data, such as a mobile phone camera.

Tips for success
1. Use a tool such as Cross the Bridge prior to this to be sure of buy-in to the 'real' problem.
2. Stick to the time scales suggested above. Th s keeps the energy and pace, allowing participants to remain in flow as best as possible.
3. Change the colour after each of the steps. Use a bright but visible colour such as orange for the solutions/ideas.
4. Follow up with a tool such as Ease Impact Grid or add straight to your plan on a page/game plan.

Roles:

Timekeeper - Keep the group to time for each element.
Scribes - Take responsibility for recording ideas
Focus - Ensure that the group is focussed on the right thing. When working on blocks don't discuss solutions and vice versa. Also during the brainstorming sections keep the group to the rules.
Rules of Brainstorming - No analysis, no discussion, no judgement, no right or wrong - record all ideas however wacky!
Reporter - Feedback to other groups, workshop, etc.

Process:

1. Decide on your goal, make sure it is phased as a goal not an issue. Group discussion five minutes.

2. Brainstorm all the blocks/barriers to achieving your goal. Two minutes.

3. Take the blocks one at a time and brainstorm all the solutions. One minute per block.

4. Review and reflect on the results. Are there common solutions? Can you propose five strategies or next steps to work towards the goal? 5-15 minutes.

Thunks

What is it?
A Thunk has been described as a question about everyday things that stops you in your tracks and helps you to look at things in a whole different light. Using a series of thunks can be a fun, interactive and collaborative way to encourage thinking.

What's the process?
Plan a selection of thunks. There are thousands of them available on the internet or in books (some of my favourite books on this topic are by Ian Gilbert) but I have provided a page of examples here.
1. Split your audience into groups of between two and five people. Tell them that they are about to be asked a series of questions, on which their group must reach a consensus on the answer within the time given.
2. For each question read, give them 30 to 60 seconds to reach an agreed decision.
3. Tell the group that at the end of the whole round, answers will be shared. (There are no right or wrong answers to many of the questions).
4. After the time allocated for each question, ask the groups if they reached a consensus and what their answer was. Then repeat for the allocated time or planned number of questions.

Review by asking what they have learnt and how it links to the themes of your session.

Possible uses
- Linking into a creative mindset.
- Breaking the ice or re-energising a group.
- Gaining consensus.
- Considering different perspectives.

Suggested resources
All you need is a pre-planned list of Thunks to suit your plan and available time.

Tips for success
Run the activity at pace and keep to short time for the groups to come to an answer.

Example Thunks:

What colour is Tuesday?
Are we man-made or natural?
Is a broken-down car parked?
Is a leaf on a tree or part of a tree?
If I borrow a million pounds, am I a millionaire?
Is there more future or past?
Does a mouse have a soul? A wasp? An amoeba?
Can a dog commit a crime?
If we borrow every single book from a library, is it still a library?
Does lined paper weigh more than blank paper?
Which is heavier, an inflated or deflated balloon?
What colour is a Zebra if you take the stripes off it?

And my personal favourite 🙂

"Is the hokey cokey really what it's all about?"

Stick to the Plan

What is it?
A flexible and thorough planning method that allows both individuals and groups to plan in detail and start with the end in mind. It requires users to be clear about the desired end result and then enables them to work backwards looking at all the detailed activity required to achieve that result.

What's the process?
1. As a group, the first step is to clearly write down the goal that everyone can live with and is unambiguous. Such as, "Plan and deliver a successful, fun and engaging one-day off-site conference."
2. This goal then forms your mission statement, for the piece of work, and on the board should be written as, "We want to plan and deliver a successful, fun and engaging one-day staff conference and to achieve this we will ..."
3. Using your defined mission statement the group should then individually write down every task that they can think needs to be done for the mission to be achieved. They should write each potential task down on a separate sticky note and it should continue the sentence in step two. For example, "Order a selection of food to suit all dietary needs" on a sticky note does not work.
4. Each group member should add their sticky notes to the board, and once completed, they should look for repetition and similarities to cluster. Remove duplicates before moving on to the next step.
5. Spend a few minutes looking for gaps in the plan as a group and add any missing items to sticky notes. This doesn't prevent items from being added at a later date if gaps are noticed or ideas received.
6. Create a timeline with 'now' being on the left and the 'event' or deadline on the far right, and work together to order the actions into the timeline. There may be many items on one day/time, which is fine.
7. Allocate responsibilities for each item. Agree on how the board will be maintained in the run up to the event. Go, do actions. Review regularly.

Possible uses
It can be used for planning almost any desired outcome. It can be used to plan the implementation of actions from a meeting. Use can be individual or group.

Suggested resources
A large board, flipchart, or blank wall. A selection of sticky notes. Pens such as board markers or Sharpies which will be clear to read. A roll of decorators lining wallpaper works really well for this too.

Tips for success
1. If some of the detailed activity still looks or feels 'big'. You can repeat the whole process using an action from the detailed activities as your goal and working through the above process again.
2. The process works as well online using a combination of platforms such as Zoom and Mural, where participants can talk, and sticky notes can be created.
3. Move or mark each item once complete, but don't remove from the board. Use the completed board to do final review and to conduct after action review as necessary.
4. Consider categories of 'To do', 'In progress' and 'Complete'.

We want to......
To achieve this we will...

Now — Completed

Cross That Bridge

What is it?
An effective collaboration tool to engage people, clarify a challenge/problem and create an urge for action.

What's the process?
1. Start by identifying the challenge, problem or objective. Write this down in your own words and agree as a team (this can be the hardest bit). Don't use bullet points, it should be written in complete sentences and should be a real issue.
2. Next, work on 'where are you now' and 'what will happen if you don't cross the bridge?' Each participant should spend some time independently on sticky notes, writing down what they think will occur if they don't dross the bridge. Again, only use complete sentences. Add all the contributions to a template on a big board or flipchart. Organise them into a sequence that tells a story and read aloud to everyone in the group.
3. Repeat for 'what will it look like and feel like when you're on the other side – what will you get?' as you have done for the previous step.
4. What's stopping you crossing the bridge? In this step, each participant is to consider first on their own, the reasons why they believe it has not been achieved or resolved yet, then add the sticky notes to the template and sequence these from left to right – furthermost left should be the items that will have a big impact if resolved and least impact further to the right.
5. Take the items from the 'Why are you not crossing the bridge?' section and use these with other tools such as radiant problem-solving, world café or Disney Imagineering .

Possible uses
- Building a business case or scoping a project
- Risk management
- Influencing and negotiating
- Changing awareness, building desire and need to change

Suggested resources
Use a template to help follow the suggested process. Have a selection of sticky notes and pens available.

Tips for success
Give people time to think on their own at the beginning of steps two, three and four. Create a large template and encourage groups together in person to stand whilst they work through it.

2a. Where are you now?

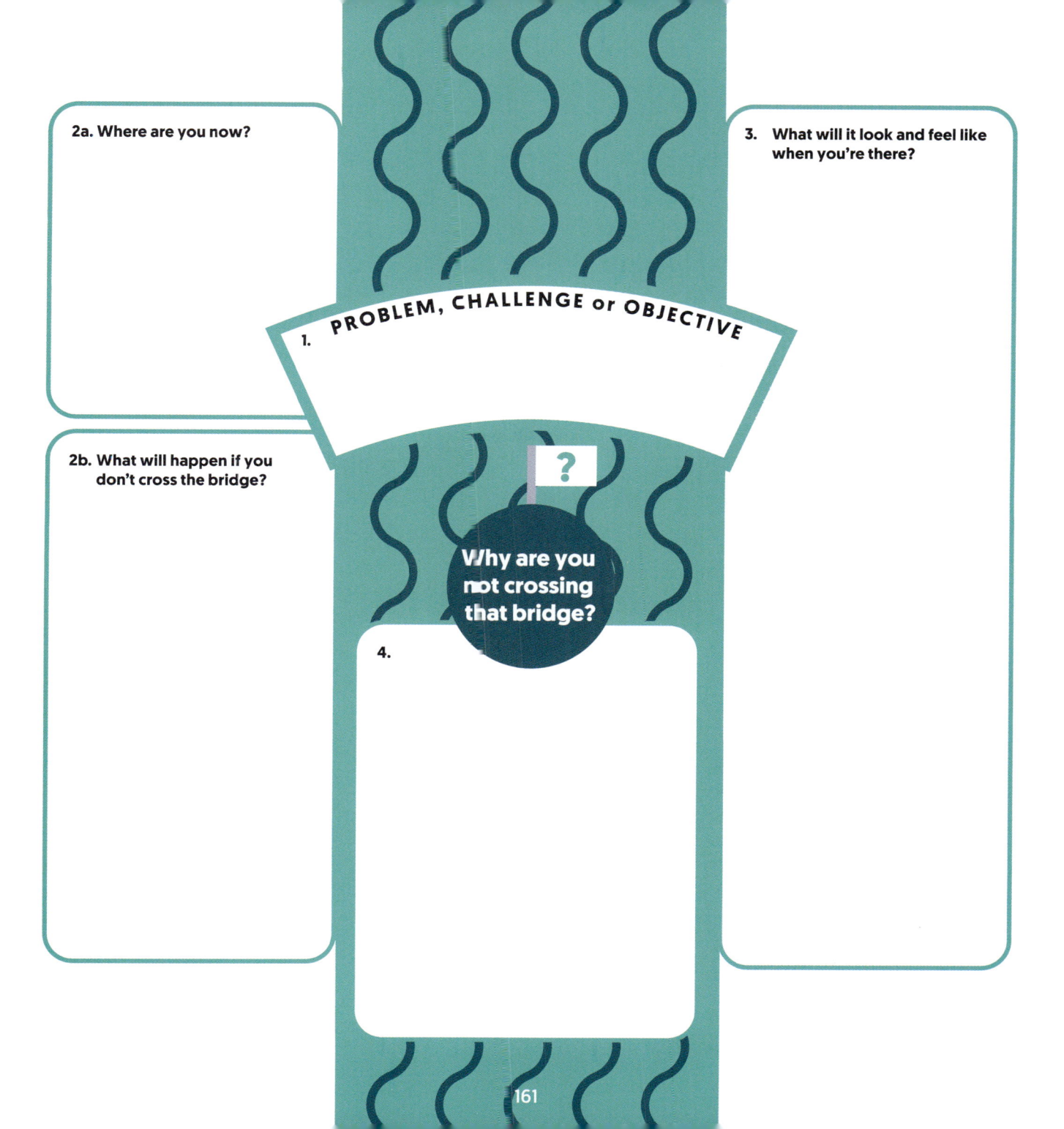

3. What will it look and feel like when you're there?

1. PROBLEM, CHALLENGE or OBJECTIVE

2b. What will happen if you don't cross the bridge?

Why are you not crossing that bridge?

4.

Tough Discussion DIES

What is it?
A structured conversational approach for engaging people wanting to solve problems and improve performance.

What's the process?
a   What I want to say... Write down what you want to say, without filters. Then look at the information and consider the real issue(s) here. What is it really that's making these feelings for you? Can it be chunked down to smaller areas to be addressed, and does it all need to be addressed right now?
b   Plan the discussion by breaking your thinking into four areas as follows:
   1   **Describe.** Describe the problem/opportunity. Consider how you can engage people and prevent building resistance. How can you describe the problem/opportunity in a non-threatening, positive and engaging way.
   2   **Information.** Provide examples and data to make it clear and unambiguous what you're talking about. Use data, examples, evidence and information to clarify what you're saying.
   3   **Engage.** Use great questions to trigger engagement and involve them in what you're saying. Check that they are clear on where you are coming from and where you want to be.
   4   **Shape.** Craft a solution together. Continue a discussion which will build a solution together. Be careful to listen to all ideas and points of view not just to deliver a solution that you've thought up in advance.
c   Use the plan to guide discussion or keep things on track. Share your planning and share with other people in the discussion. This will help separate the people from the problem and reduce the risk of anything being taken personally.

Possible uses
- Performance management/reviews
- Tackling challenging/difficult behaviour
- Conflict resolution
- Engaging people with change
- Problem solving

Suggested resources
Use a template to help prepare for the discussion.

Planning notes

Describe
Describe the problem/opportunity.

Information
Provide examples and data to make it clear and unambiguous.

Engage
Use great questions to trigger engagement and involve them.

Shape
Craft a solution together.

Disney Imagineering

What is it?
Disney's thinking and ideation technique bring together three different strategies in a way where all three must be used to create a positive effect: the dreamer, the realist, and the critic. A dreamer without a realist is often unable to translate fantasies into tangible reality. A dreamer and critic can become engaged in constant conflict. A dreamer and realist can create things but find that a critic helps evaluate and refine the final product.

What's the process?
1. Set up three areas and a central space to brief the whole group. It could be separate rooms, or it could be corners of a particular room or space. Be clear on the topic to be used for idea generation – new products, smarter ways of working, making more money, whatever...
2. Ensure there are plenty of paper, pens, whiteboards, etc., in each area to record discussions. Maybe magazines, LEGO® Bricks or playdough too.
3. Brief the group that they will spend time together in three separate zones – The Dreamer, Realistic and Critic. There are rules and a separate brief for each zone. Decide on the time available to split the three zones (20-30 minutes each is a good time).
4. Allocate a gatekeeper for each zone who will help the group focus and stick to the guidelines for the zone. Move to each area in turn, sticking to the time agreed and brief the following on arrival in each zone:
   DREAMER. A dreamer spins innumerable fantasies, wishes, outrageous hunches and bold and absurd ideas without limit or judgment. Nothing is censored. Nothing is too absurd or silly. All things are possible for the dreamer. To be the dreamer, ask: If I could wave a magic wand and do anything I want, what would I create? How would it look? What could I do with it? How would it make you feel? What is the most absurd idea I can conceive?
   REALIST. The realist imagineers the dreamer's ideas into something realistic and feasible. They would try to figure out how to make the ideas work and then sort them out in some meaningful order. To be the realist, ask: How can I make this happen? What are the features and aspects of the idea? Can I build ideas from the features or aspects? What is the essence of the idea? Can I extract the principle of the idea? Can I make analogical-metaphorical connections with the principle and something dissimilar to create something tangible? How can I use the essence of the idea to imagineer a more realistic one?
   CRITIC. The critic reviews all the ideas and tries to punch holes in them by playing the devil's advocate. To be the critic, ask: How do I really feel about it? Is this the best I can do? How can I make it better? Does this make sense? How does it look to a customer? A client? An expert? A user? Is it worth my time?
5. Take your ideas and turn them into a plan using your preferred or most appropriate planning and decision-making tools.

Possible uses
It is ideal for when there is a need to generate new ideas and implement action when ideas are agreed on.

Suggested resources
Three separate areas in which each strategy can be applied. The move from one place to another helps with mindset in each stage.

Tips for success
Plan to use this tool with the senses in mind. Set up spaces to reflect each of the three areas. Consider background music, sweets, whiteboards, bean bags, and bean bags.

ACTION DREAMER REALIST CRITIC

Fluctuating Feelings

What is it?
A tool for engaging all participants in reviewing their feelings following an event, project, or period of time.

What's the process?
Plot the template onto a suitable surface (whiteboard, flipchart, online template, etc.) Note the time scales of the event that you wish to review – this could be hours, days, weeks etc.

Give each person in the group a different coloured pen (if not possible, use a different pattern or be prepared to annotate with initials or first name). Ask each person to draw a line that represents their feelings (positive and negative) over the timeline specified. During this step, ask members not to discuss, make observations or comment.

Discuss to review and identify learning. There may be particular times when everyone was on a high or low – ask what was happening and why? There may have been times when certain members of the group where completely opposite to others – discuss why this was. Could it have been avoided? What is acceptable? How can you support each other etc?

Explore what needs to be done to apply learning from this. It may involve using an action planning tool such as Stop Start Continue or Bin Bank Build.

Possible uses
- During the planning of an agenda or workshop.
- To review any type of event or activity.

Suggested resources
Template pre-printed or drawn up in the moment.
Multiple coloured pens.
Sticky notes.

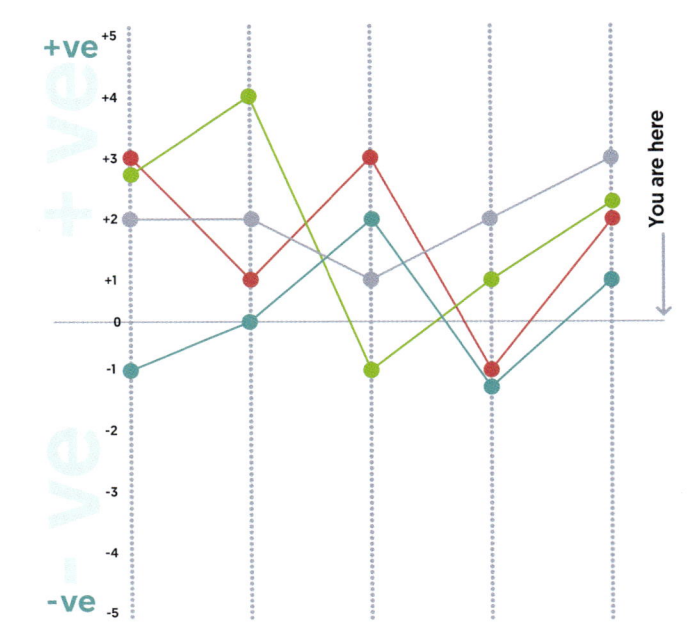

- John
- Ash
- Sam
- Louise

+ve

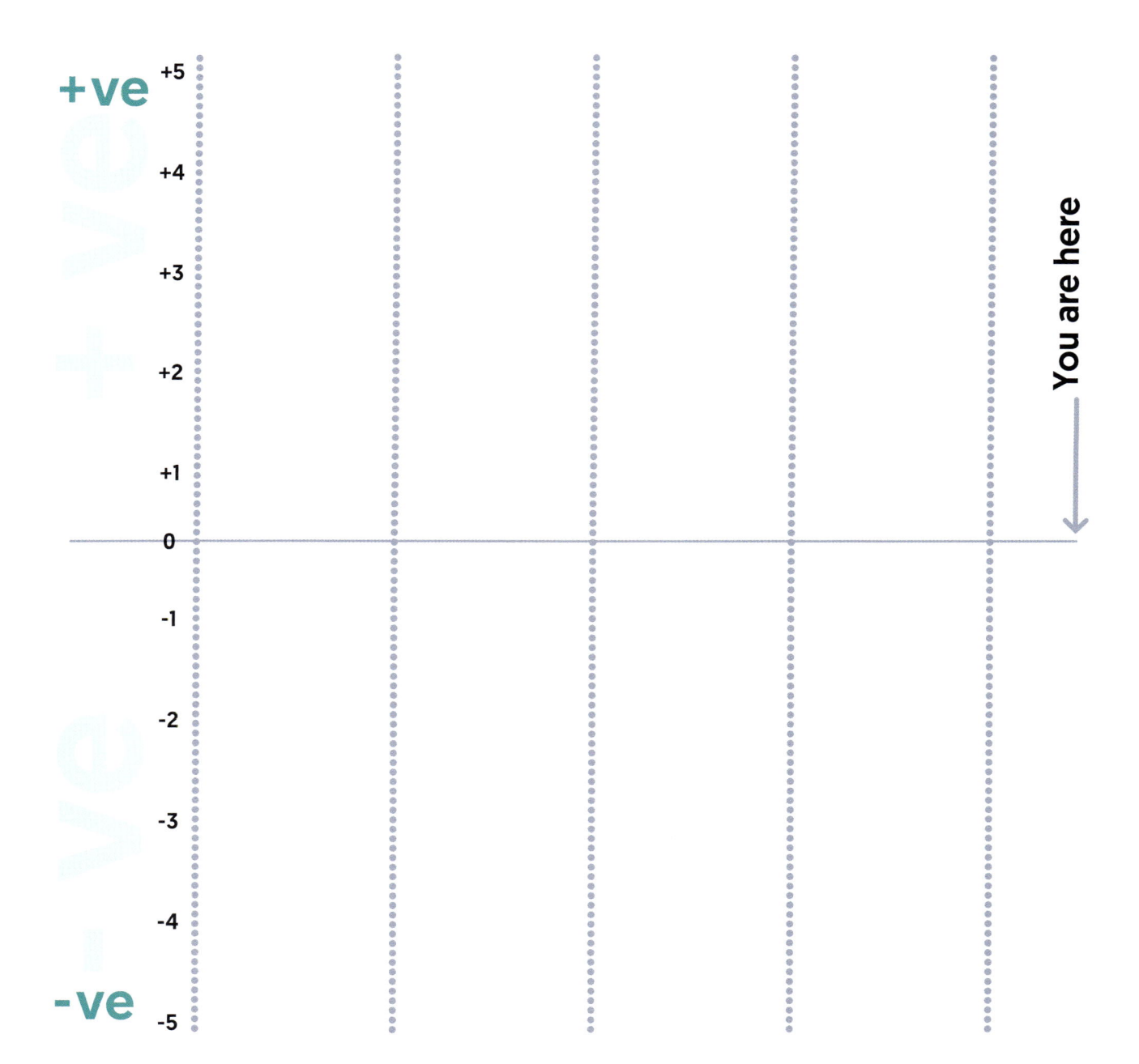

+5
+4
+3
+2
+1
0
-1
-2
-3
-4
-5

-ve

You are here

S-WOT's Your Story?

What is it?
A visual review process that uses storytelling to gather all the information. It involves everyone and provides a structured and familiar output.

What's the process?
Before you start the activity, draw up or print a copy of the template on the largest possible board or sheet of paper you can find. You may want to keep the 3 x 4 grid covered until everyone has told their story.
This, like many of the tools, works best when individuals have a chance to reflect before the group work together. If working with a team for the first time using this tool, do the first step together in silence. If you're familiar with it, ask the group members to complete step one in advance and stress its importance.

1. Each individual should write down their view of the event being reviewed (tell their story), with each key item on a separate sticky note as THEY saw it. They should be encouraged to include a mix of how they felt, what they did, saw and heard. Not just the outputs and outcomes.
2. Discuss and share the stories. You could do this one by one, as a general group discussion or theme by theme.
3. Reveal the 3 x 4 grid and move all sticky notes into the areas based on the row's descriptor.
   Intentionally Successful
   We tried, but it failed
   Unintentionally Successful
   We didn't see that coming
4. Consider the whole board and generate actions based on the following:
   Intentionally Successful – **STRENGTHS** – How do we keep these alive?
   We tried, but it failed – **WEAKNESSES** – What can we do differently next time?
   Unintentionally Successful – **OPPORTUNITIES** – Why did this happen and how can we repeat it?
   We didn't see that coming – **THREATS** – What can we learn from this? How can it be avoided in the future?
5. Take the actions and turn them into a plan.

Possible uses
It can be used in many areas, during meetings and workshops to review a sprint, a piece of work, a project, an activity or even a whole year for the team.

Suggested resources
Lots of sticky notes, suitable pens, flip chart, whiteboard, or large facilitation board. If doing this in an online setting, a template pre-prepared with the 2 x 2 grid.

Tips for success
In steps one and two, individuals should be comfortable that they are telling their story, and it won't be challenged or disagreed with unless the facts are inaccurate.

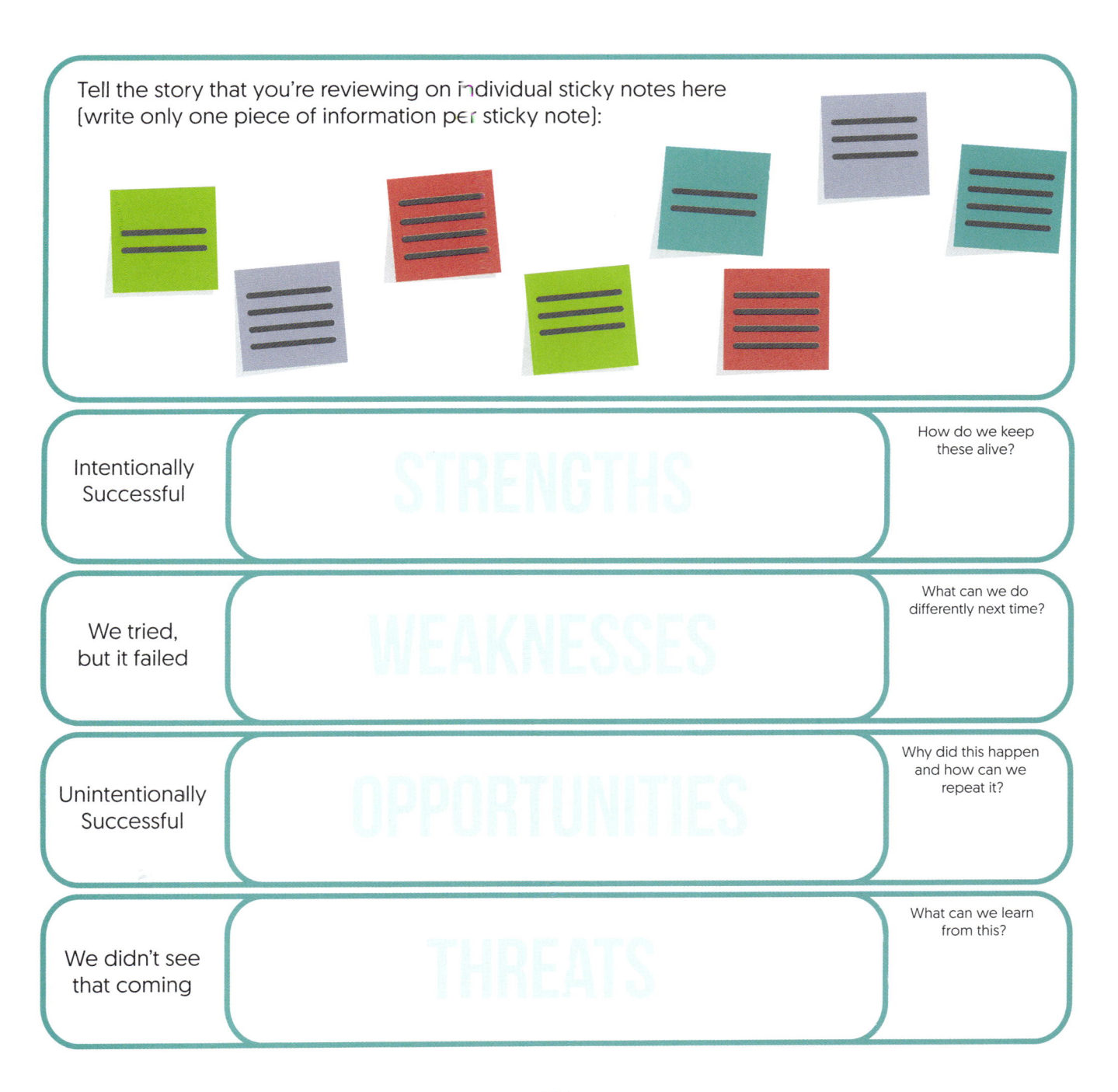

Tell the story that you're reviewing on individual sticky notes here (write only one piece of information per sticky note):

Intentionally Successful	**STRENGTHS**	How do we keep these alive?
We tried, but it failed	**WEAKNESSES**	What can we do differently next time?
Unintentionally Successful	**OPPORTUNITIES**	Why did this happen and how can we repeat it?
We didn't see that coming	**THREATS**	What can we learn from this?

NICE to Speak

What is it?
A way to encourage everyone to contribute to meetings and a tool to confirm understanding.

What's the process?
NICE to Speak works well with a meeting for up to 20 people (depending on your agenda) and is equally effective face-to-face or online sessions.
1. Create a list of participants' names or initials. This could be in the margin of your notepad or on a separate sheet of paper.
2. Observe meeting attendees and make a mark against their names when they contribute. This will give you an indication fairly quickly as to how close you are to a 100/100 meeting.
3. At a variety of appropriate times, use the following process/acronym to engage quiet meeting attendees:

    N – Name. Pick a person who hasn't contributed much or at all so far. You may choose to do this randomly or by role/relevance to the agenda item.

    I – Introduce and involve that person. Ask great questions directly to the intended person. It could be as simple as, "Mike, what are your thoughts so far?" or "Helen, what's the best part of this idea?" They need to be open questions that will get more than a Yes/No response. You may want to ask more specific questions such as, "Pete, how will this affect your area?" or "Sam, what else can we do here?"

    C – Check and confirm understanding. Use questions to encourage playback of information or confirmation of agreed actions. It could be, "What actions have we agreed on so far?" or "When will this be effective?" and "Who is doing this?"

    E – Encourage further involvement. Really listen to their responses, challenge productively and thank them for their contributions. Encourage them to continue to contribute to the meeting.
4. Use constantly throughout the meeting. Try to play to the strengths of team members if you know them and use language that will engage them better.
5. Review effectiveness and keep practicing.

Possible uses
This exceedingly simple tool can be used to help key meeting roles in the following ways:
- Help monitor contributions from members of the meeting. Use it to note when a participant contributes.
- Used to consciously bring people into the meeting who haven't had much airtime. This could be because they are generally quiet, disengaged or have been overpowered by more dominant meeting members.
- Gather feedback on the discussions or confirm that the information has landed.

Suggested resources
All you need is notepad, pen or a copy of the agenda with the attendees names on.

Tips for success
- Use this regularly and make it your own. Once it becomes a habit in standard/traditional style meetings, you will engage more meeting attendees.
- Try to do it naturally, so it doesn't look like you have a script or a plan to ask people questions.
- Develop a range of great coaching questions to use across the NICE model.

Masterminding

What is it?
Masterminding is a safe, collaborative, group coaching process. Based on and adapted from the work of Hungarian psychoanalyst Michael Balint. It is designed to be a psychologically safe way to share/own problems, retain confidentiality and engage others' knowledge, skills and experience in helping solve your problems.

What's the process?
The starting point is to ask each attendee to either come armed with their own challenge/problem or give them time at the start to decide on what they'd like to work on. I often ask, "What's keeping you awake at night?" or "What problem would make a real difference to you and your team if we help you find a solution in this session?" They must then turn this into a question (often best started with What, How or Why) which they will pose to the group on their turn.

Once individuals have had time to select their question, the following steps should be followed:
1. In groups of no more than eight (ideally between four and seven), invite one member to pose their question/challenge that they want help with. There should be no set sequence to this, but ideally the first should be a keen volunteer to help set the pace.
2. Once clear on the question, the remainder of the group can use between two and three minutes to ask fact finding questions to build their understanding of the situation, "How long has it been going on for?" or "Who is involved?" or "What has already been tried?" and "What will success look like?" This time should not be used for loaded or leading questions such as, "Have you asked Julie?" or "Have you tried an Agile approach?"
3. At the end of the questioning phase, the owner of the question should disconnect themselves physically from the group (move out of the circle or turn off camera) prepare to take notes.
4. The remainder of the group should now spend an allocated period of timing discussing the question and what they would, could or have previously done to solve the problem? Sharing ideas, asking each other questions and offering different points of view is key to giving the owner of the question lots of possibilities. I find that around seven minutes works well for this, longer can be given if the time is available, but the time must be agreed at the start of the session.
5. At the end of the main group discussion, bring the owner of the question back in to the group, welcome them back and ask for their insights. The key here is not to offer a full summary or replay the last seven minutes, but to share up to two actions that they will take away or key insights that they are going to explore in more detail.

Rotate this process for each member of the group. Ideally they will each have a turn.

Possible uses
- Problem solving
- Idea generation
- Group coaching

Suggested resources
All you need is a circle of chairs if face to face and note pad/pen for each attendee.

Tips for success
Groups sizes of four to seven work well for this. Timings need to be reflective of the group size and time available, but do not rush or leave someone having partial answers to their challenges.

When working on-line or face-to-face, the owner of the questions should disconnect themselves from the main group by turning their back or turning their camera off and not contributing further to discussions.

If facilitating in support of a group, help them focus by enforcing rules around framing the challenge, questioning and feedback.

Action learning - iceberg

What is it?
A tool for reviewing and learning. A simple metaphor to help make learning effective and memorable.

What's the process?
The task activity, outputs, and outcomes, are the bits that everyone sees, and like the iceberg, there is so much more going on below the surface. It is important that this process is used to also look at the methods, feelings, and behaviours.

1. Prepare some simple templates on flipchart or your online platform for each group that will be working on the review. I would suggest that group sizes of no more than eight are good to engage everyone. The template works well if split between 'What went well..' and 'Even better if...'
2. Start the conversation by discussing what is to be reviewed and managing expectations of the scope of the discussion – is it an event, project or period of time?
3. Discuss as a group what went well and how it would have been even better if. Ensuring as much information is captured on the board as possible. Note that the 'Even better if...' aspect is the start of a statement and is in the positive frame. For example, instead of writing down that supplier X delivered late on three occasions, you would re-frame it to even better if 'suppliers delivered ahead of schedule giving us contingencies'. That way you have a clear goal or suggestion to solve a problem, and it's not just a side of flipchart full of moans.
4. Ensure that you are discussing more than the task. You should review your methods, behaviours, and feelings.
5. Take some time to look at and discuss the comments to see why things happened? What made it a success? What caused it to fail? You can often link this to theory, such as behavioural profiles, user manuals, project handbooks, etc. This can help you understand how you can improve.
6. Create a simple action plan to improve or continue your success. Using a sheet of flipchart paper, you can agree on a list of individual or team actions to Stop, Start and Continue.

Possible uses
This process tool can be used to review any activity or action. It is a great starting point when you are looking to challenge existing ways of working or product offerings. It's also a very effective way to review a meeting at the end to ensure you're getting the best out of the meeting.

Suggested resources
Flipchart or whiteboard, pens and sticky notes.

Tips for success
- Become comfortable being uncomfortable. Do this regularly and try to get better at it each time. It will become a rich and effective process that will also save time.

Review of what happened

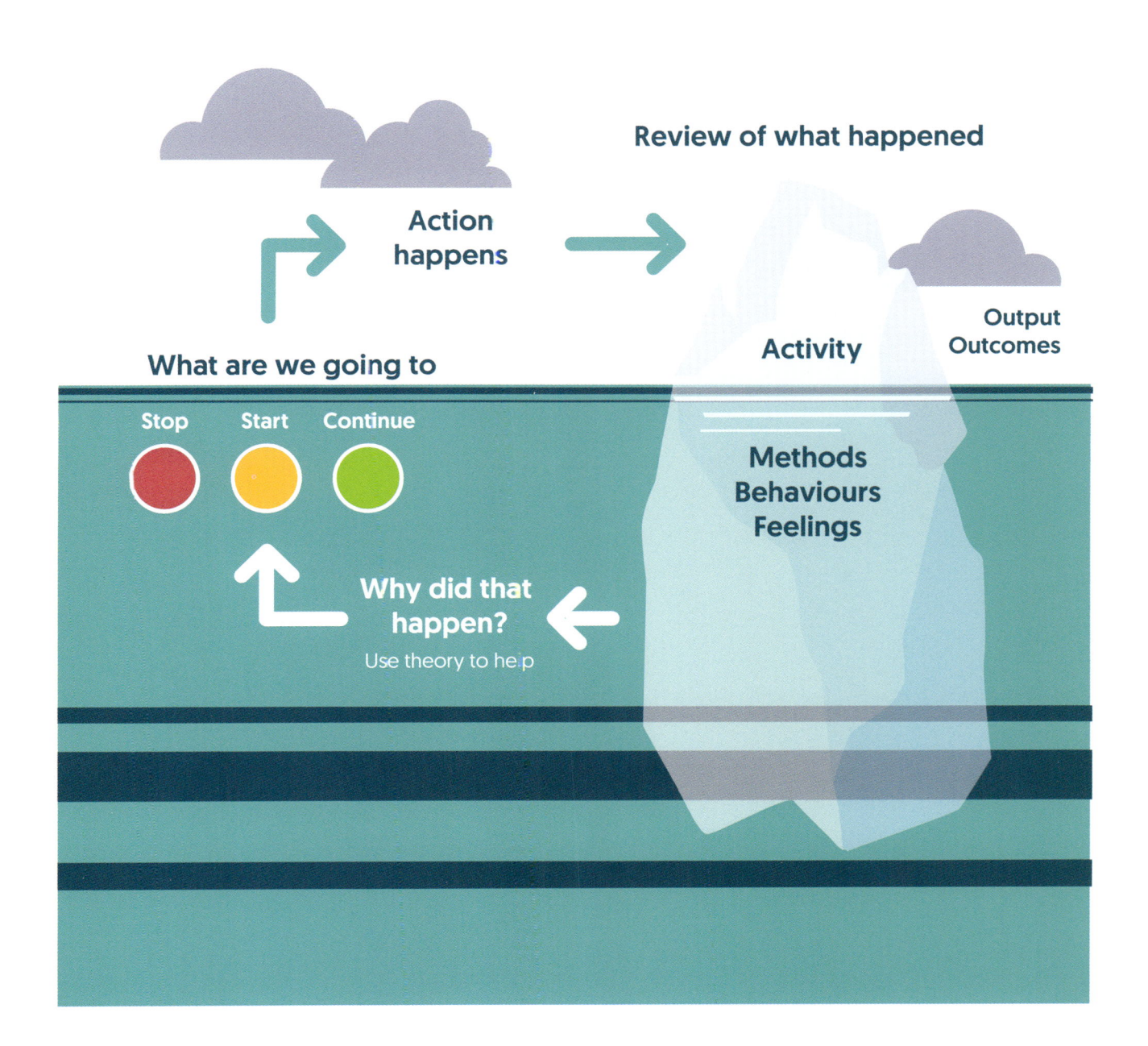

Action happens

Activity

Output
Outcomes

What are we going to

Stop   Start   Continue

Methods
Behaviours
Feelings

Why did that happen?
Use theory to help

Ease Impact Grid

What is it?
A simple and effective tool for prioritising actions.

What's the process?
1. Start by ensuring your template is drawn up and visible. In a team setting, it is best in a large format so everyone can gather around.
2. List your key action points or things to be done and number each item. This could be on a separate sheet of flipchart paper or alongside, but everyone should see them and be able to articulate their understanding of them when asked.
3. Populate the grid based on its ease and impact of doing the action. This could be written straight onto the template, or a number on a sticky note could work, allowing you flexibility if necessary.
   a   Quick wins – easy to do with a high impact
   b   Longer-term plans – hard to do with a high impact
   c   Low-hanging fruit – easy to do with a low impact
   d   Disregard if possible – hard to do with a low impact
4. Allocate resources, names or teams to an action and time scales. Quick wins would be first followed by Low Hanging Fruit or Long-Term Plans depending on resources and need.

Possible uses
To develop individual or team action plans. It can also be used as a starting point before developing and populating a one-page strategy or gameplan.

Suggested resources
Printed template, the template is drawn onto a flipchart/whiteboard or set up on your online platform. Pens and sticky notes

Tips for success
Link with actions on your strategy or game plan in order to fully align to projects.

1. My key learning points...

1

2

3

4

5

6

2. My prioritised list...

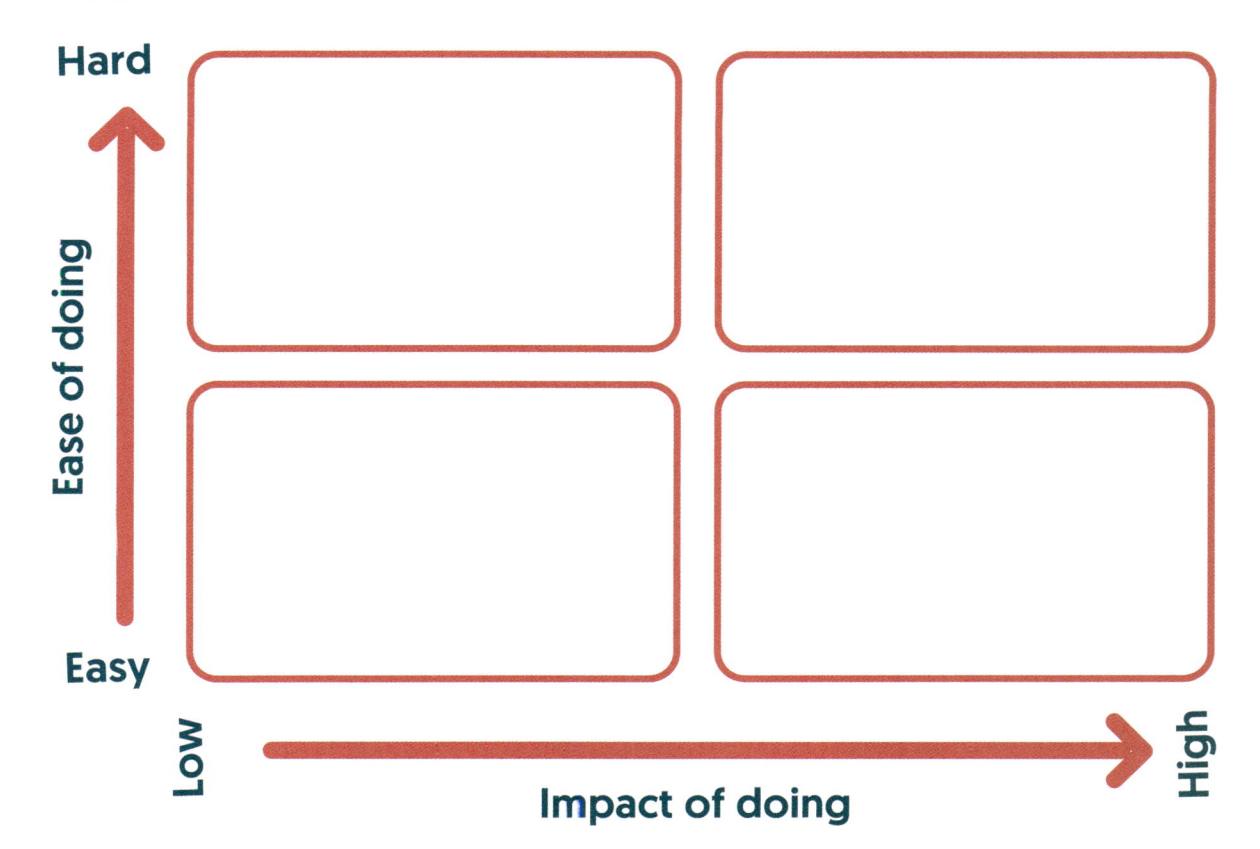

Ease of doing: Easy → Hard

Impact of doing: Low → High

DFV (Desirability, Feasibility, Viability) Analysis

What is it?
A tool to help refine the number of ideas/actions based on their Desirability, Feasibility and Viability.

What's the process?
Be clear about the problem you're trying to solve and use appropriate idea generation or problem-solving tools to create options. Then:
a) Walk through the three circles as follows:
1. First, be clear about the desires of the audience you're designing for – what are their needs? Then look at your ideas through this criteria as a lens. If your idea is not desirable, ditch it.
2. Once you've identified the desirable ideas, explore their feasibility and viability. What is technically and organisationally feasible? Which ideas can be financially viable? Do your ideas rate against your audience's criteria (cost, volume, pace, etc.) Keep the best and ditch the rest.
3. By now you should have a section of ideas that overlap the DFV circles which you can take further for development as appropriate.

Possible uses
This tool can be used in design, decision-making, problem-solving, project management, gaining insights, idea generation and evaluation.

Suggested resources
Have a copy of the DFV template available. Lots of pens and sticky notes from the idea generation aspect of your session.

Start Here

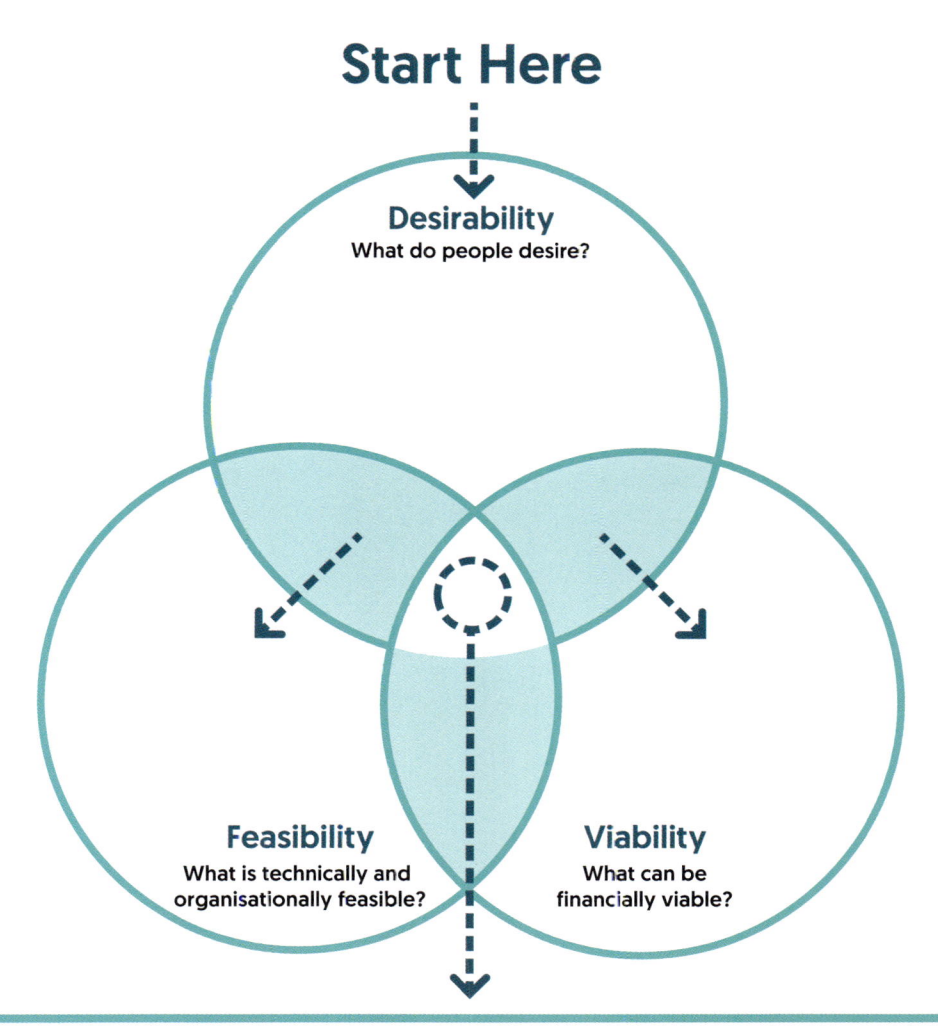

Desirability
What do people desire?

Feasibility
What is technically and organisationally feasible?

Viability
What can be financially viable?

Add to this box all overlapping solutions that are **Desirable, Feasible** and **Viable...**

Harvesting Ideas

What is it?
Harvesting is a way to collate ideas, identify themes and synergies and recognise duplication.

What's the process?
1. Using your chosen tool/approach collate your ideas on separate sticky notes (this could be the result of World Café or Radiant Problem Solving, etc.) – one idea per sticky note.
2. Allow group members some time to absorb the ideas and take it all in. Look for patterns/themes that you can group the ideas into.
3. Move sticky notes into themes/patterns identified and discuss as you do it. Note: this is not an opportunity to dismiss or evaluate any ideas.
4. Stand back and look at the ideas again. Ask:
   a. Can any of the ideas combine to make a better idea?
   b. Is there anything missing? – add a new sticky note if you think of anything.
   c. Does anything stand out? If so, what and why?
   d. Do any ideas need further clarification or development?
5. After the harvest, use another tool/process to help evaluate and prioritise ideas.

Possible uses
It's a really useful exercise after lots of ideas have been generated. It can:
- Summarise and group the ideas
- Stimulate a final creative surge of energy for new ideas
- Prepare for final evaluation and prioritisation

Suggested resources
The bigger the better. Ideally using large sticky notes or the sticky note option in your online platform will help with visualisation and sorting.

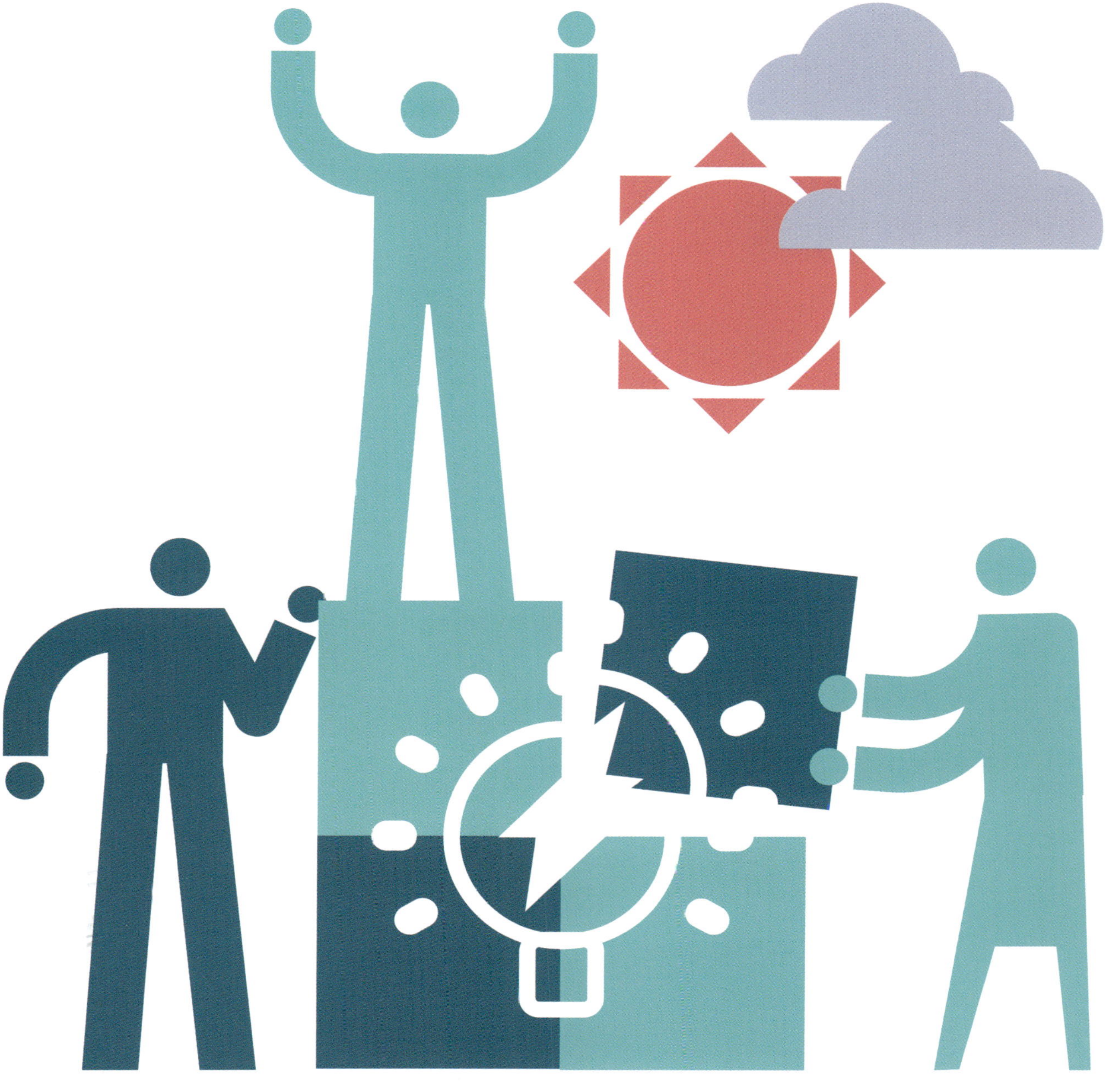

Blob journey

What is it?
A visual tool to identify how people feel about a project, task, role, or event. A great way of checking in with people, ensuring 100% inclusion in the process.

What's the process?
This can be done as printed images for personal use, projected onto a whiteboard, or shared as a slide during an online presentation/workshop.

Spend a little time crafting the question you want them to answer. Ask individuals to circle, colour in or place a sticker on the character which best shows how they feel in answer to your question. For example, 'when you were told about the changes ahead, how did you feel?' Give them a minute or two to scan the diagram, choose a character in answer to the question and think about why they chose that particular blob.

Then go around the group, asking them to identify their chosen blob and explain why they chose it. For example, with the character marked **A** left, they may say that "they can see the end result, feel happy about their involvement in it and are excited about sharing the results".

It is important that the group understand the rule that a person's choice is the correct choice as it's their personal answer to the question and is not to be challenged or disagreed with.

If appropriate, keep the diagram and use it to review progress or to plan support throughout longer projects. How people respond will give leaders insights into what they need to do to provide support or things to monitor.

Possible uses
This could be used in many types of meetings, including:
- Team check-in
- Project review
- Scrum meeting
- Face-to-face or online development workshop
- Experiential team development
- 1-to-1 coaching

Suggested resources
Printed version per person or large print for the group. Or as a blank image on a slide in the chosen platform for online presentation. Pens, sticky notes, or dots if face-to-face.

N.B., I have included the blob journey here, but there are many available to purchase. Popular versions include the Blob Tree, Bridge, River and Needs. Topical and seasonal versions such as Blob Olympics, Blob Christmas and Blob Classroom are also frequently available.

Tips for success
1   If using face-to-face, print as large as possible (A1 works well) and maybe even laminate for regular use.
2   Keep versions marked by teams for review and to help with coaching a team or individuals through change or personal development.

Adapted from the work of Ian Long and Pip Wilson

Global CV

What is it?
A team activity used to get to know each other better, act as an ice breaker, provide some fun and identify strengths from experience. Looking at 'what got your team here' is a very effective way of getting to know each other and building vulnerability-based trust.

What's the process?
1. Invite everyone to use the allocated resources to draw a visual representation with as few words as possible and that shows every job they've ever had. You could start with a short drawing workshop or showing a Ted Talk – Dan Roam and Graham Shaw have some good resources.
2. The team members should include paid and unpaid jobs, volunteering, early career, family roles and more recent jobs. They may want to spend a couple of minutes thinking about it and writing a list before getting artistic. You should allocate around 15 minutes for this part.
3. You can choose whether or not each person adds their name to their image or whether you want to make it part of the fun. Use the remainder of your allocated time (I'd suggest around 20 minutes for a team of around 10 – 15 people) to walk around the room with each image and discuss who's done what. Encourage people to talk about their roles. Ask each other and be inquisitive about things like what skills they had in those roles? Or what made it fun?

Possible uses
As an icebreaker or team energiser in an event where you want to build trust, get to know each other, and have some fun. It can be used at a time in the day to change the energy of the group as appropriate.

Suggested resources
a. If doing it individually on paper, you would ideally have some A3-sized paper per participant or a sheet of flipchart paper. Some suitable coloured pens for the paper type and size.
b. If doing it collectively, allocate an area of some whiteboards to each person and ensure they have plenty of different coloured pens.

Tips for success
Leave the images on a wall in a shared space for the duration of the meeting and watch people keep returning to them during breaks. You will find that they continue to ask each other questions and building relationships.

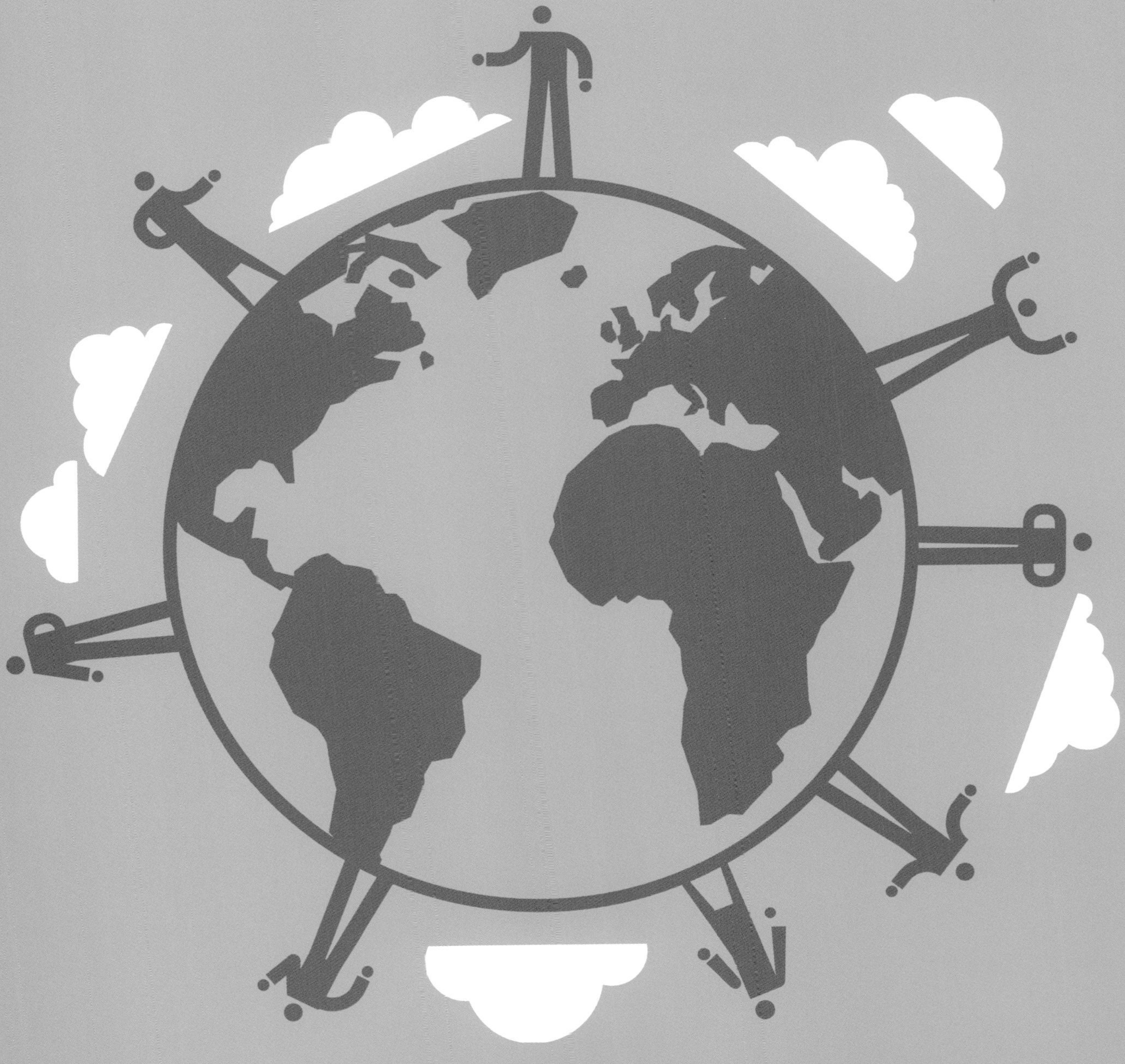

Shapes

What is it?
Shapes is an icebreaker that creates a fun energy and insights into each other before a workshop or meeting. It is based on work done by BUPA Healthcare in the early 2000s.

What's the process?
1. Draw the shapes shown on the following page onto a flipchart, whiteboard or have them prepared on a slide. Cover them up until you introduce the activity.
2. Explain that you are about to reveal some shapes. Once shown, they are to choose a shape, their favourite shape. Ask them not to overthink it and preferably their choice will be the first one that jumps into their mind when looking at the shapes.
3. Ask them one shape at a time to identify which they chose by a show of hands or moving around the room to group people by shape. Then explain the following meanings of each shape:
    i. Square: Perfectionist, If it's worth doing, it's worth doing right. Note the four identical length sides, 90 degree corners, the ability to equally split a square.
    ii. Triangle: Natural Leaders, Controlling, get stuff done. Triangles get to the point, drive action and get results.
    iii. Circle: People watchers. Circles always look out for each other, ask how they're doing and like to make connections. They can often get caught watching people – like at a train station.
    iv. Rectangle: Change agents, change things for sake of it. They are good at change, are often cheer leaders for change and will support people through change. They may also like to freshen things up from time to time – maybe like re-arranging furniture at home or organising kitchen cupboards.
    v. Squiggly Line: Creative Thinkers or Nutters. Since when has a squiggly line been a shape? Those who choose squiggly lines are great at thinking outside of the box and coming up with ideas that no one else would have thought about.
4. Allow some time for reflection and discussion to see how many of them find the brief descriptions accurately reflect them. You could also ask them in groups to create a list of 'strengths of each shape' or 'ways to get the best out of each shape'.

Possible uses
Shapes can be used as an icebreaker, energiser or a way to change the mind state of attendees. It is also a great conversation start and simple way for people to begin to understand each other in a team development type session.

Suggested resources
- Flipchart paper with the shapes drawn up. Or powerpoint slide with images.

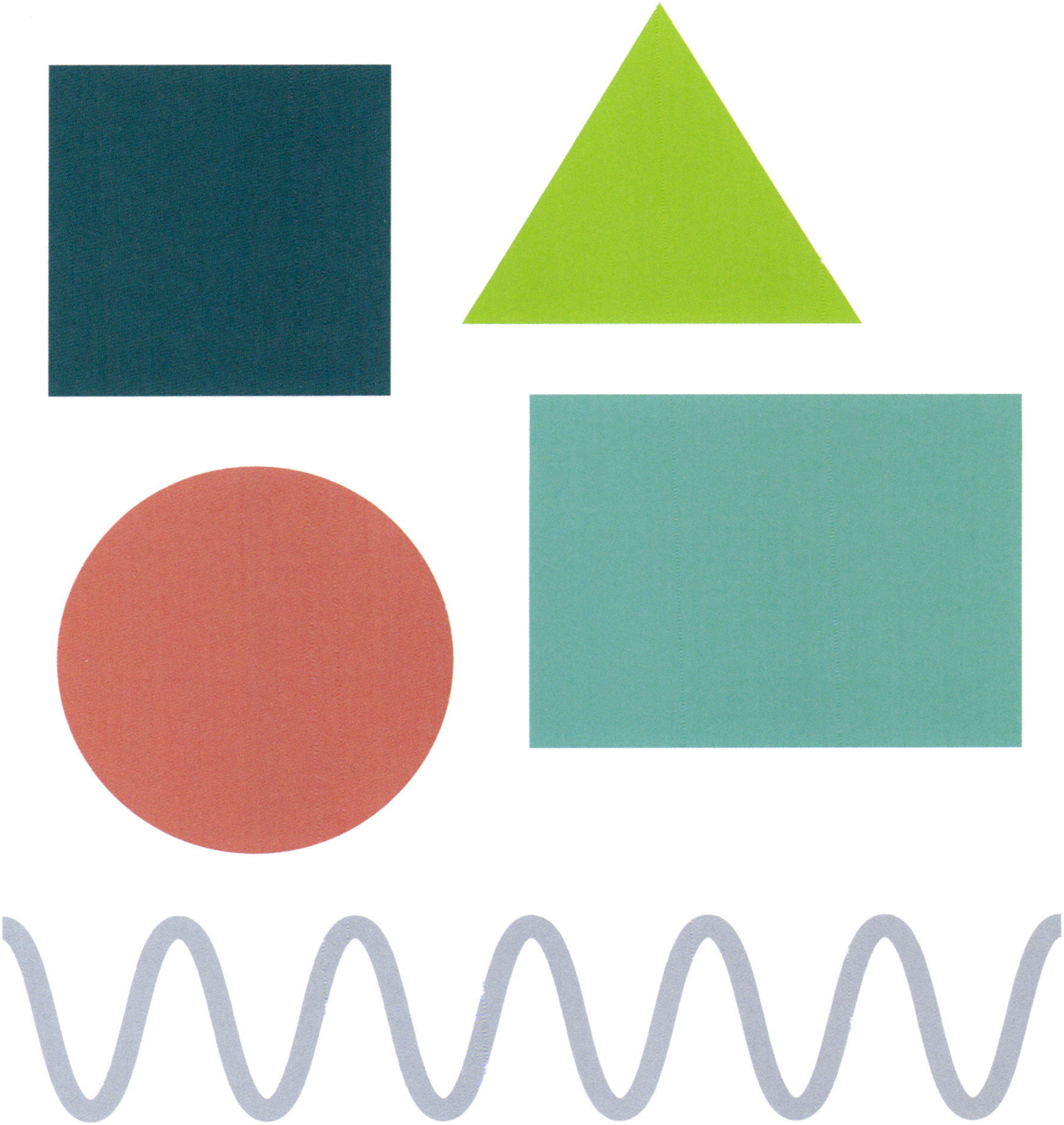

Gaining consensus

What is it?
A tool to allow several people at once to explore and gain consensus on an issue, in an inclusive and quick way.

What's the process?
1. Divide people into groups of ideally four, but three to six will work.
2. Place the flipchart paper on the table in front of them, draw a circle in the centre and label this 'Consensus'.
3. Divide the remaining page into as many sections as there are people. Each person should be sitting by their section of paper.
4. To begin with, everyone has five minutes to write their thoughts/ideas/questions on their own section of paper – this should be done working alone without discussion.
5. After this time, one person starts by sharing one of their thoughts, and the group discuss this and agrees – if consensus is gained, then the idea is written in the centre circle.
6. Moving around the group in order, each person shares a new thought or idea until all have been heard.

Possible uses
Consensus gaining can be used to narrow down options, gain and identify common ground and help ensure everyone is on the same page. It can be a good way to diffuse or prevent conflict.

Suggested resources
- Flipchart paper
- Marker pens
- Tables that people can sit around

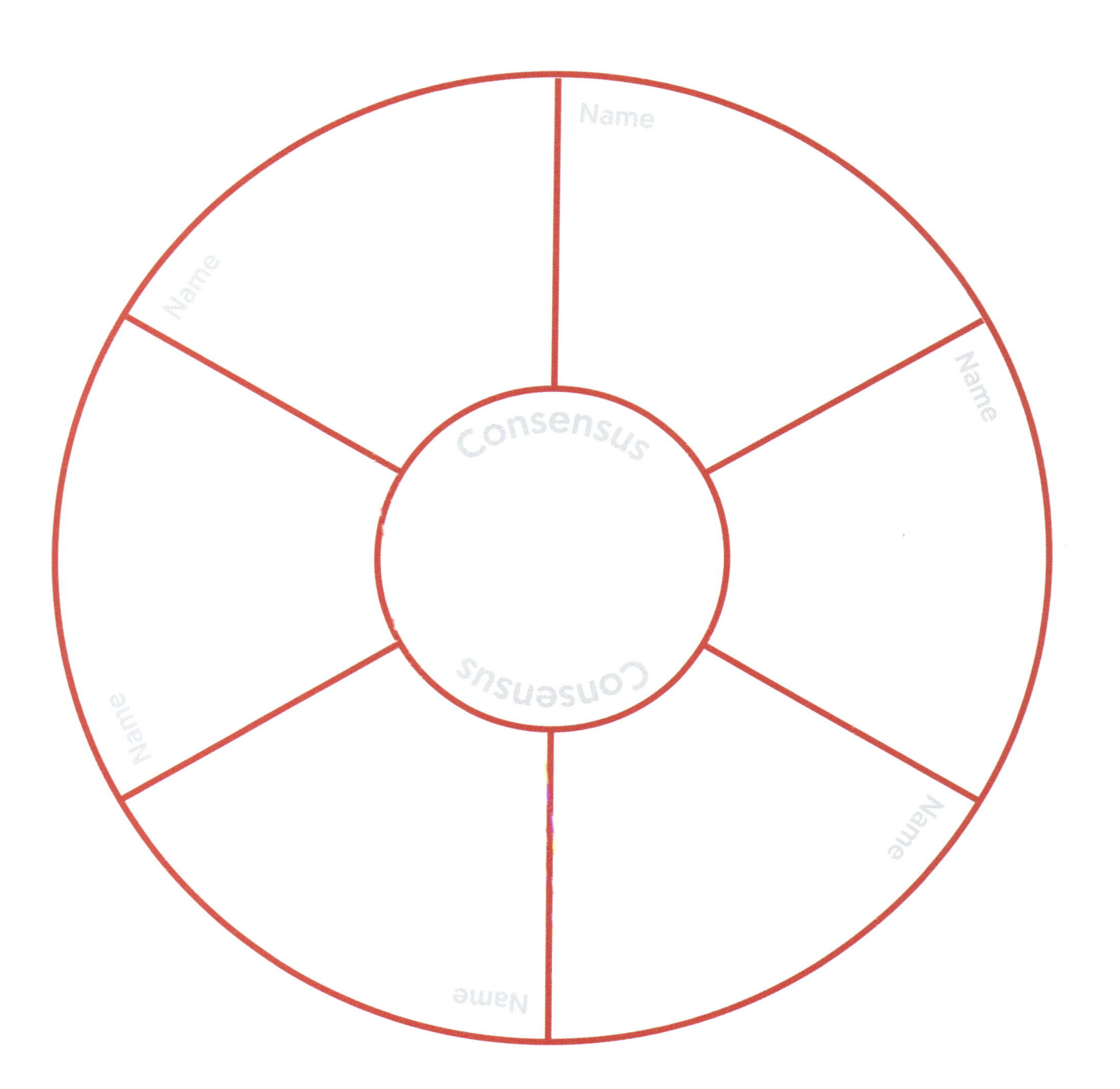

Team Manifesto

What is it?
The Team Manifesto is a great way to set up or re-establish a team and prepare them for success. It aims to build clarity, gain buy-in and create clear accountability for what the team will do and how they will do it.

What's the process?
The Team Manifesto can be developed in hours or days. Depending on the team and its function, you will choose your own timescale for developing this. The Team Manifesto consists of six topics, each of which can be developed as a discussion or using a particular tool/process. They are:

Purpose – Principles – People – Process – Performance – Pride

Here's a little about each:

Purpose — What is your purpose? Not the company's mission or vision statement but the purpose of the team who the manifesto is for. This should be clear, unambiguous and bought into by the team (ideally created by everyone). Keep it to one sentence where possible.

Principles — What's really important to us? I would suggest three or four guiding principles that will help team members make decisions, each with a brief explanation/description. There are many ways to discover these, but certainly get the group to come up with their own first, then in small groups and then finally as a whole team.

People — Who is the team? What do they do, and how do they do it? A list or table of roles is a good starting point and can be added to with tools such as Mad – Sad – Glad, or a profiling tool like Facet5, Lifeorientations® (LIFO®) or another chosen model.

Processes — How will we work together? What is our drumbeat (meeting schedule)? Any decision-making processes and working practices?

Performance — What will happen when we've succeeded? How will we know? What are your top key measures? Your strategy may be referenced here, but don't get bogged down in the detail.

Pride — What do you want to be famous for? This part is a great way to imagine your future. A visioning exercise such as Cover Story is a brilliant addition here to encourage people to think big and imagine success.

Possible uses
Use the Team Manifesto to summarise what and how your team will work.

Suggested resources
Tools appropriate for each of the topics. If using one template, have it drawn up in your preferred style and work through them as a team.

Tips for success
Spend time together as a team, away from the office/department. A draft can be created in a few hours or a rigorous approach can take two full days together. It's always time well spent.

You could also work through it matched with other methodologies such as a LEGO® Serious Play® (LSP) Real Time Strategy workshop for the team or a series of Grove Graphic Templates such as Game Plan, Cover Story, and Five Bold Steps Vision.

Purpose	Principles	People

Performance

Process	Pride

World Café

What is it?
The World Café methodology is a simple, effective, and flexible format for hosting large group dialogue.

What's the process?
World Café can be modified to meet a wide variety of needs. Specifics of context, numbers, purpose, location and other circumstances are factored into each event's unique invitation, design, and question choice, but the following five components comprise the basic model:

Setting: Create a 'special' environment, most often modelled after a café, i.e., small round tables covered with a paper tablecloth, coloured pens, a vase of flowers, an optional 'talking stick' item. There should be four or five chairs at each table depending on the group size and the number of questions.

Welcome and Introductions: The host begins with a warm welcome and introduction to the world café process, setting the context, sharing their café etiquette, and putting participants at ease.

Small Group Rounds: The process begins with the first of three or more rounds (length of time chosen by the facilitator) of a conversation conducted by the small group seated around a table. At the end of the round, the group moves onto the next table in the sequence. They may choose to leave a person on the table as the 'table host' for the first minute or all of the next round to update the incoming group on what happened on the table in the previous round.

Questions: Each round is prefaced with a question designed for a specific context and desired purpose of the session. The same questions can be used for each round, or they can be built upon each other to focus the conversation or guide its direction.

Harvest: Afterwards, the small groups or individuals are invited to share their insights or results from their conversations with the rest of the larger group. The results can be shared in various ways, and actions can be explored using other tools in this toolkit.

Possible uses
- Any meeting that requires group debate and collective decision making.
- Can be used as just one part of a larger meeting.

Suggested resources
- Paper tablecloths, banqueting roll or large sheets of paper.
- Mixture of coloured pens/markers
- Sweets and snacks
- Music and speakers

Tips for success
1. Consider the questions carefully. Craft them so that they are suitably ambiguous and not too rigid. Consider including questions about what's good, not so good, the benefits if improving/changing and what others might be able to do for you.
2. Don't take the layout for granted. A good layout, snacks, resources and music add to the experience and help create the right energy.

Open Space Technology

What is it?
Open Space Technology is a tool for running meetings or aspects where the participants create and manage the agenda themselves.

What's the process?
Identify a need within your agenda for the attendees to take control of the content. Explore the process explained earlier in the book and begin setting up of your spaces, Open Space programme and templates. Throughout the earlier stages of the event, gather ideas and potential topics that can be shared as options when you introduce the open space activity. Having a small selection of topics and hosts primed throughout the event maybe worthwhile to create initial buy in and engagement.

When the time comes, take the time to explain the process and break it down into stages:
1. Introduce and overview the process.
2. Invite topics.
3. Invite hosts for chosen topics
4. Fill the template with topics in timeslots.
5. Invite attendees to choose the topics they wish to join in on.
6. Follow your timings and have great discussions.

At the end of your open space session, invite hosts to share key aspects and findings of their discussions, such as lessons learned, actions agreed upon, and concepts being taken forward.

Possible uses
A great way of using a large amount of time (usually two hours plus) to engage with the attendees of a course, conference or workshop. Especially useful in putting the agenda on to them and giving attendees a chance to explore topics that have arisen during the earlier aspects of your event.

Suggested resources
Sticky notes, flipchart, multiple locations suitable for hosting different discussions, template similar to the one below for people to populate

There's more detail on this particular tool earlier in the book. Take some time to explore that section in detail.

	1 – Breakout room A	2 – Blue chair corner	3 – Dining area	4 – Breakout room B	5 – Table with flowers on
Opening	All together to set the scene and gather ideas					
10am to 11am					
11am to 12pm					
Lunch					
1pm to 2pm					
Closing session	All together to harvest ideas/summary				

Mad Sad Glad

What is it?
Mad Sad Glad is a useful tool to help you understand team members. It also guides you in how you communicate with each other and interact in the best way to achieve a positive team climate.

What's the process?
1. Invite team members to a workshop or meeting, and be sure to share the purpose of the session so they can prepare.
2. Explain why this is useful and what the benefits are of doing it, and what it can overcome. Use real-life examples to illustrate, if possible, how knowing these things build trust, understanding and help create effective ways of working.
3. Ask each person to think about what makes them Mad, Sad and Glad in the given context. It could be work in general, projects or a specific team environment.
4. Record on the table either directly or using sticky notes. It's better in a workshop scenario to use large sticky notes or write big enough on a whiteboard for people to stand around and discuss.
5. Allow time for attendees to read and ask questions. It's key to set the scene that the contents of the table are fact. They are the things that people find make them Mad, Sad and Glad; therefore they are not open to challenge or disagreement.
6. There should be no need to go through each item individually. Each person should be able to use their intuition and knowledge of each other to respond appropriately to the chart.
7. Use regularly as a review tool to ensure you are working well together.

Possible uses
Areas it can be used are:
- Building trust
- Building awareness
- Project set-up workshops
- Reviewing
- Understand why people are behaving like they are
- Creating a positive work environment
- Team building

Suggested resources
A chart drawn up on a whiteboard, flipchart or set up on your online platform. Pens and sticky notes.

Tips for success
Not only can this be used for your own team, but it can be a part of other aspects of work. It could be shared with key stakeholders to help work as effectively as possible. It also could form a great part of the Team Manifesto in the People topic.

	SIMON	VICKY	TIM	LESLEY
What makes you MAD	Avoidable surprises. Problem stating. Inaccurate/incomplete data. Not going extra mile for our customers. Not caring about losing good people.	Surprises. Missing deadline requests without explanation. Being missed out of the loop. Having agreed to plan then not completing. Only getting part of the information.	Digressing. People spending too much time on themselves. Lack of structure at meetings. Lack of 1:1 time. Lack of trust in my ability. Lack of direction. Given tasks that aren't followed up.	Being excluded when I could help. Deadlines being missed. Not being responded to. Surprises. Not doing what was agreed or re-negotiating. Festering in the negativity.
What makes you SAD	People who don't care. Working too hard + long hours. Spending lots of time on underperformers instead of high performers.	Doing things the same. Missing opportunities. Missing deadlines. Missed expectations. Dissatisfaction over "trivia". Complaints.	Lack of time. Lack of time to 'develop team'. Lack of 'Open Forum' time. Lack of social aspects. Work/Life Balance.	Not being used as support. Not being consulted. Things not working well. Irritating people when it's not my intention. If team didn't see benefits of what striving to achieve.
What makes you GLAD	Manage my expectation and keep me informed. Ask me to make decisions having all info and facts. Create a plan, do + get results. Using initiative. A good debate + dialogue. Having a laugh.	Achieving deadlines. Seeing teams develop. Compliments. Getting external recognition. Getting internal recognition. Being the best. Problem solving not stating. Being creative.	Support. Reassurance. Advice/Guidance. Friendship. Using different strengths. Knowledge base. Positive, enthusiastic caring people.	Getting together + agreeing way forward. Working together to solve challenges. Making a difference. Having fun. Recognition.

BIRDS Review

What is it?
A BIRDS Review is a very simple and effective way of encouraging meeting attendees to consolidate their learning and actions.

What's the process?
1. Explain to the group the headings of the acronym BIRDS:
   Breakthroughs – what breakthroughs in thinking have you had during the session?
   Ideas – have you got any ideas that you will look into? If so, what?
   Reminders – what have you been reminded about that you knew, but had forgotten?
   Decisions/Do Now – what will you do straight away as a result or what actions have you listed?
   Still needs answers – what questions has this raised that still need answering now or later?
2. Ask attendees to either:
   1. Share one item from the list
   2. Consider all parts of the BIRDS Review, make notes and prepare to share with the group – collectively or in small groups.
   3. Or the meeting chair could use the five letters randomly to check-in with attendees, i.e. ask Paul to share an idea that he has had during the meeting, or Jodie to remind us of any actions (Decisions/Do Now) agreed so far?

Possible uses
- BIRDS Review can be used at different points in meetings and workshops to conduct a review or maybe at the end to gather thoughts and confirm actions.

Suggested resources
You can run this as a discussion or an activity. It's worth having the BIRDS acronym on a slide to help guide attendees and maybe even a selection of sticky notes to gather answers if you want to.

BREAKTHROUGHS
IDEAS
REMINDERS
DECISIONS/DO NOW
STILL NEEDS ANSWERS

Story Dice

What is it?
A pack of dice which contain an image or icon on each side. There are several producers of these types of dice, most popular are Rory's Story Cubes, which are also available in different topics and categories. These are a fun and inclusive way of telling stories, reviewing activities, and generating ideas.

What's the process?
The use of Story Dice, encourage the use of metaphor and develop skills of storytelling and creativity. There are many different ways of using them, but here's one of my favourites.
1. Pick a number of dice between three and nine (There are nine in most sets, some sets are bolt on packs of three).
2. Decide and brief the group on the topic. It could be to review an event, describe team strengths, explain the benefits and features of a product.
3. Each person is to roll the dice in turn and using the images that land face up, tell the story of the chosen topic from their view.
4. Multiple rounds can be undertaken to break a topic down. In a project setting for example, the first round could be features of the project, the next round team strengths in the project, third round things to improve the project, and so on as you need.
5. Informally gather thoughts and ideas for use as necessary.

There is one rule – there are no wrong answers.

Possible uses
This can be used for activity, event, project, or team reviews.

Suggested resources
One or multiple packs of Story Dice an open mind and a sense of humour.

Tips for success
These resources are small, keep a set close by to add to a meeting or workshop when you want to change the energy or pace and try something a little different.

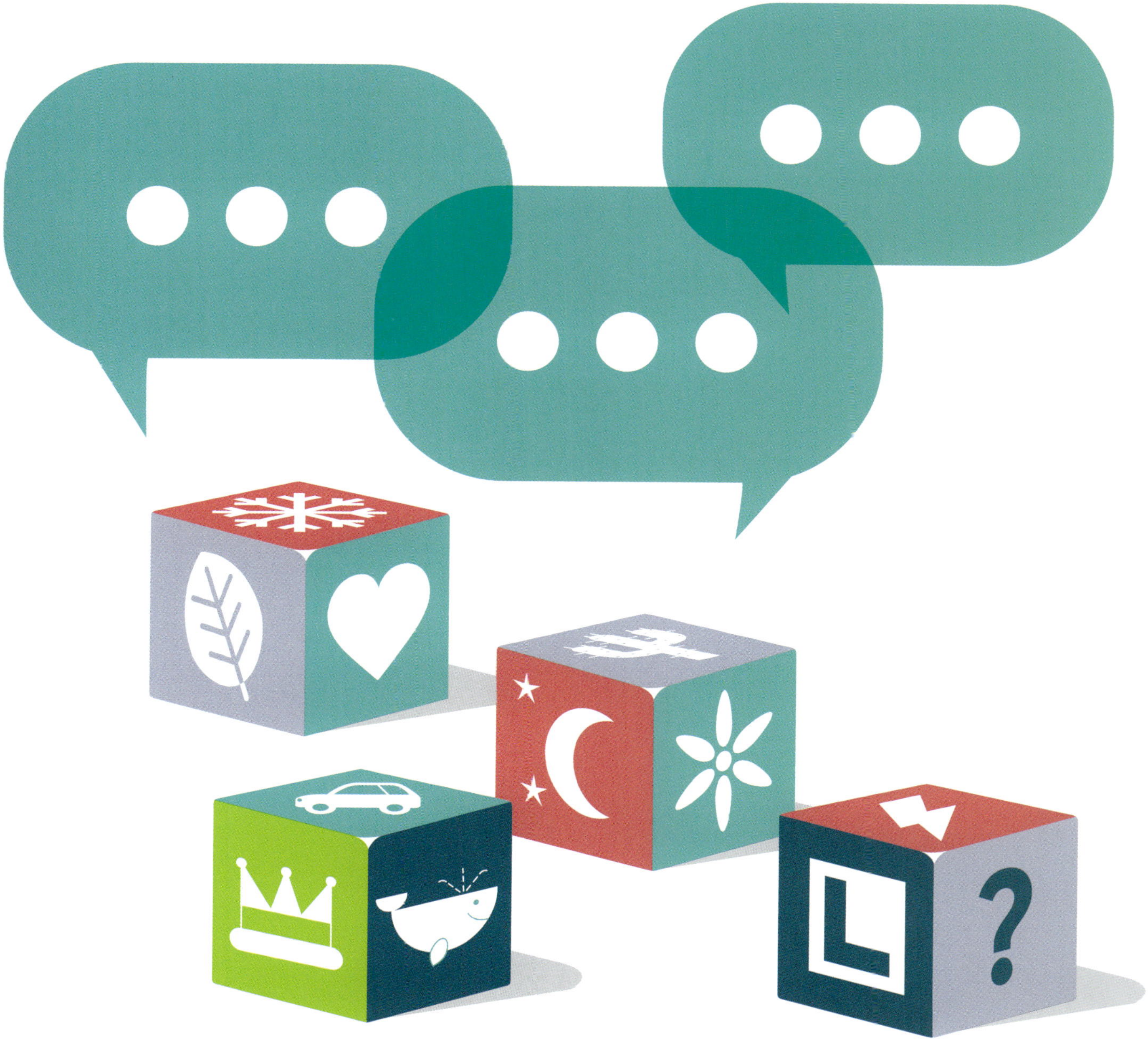

Hopes and Fears

What is it?
- It is a tool that ensures buy-in to any workshop or meeting.
- It's a short exercise to help members of a team share their perspectives on a task/project and build a common understanding of goals and potential problems.
- It's a way to answer the question, "Do we share the same idea of what's supposed to happen here?"
- It emphasises the value of each person's contribution, encouraging greater trust and understanding within the team.
- It allows you, as the facilitator, to kill any risks at the start.

What's the process?
An exercise which will highlight shared understanding and allow discussion and create buy-in. It's better to express thoughts so they can be discussed and addressed where possible. Setting the right tone of relaxed discussion at the start is very important.
- Ask the group members to consider their hopes and fears concerning the topic/task in hand.
- Give them around five minutes to jot down their thoughts individually. This element is key as individual thinking lends itself to different styles and it prevents people from being swayed by others.
- Ask the group to write these up on flipchart paper, headed 'Hopes'. By writing them up on the flipchart, they provide a neutral focus point for the group, so the hopes become shared by all of them.
- Don't discuss it for the moment. Then ask for the 'Fears', writing them up on flipchart paper headed 'Fears'.
- Now go back to the Hopes and discuss further how you can ensure these are fulfilled as a team.
- Then move to the Fears and discuss how the team can avoid them. These are risks that need to be eliminated as swiftly as possible.

Possible uses
- At the start of meetings, training or workshops.
- Great in the first stages of the team/project forming. This is when people are likely to have the greatest difference of opinion about what they should do.
- If unrealistic or inappropriate hopes are identified, they're less likely to become frustrated if they're discussed.
- It helps individuals to learn about one another, which will help them to communicate more effectively.
- Use for an existing group, where they are beginning to explore something new. For example, a discussion around a change to be implemented, or a project to be kicked off.

Suggested resources
Flipcharts, pens, and sticky notes.

Tips for success
Group dynamics can help make this flow well. Small groups could be split into half and in turn take Hopes or Fears for around six minutes and then swap. Larger groups could have a flipchart with both Hopes and Fears written and then nominate a spokesperson.

For this session/meeting/negotiation what are your greatest?

My Greatest Hopes	My Greatest Fears	How can we turn these hopes to reality and kill our fears?
Group Greatest Hopes	**Group Greatest Fears**	

Magic Cane

What is it?
A short team challenge (though I've seen teams take a long time to complete it) that can be used with a serious intent to break the ice, change the energy, explore team working or make a key learning point. Teams are given a magic cane (sometimes referred to as a helium stick), which they must lower to the ground using just their index fingers.

What's the process?
The chosen length of cane is rested on team members' index fingers. The start position is for team members to stand opposite each other with their elbows tucked into their sides, their hands facing forwards, with both their index fingers sticking out. Before letting go of the cane, the facilitator should explain the purpose and the rules:

Purpose – to lower the cane to the ground as quickly as they can by following the rules.

Rules – 1) team members must maintain contact with the cane at all times using only their index fingers.
2) fingers cannot be hooked around the cane or clamped. The cane can only sit on top of their fingers.

If any of the rules are broken, the challenge will be re-started.

NB. At the start of the exercise, when the facilitator lets go of the cane, it will likely rise, like 'magic'. It will then take good communication, coordination, and concerted team effort to succeed.

Possible uses
It can be used to show the importance of working together as a team. The activity can help reinforce communication, co-operation, leadership, and problem solving.

Suggested resources
A length of garden bamboo suitable for each team member to have between 50cm and 100cm space per person. Multiple lengths can be taped together using strong 'gaffer' type tape. Or a larger team can be split into groups of between four and seven with a 2m length of bamboo each.

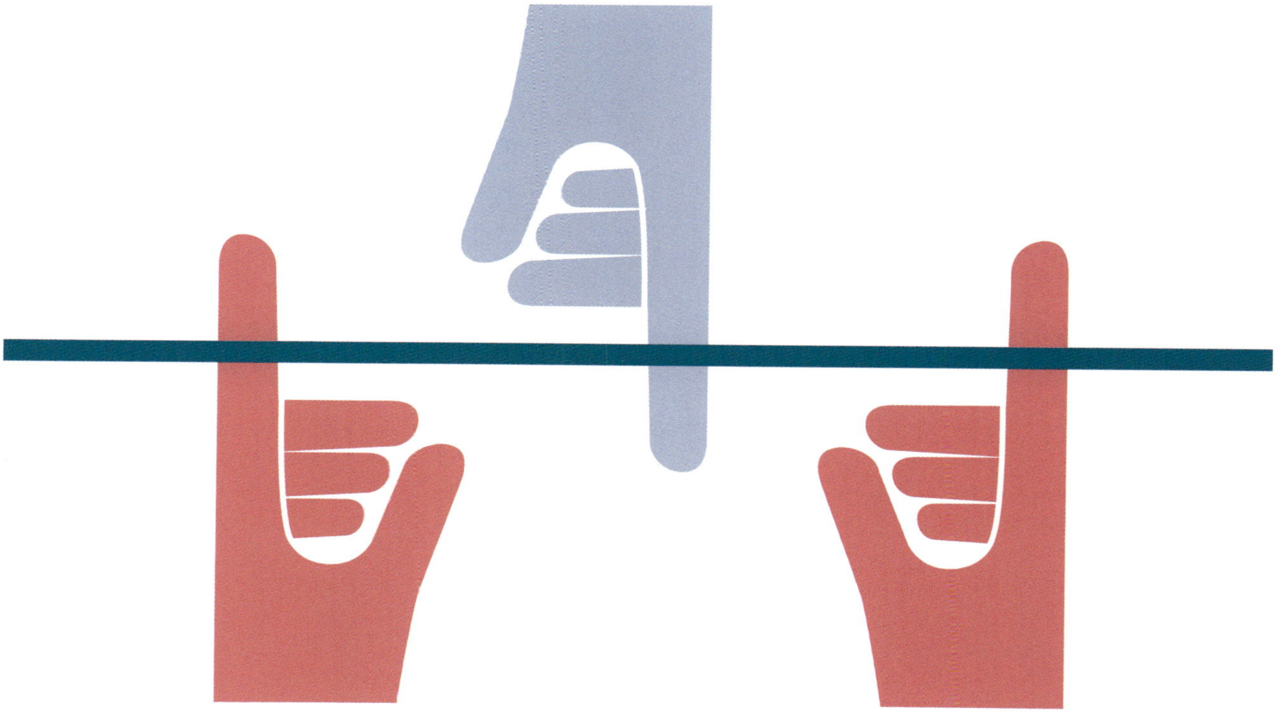

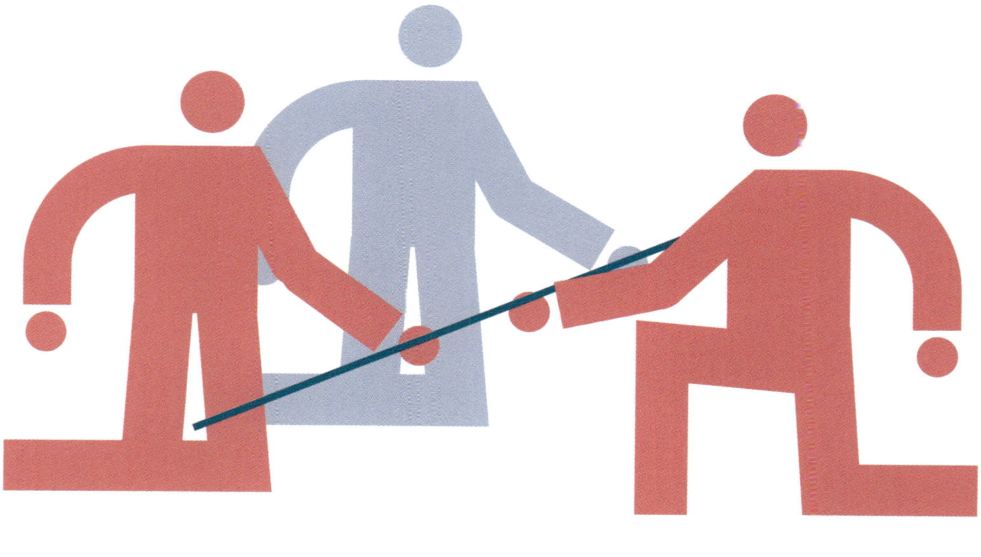

Team Juggle

What is it?
A fun team energiser-type activity with several potential key learning points. A great way of re-energising a group, changing the state, and introducing a key aspect of a workshop or meeting.

What's the process?
This works well in one group of up to approximately 20 people or in smaller groups of six or more. Assemble your group(s) in circles and brief them as follows:
1. Your objective as a group/team is to get as many of these juggling/tennis balls moving around the group in the same sequence at once as you can without dropping them. You must pass the ball to the same person each time. Start with one ball and establish a sequence. The sequence is complete when everyone has had the ball once and it is back with the person it started with.
2. Once the group has completed step one, explain that you will introduce more balls as the exercise goes on. Start the sequence again and gradually increase the number of balls. You are trying to get as close to one per person as possible. (A good time to consider the team's capacity and what happens if 'the ball is dropped').
3. You can periodically stop the group and ask what's working well or what can be better.
4. If the team are working well together, a good challenge might be to get your chosen number of balls being juggled for 90 seconds without any being dropped.

Possible uses...
- Changing the energy or state of the group dynamic.
- An Icebreaker at the start of a session or after a break.
- Learning point exercise for areas such as:
- Trust – knowing your job and doing it whilst others do theirs.
- Change – reaction to changing direction.
- Working at capacity – having too many balls in the air.

Suggested resources
You will need enough juggling balls for each person to have one each, plus a few spare ones. Koosh balls or tennis balls will do the same job.

Tips for success
1. Choose the amount of time and number of balls to suit your available time and desired outcomes.
2. You can add complexities like reversing the order if the team are doing well or you want to theme the message around change.
3. If a team is struggling, you may introduce a leader or manager role who provides instructions or a drumbeat, saying 'throw' or 'now' etc., to which the group should act.

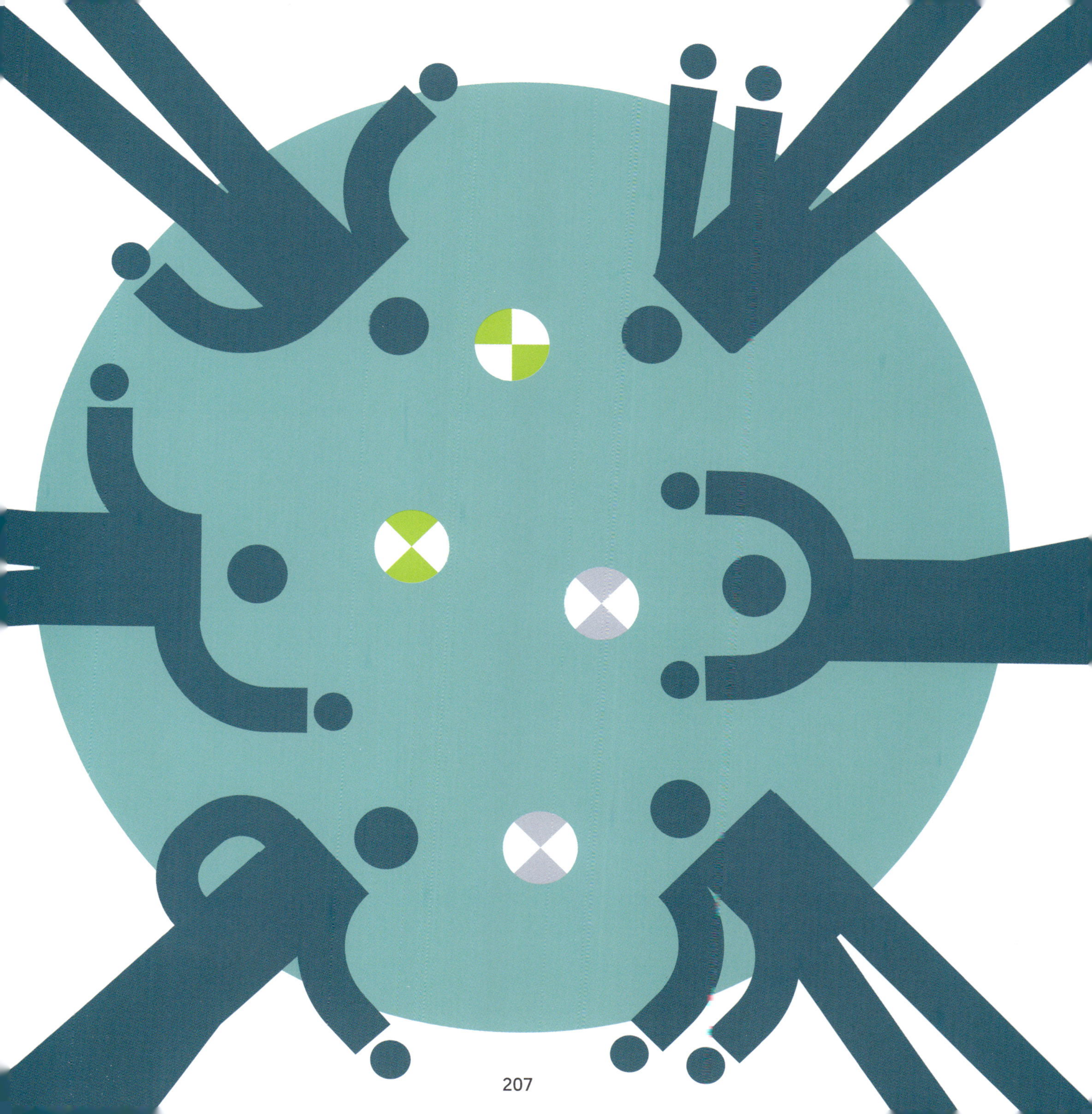

Marshmallow Tower

What is it?
A great team development activity to engage in a fun way, explore leadership, teamwork, time management, competitiveness and much, much more.

What's the process?
For groups of between four and seven participants, layout a set of resources for each group. A group should have the following:
- Around half a packet of uncooked dry spaghetti pasta.
- An equal number of marshmallows.
- One sheet of flipchart paper to design with and build their tower on.

Set the scene for the groups, by giving them an amount of time to suit your agenda (20 to 30 minutes works well) and telling them they are to build a tower as tall and stable as possible using only the spaghetti and marshmallows in the time allowed. The structure must be built on a sheet of flipchart paper (this helps you as a facilitator to tidy up).

You may choose to allocate them some time to design, during which they cannot construct – this will depend on your session objectives.

At the end of the time, groups are to step away from their tower whilst its height is measured.

Announce a winner as appropriate and review based on your session objectives using a review tool such as Action Learning, Mood-o-gram, Blob Journey or Action Replay.

Possible uses
This short, fun activity can be used as part of your meeting/workshop to:
- Change the energy
- Learn a skill/behaviour
- Provide a shared experience for the group/team
- Assess a key point in a workshop or course

Suggested resources
You will need the following:
- Dry uncooked Spaghetti and marshmallows – enough for the number of groups you have
- Flip chart paper – one sheet per group
- Pens for design
- Ruler or tape measure
- Pens, sticky notes, templates, and flipchart as necessary for your chosen review

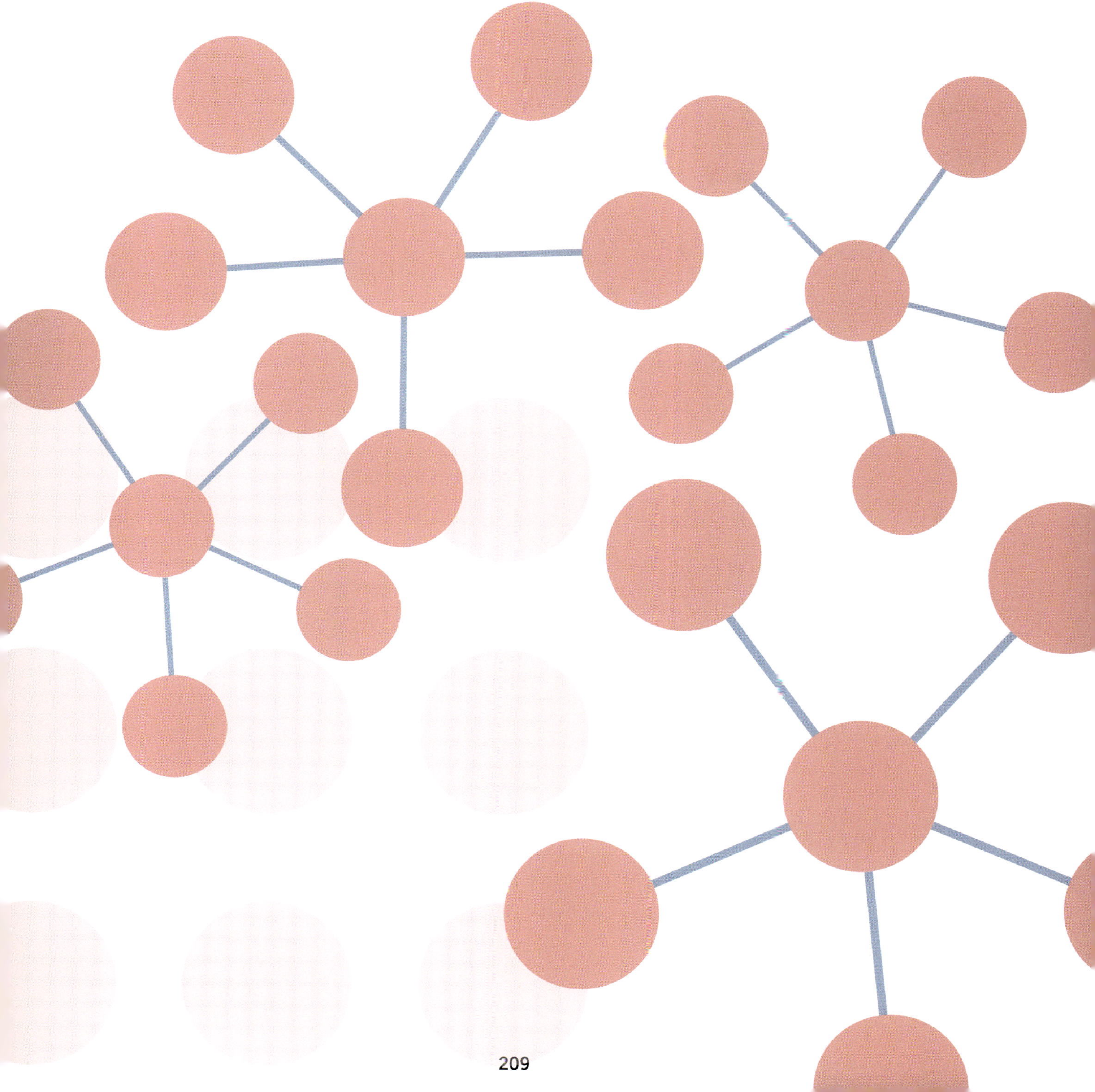

The Lego® Duck

What is it?
A simple yet hugely impactful short activity to demonstrate the power of diversity and introduce stories and metaphors.

What's the process?
1. Give each group member a set of the six duck bricks and tell them they have one minute to build a duck. When everyone has built a duck or the minute is up, stop the group and comment on how awesome the ducks all look.
2. Point out that there is no right or wrong answer. If a builder says they've built a duck, that's what it is. Ask them to look around the group at everyone else's build and see if there are any the same or similar. The likelihood is that all ducks will be different. This is a great opportunity to point out the following:
   a. When it comes to solving problems, there are many ways of doing so, even when everyone has the same resources. Getting as many ideas as possible when trying to solve problems/challenges is key.
   b. We all think differently, often down to our understanding of the questions or our frame of reference (in this case, what we believe a duck is). Whilst everyone had the same amount of time, resources and briefing, everyone built a different duck.
3. You could quite easily finish the activity here, and having fun with a serious intent would have been achieved. However, why not try this;
4. Ask the audience/group to modify or rebuild their duck using the same resources and 2 minutes only in answer to a question related to your session. It could be to review the meeting/course so far, and maybe to show their superpower on the topic or, see examples.
5. Ask the group to share their modified duck and its meaning. This could be done as a whole group if you have small numbers, it could be by table or simply with the people sat next to them.

Example questions – modify your duck to show:

How you feel about the meeting/ project to date.	Your superpower in the team you currently work.	Your biggest current workplace challenge.
What's important to you in work.	The top strength of another member of your team.	Something you can do to improve colleague engagement.

Possible uses
- When you want to change the energy in the room
- To identify and make a point about different thinking
- To explore answers to a question or review

Suggested resources
LEGO® duck bricks (x6) per person – can be sourced separately or purchased in any of the following LEGO® sets – 2000416, 30503 and 30541

Tips for success
If participants say they don't know what to build, reply with the phrase – 'don't worry, your hands do'.

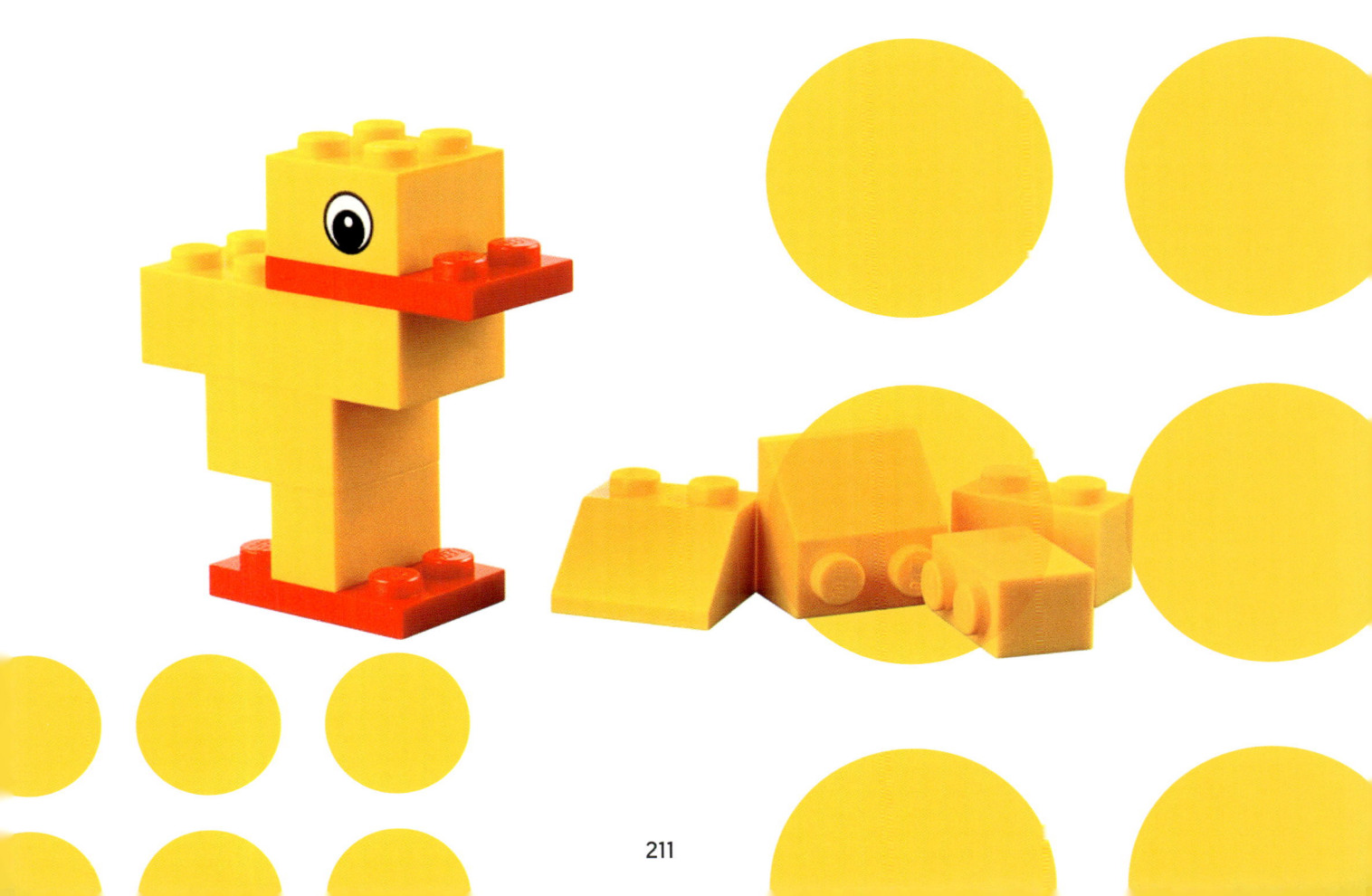

Brick Tower and Their Best Self

What is it?
A team activity which can be used create ideas, review work/meetings, gather feedback and learn about each other.

What's the process?
1. Give each person a set of LEGO® bricks (each person should have the same bricks (a set with 50 to 100 pieces works well). Ask them to open the set and place all parts on the table. (Feel free to observe behaviours at this point, but don't comment). You may see people start to fiddle with bricks, they may put pieces on the table away from their body, or they may start to lay them out in a logical way, i.e. in colour, shape or size order).
2. Tell them they are about to be given a challenge, and they will have only two minutes to complete it. Then ask them each to build a tower, using only the resources they have been given and include a couple of criteria, such as must have green at the base or have a flag on top, etc.
3. At the end of the build time, ask the group to place their tower on the table and look around to see if there are any similar structures. They will all look very different and have many different features, shapes, etc.
4. Ask group members to share something about their tower and why they chose to build it the way they did. They will often describe their build using language that matches their strengths (see the section on LIFO® in this book), a stable tower that looks good, or a pretty and inviting tower which includes a Minifigure, maybe the tallest tower or even one that has used up all of the pieces so that they could 'win'. This also helps to start with storytelling techniques.
5. Use these descriptions to help link to your session – maybe looking at behaviours/strengths and how they can be best used.
6. Ask the group to modify their tower to show the answer to a question you wish to explore in your meeting/workshop, if your focus is team building, they could build to answer questions such as:
    a. What are your strengths that play out in this team?
    b. Who are you best connected within the team, and what traits of theirs help you most?
    c. What are your best conditions to work in?

Possible uses
This activity can be used for team building, learning about each other, as an energiser or icebreaker in a meeting/workshop.

Suggested resources
A small set of LEGO® bricks per meeting participant. It's key that everyone has the same selection of bricks. There are many options out there. Some options could be:

LEGO® Serious Play Window Exploration Kit/Fiddle Bag set 2000409. Or any of set numbers 10403, 10706 or 30588; maybe even Ikea Bygglek set.

Tips for success
Set a few rules during building, like there are no wrong answers, don't over think – just build something, and building time is quiet time.

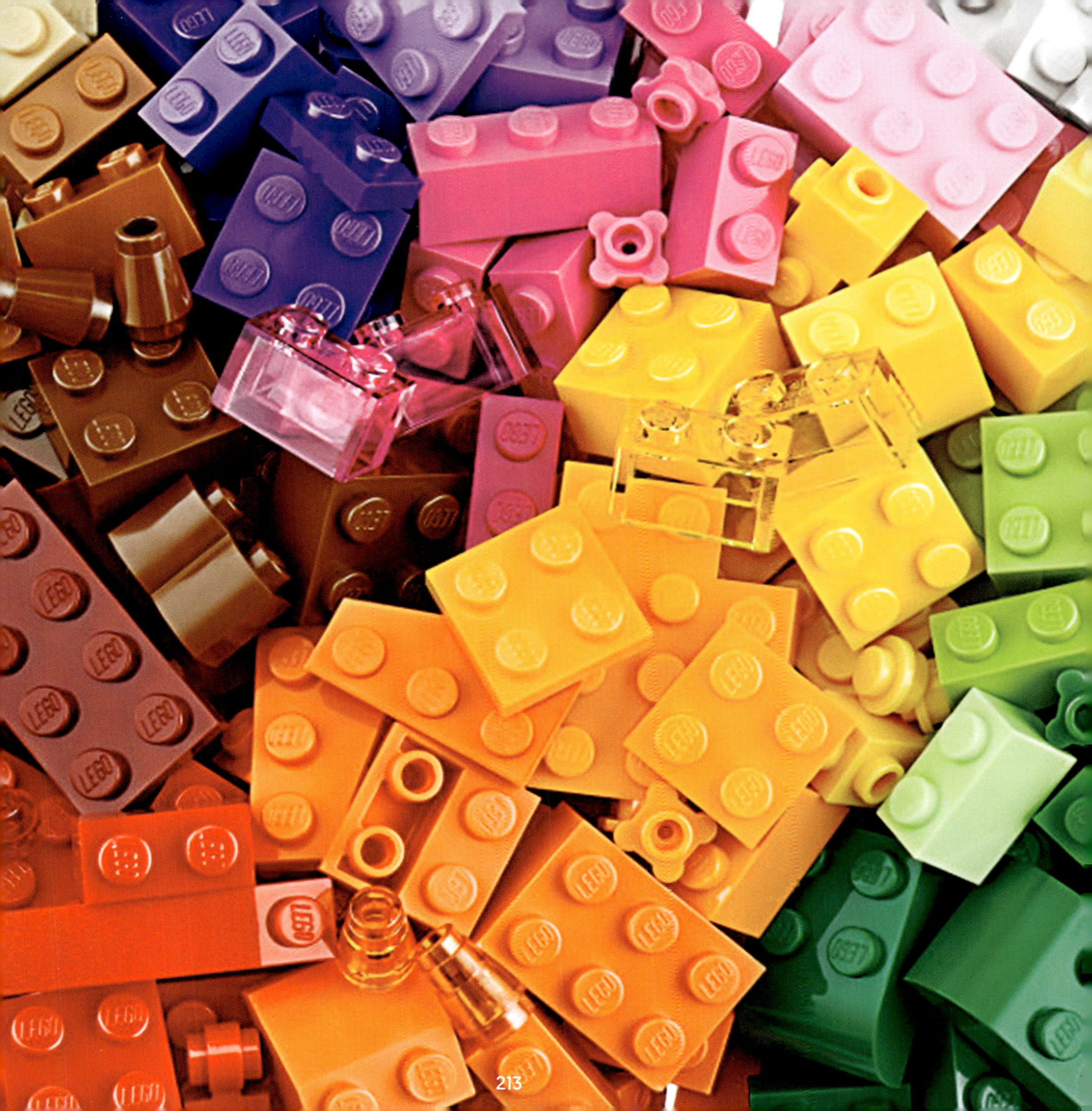

OARRs Agenda Template

What is it?
A visual agenda template to use collaboratively when creating your plan.

What's the process?
On-screen, if an online workshop or large printed/drawn-up template is prepared for the start of your meeting.

Work through the OARRs sequence to create buy-in and accountability as follows:

Outcomes – agree as a group what outcomes you want from the meeting. A good idea is to ask attendees to do this individually and then add them using sticky notes to the template. Discuss, cluster, and agree outcomes as a group for the session.

Agenda – create an agenda for the session designed to achieve the agreed outcomes. Write key agenda items as questions. Don't forget to include breaks, refreshments, and items/approaches to produce the desired energy.

Roles – discuss any roles that you need to have fulfilled in order to achieve what you want. Do you need timekeepers, scribes, gatekeepers, etc?

Rules – de-risk the meeting by setting and agreeing on simple ground rules that prevent the meeting from being de-railed. Rules could cover behaviours, contributions, tech, distractions, etc.

Possible uses
OARRs can be used to set up the right environment in monthly meetings, workshops, training courses, problem-solving sessions and much more.

Suggested resources
Template (printed or online) as big as possible. Pens, markers and sticky notes.

OARRs Agenda Template

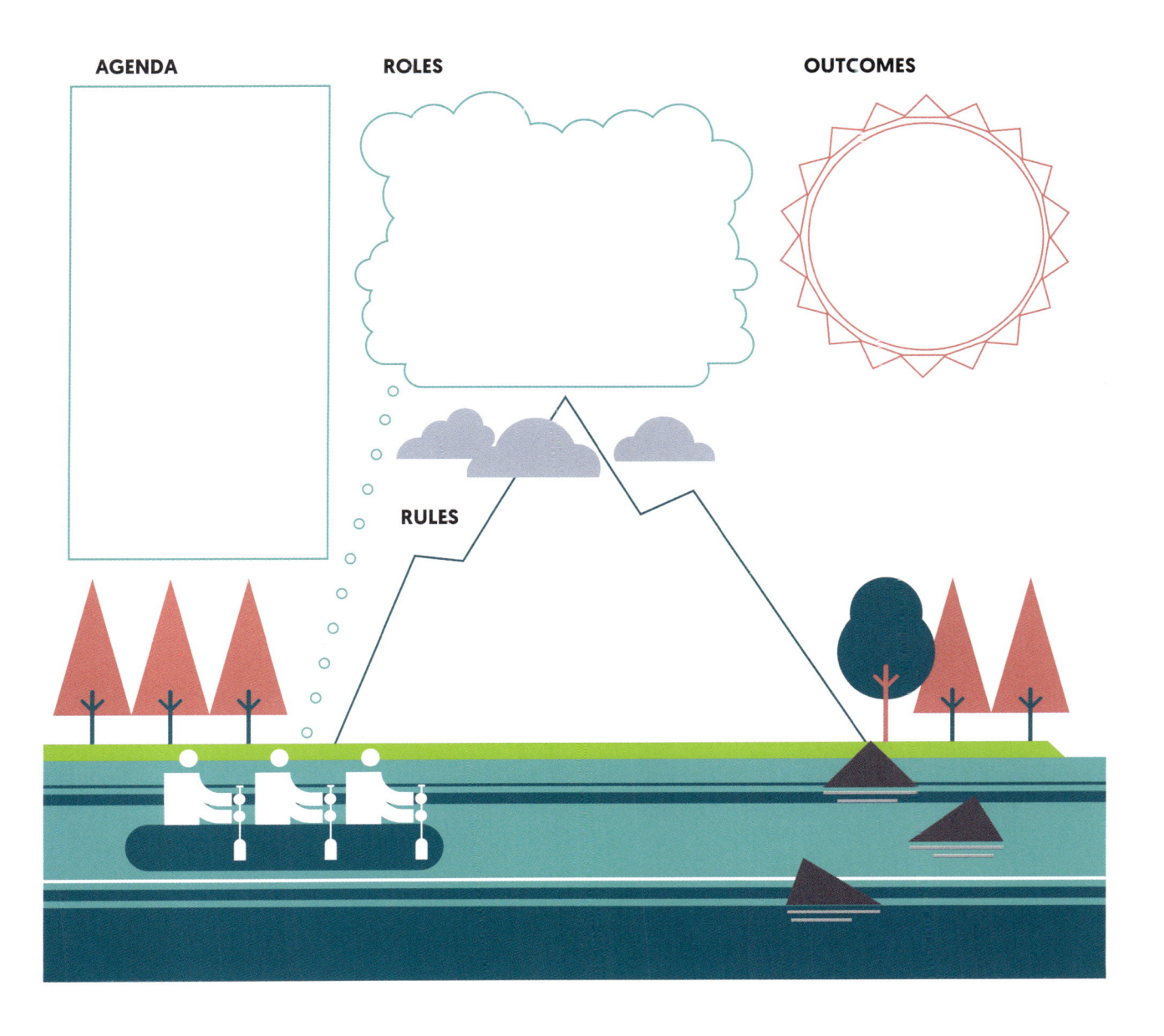

AGENDA

ROLES

OUTCOMES

RULES

215

Tactical Meeting Agenda

What is it?
A template to adapt and adjust to suit your environment for quick, high-energy tactical regular team and department meetings.

What's the process?
1. **Lightening Round Notes.** (Five - ten minutes) – each team member is to list and share their top three things on their plate for the coming day/week, depending on meeting frequency. This should take no longer than one minute per person, even with a couple of follow-up questions. The meeting lead or relevant other team members should note anything that needs further discussion.
2. **Key Metrics Review.** (Five to ten minutes) – Review the key metrics of the business, department or team and note the current status of each. These metrics should be those which the team have previously identified as critical for your success.
3. **Tactical Agenda Items.** (30 minutes) – Discuss the potential tactical issues to be covered, assign an order for the discussion and dive in. These issues may have come up in the Lightening round or the key metrics review. Using problem-solving tools such as radiant problem solving or Five Whys may be appropriate to help answer an item or provide focus.
4. **Cascading Messages.** (Five minutes) – Discuss what, if anything, each team member should communicate to their direct reports following the meeting and agree on a time frame for that to occur.
5. **Decisions/Actions.** (Five minutes) – Ask one team member to chart the decisions and actions committed to during the meeting. Team leaders should note these as well.
6. **Potential Strategic Topics** – As you progress through your meeting, use this area to note topics that you need to cover during a strategic meeting. Be sure to resist the temptation to resolve these issues right away.

Possible uses
It can be ideal for daily stand-up meetings, scrums, team check-in and any short, tactical meeting that needs to be fast-paced.

Suggested resources
It's good to have a template available and also a copy of the previous tactical meeting agenda to review. Templates can be individual copies or large printed versions on a wall that the group stand around. Large templates force the group to stand and create great energy. Pens/markers as necessary.

Template Example

1. Lightening Round and Check-in	2. Key Metrics Review Goal / Metrics 🔴 🟡 🟢	3. Tactical Agenda Items Order topics • • • •
4. Cascading Messages	5. Decisions, Actions & Check-out	6. Potential Strategic Topics

Adapted from Patrick Lencioni's *Death by Meeting*

Power of Synergy

What is it?
Power of Synergy is a short exercise to show the power of working together as a team to find a solution. The end result shows that the sum of teamwork is greater than the parts of the team.

What's the process?
1. Team members start by working individually on a given question (no internet access allowed). A good example could be 'to name all the James Bond films ever made'. (Answer to save research on the next page).
2. Give them five minutes to come up with as many as they can individually. Typically, each individual will come up with a handful of answers. You can ask them to shout out the number of answers they have (but none of the titles).
3. Ask them to pair up and share their list with a partner. What is their combined list, and how many have they increased by?
4. Continue to increase the size of the groups – either until a group has come up with all of the films or the groups are working as one. You'll often find they get close to the final number.

Possible uses
A great activity to highlight the need for diversity and collaboration to find a much better solution.

Suggested resources
Just a list with the answer to your question.

Tips for success
If you have a large group (maybe 25+), you could make it a competition and finally have two large teams working together.

Other possible topics or questions that would be fairly generic and not too specific could be:
- Olympic games (summer, winter or both)
- African countries
- Countries in Latin America

Power of synergy example – James Bond Films

Dr. No (1962)
From Russia with Love (1963)
Goldfinger (1964)
Thunderball (1965)
You Only Live Twice (1967)
On Her Majesty's Secret Service (1969)
Diamonds Are Forever (1971)
Live and Let Die (1973)
The Man with the Golden Gun (1974)

The Spy Who Loved Me (1977)
Moonraker (1979)
For Your Eyes Only (1981)
Octopussy (1983)
A View to a Kill (1985)
The Living Daylights (1987)
Licence to Kill (1989)
GoldenEye (1995)
Tomorrow Never Dies (1997)
The World Is Not Enough (1999)
Die Another Day (2002)

Casino Royale (2006)
Quantum of Solace (2008)
Skyfall (2012)
Spectre (2015)
No Time to Die (2021)

2 Non-Eon films
Casino Royale (1967)
Never Say Never Again (1983)

Power of synergy example – Olympic sports

The 63 IOC Recognised Non-Olympic Sports

Combat Sports, 3
Karate
Sumo Wrestling
Wushu

Independent Sports, 30
Aerobics
Ballooning
Glider Racing
Hang Gliding
Skydiving
Ultra-light Aircraft
Formula 1
Karting
Motorcycle Racing
Power Boating
World Endurance Champ
Word Rally Champ
World Rally Cross
World Touring Car Champ
Apnea
Artistic Roller Skating
Bowling

Dance Sport
Finswimming
Freestyle Frisbee
Frisbee Golf
Ice Climbing
Life Saving
Orienteering
Ski Mountaineering
Speed Roller-skating
Sport Climbing
Surfing
Underwater Orienteering
Water Skiing

Object Sports, 28
American Football
Bandy
Baseball
Bocce
Carom Billiards
Double Disc Court Frisbee
English Billiards
Floorball

Guts Frisbee
Inline Roller Hockey
Korfball
Lawn Bowls
Netball
Pelota Vasca
Petanque
Polo
Pool
Racquetball
Snooker
Softball
Sport Bowls
Squash
Tug of War
Ultimate Frisbee
Underwater Hockey
Underwater Rugby

Mind Sports, 2
Bridge
Chess

Parking Lot

What is it?
A simple and effective way of keeping meetings on track whilst capturing questions, ideas, and other points to be discussed.

What's the process?
1. Draw up a simple template on a flipchart or a section of your online platform.
2. At the beginning of the meeting, get agreement that we'll do our best to keep on track and focus on the agenda, yet important questions will not be ignored. Make it clear that anyone can add to the parking lot throughout the meeting, but you have allocated one person to capture these and ensure they're not missed.
3. During the meeting, if a topic or question is raised, that is not appropriate for that time or agenda item, capture it on a sticky note or card and add it to the template. This is down to yours and the group's judgement, but really can help to keep focus. It could be worthwhile adding the name or initials of the person who raised the point so they can pick up where they left off at the right time.
4. At the end or appropriate time, i.e. after a break or lunch, review the items in the Parking Lot. Decide how they will be tackled based on the purpose of the meeting or the time available. This may mean that some are discussed then, but others are added to the agenda for a different meeting or taken as a separate meeting need altogether.

Possible uses
Great to use in any meeting but especially useful in longer meetings and workshops.

Suggested resources
Flipchart, pens, sticky notes or cards, and spray adhesive.

Tips for success
- Always follow up with the items even if they're not discussed at that meeting. Don't let people think their points are not relevant by letting them go unanswered.

Parking Lot

Recipe for Success

What is it?
Recipe for Success is a simple exercise that takes the well-known idea of creating a recipe and uses it to imagine the team's next steps or how they will work together.

What's the process?
Either on one large template or three separate flipchart sheets, create a template with the following headings:
- Ingredients – What ingredients do you need?
- Image – What does success look like?
- The Process – How do you make it happen?

In groups, give them around 30 minutes to work through the template. Depending on your objectives, you may wish to give them more or less time.

I would suggest the groups work on them in order of, Ingredients, Image and then The Process.

On completion, groups should present their recipes back to the larger group. This will identify lots of similarities, share metaphors and create buy-in.

Possible uses
A great way of consolidating learning from a team day, actions from a planning meeting or visioning success following a strategy meeting.

Suggested resources
Big boards or flipcharts per group (It's a good idea to have groups of four - seven people). Sticky notes and coloured markers are needed too. It's also a good idea to have some old lifestyle-type magazines or food magazines, scissor and glue to create their own images/collages – not a must, though.

Recipe for Success

Ingredients

Image

Process

Quick Coaching

What is it?
A super-effective method for improving personal achievements and growth, based on the work of Nick Drake-Knight. This simple tool builds confidence, accountability, and individual results.

What's the process?
1. Start your conversation by building self-esteem, asking them about what is going well and working for them. Be curious. Ask questions such as, "What are you doing? How does it feel when it's going well? Where are you achieving the most right now?"
2. Explore what is possible by building on their strengths and what is working. Ask questions and listen. Encourage them to think big, asking, "What else?" Use the answers from the previous step to build the possibilities and excitement.
3. Work with them to co-build a solution to implement their ideas. Ask what support they need from you. Use questions to get them thinking about simple steps, resources, timescales, and other support.
4. Challenge them and check they are committed to making it happen. Ask them, "How they will know they are successful? What will it look like, feel like? What will people be saying?"

Possible uses
This is a great tool to use in many conversations, but specifically, it can be used for:
- Building accountability and commitment
- Solving problems
- Creating new ideas
- Creating new behaviours and ways of working

Suggested resources
No specific resources are needed for this tool.

Tips for success
- Use powerful coaching questions that get the other person thinking and challenging them.

What's working?

What are you doing that's working?
How does it feel when it's going well?
Where are you achieving most right now?
What support are you getting?

What's possible?

How can you use what's working to achieve more?
What would 'more' look like for you?
What's next in your journey to success?

How are you going to do it?

When are you wanting to do this by?
What resources, support, etc, do you need?
What are your first steps?
Are there any things that might get in the way of taking these steps?

How do you know you are successful?

What will it look and feel like when you've been successful?
What will people be saying when you're successful?
What will you get on completion?

About the Author

Martin is a UK-based facilitator. Spending over 20 years delivering experiential training to many organisations across all sectors. His passion for effective and impactful collaboration comes from his combined experiences in his work life, volunteering roles, and hobbies. Martin's client work covers team development, leadership, strategy, change management, coaching and much more.

Like so many of us, Martin has experienced poorly run meetings and attended badly structured conferences. He has also been fortunate enough to attend some truly inspiring events, where learning has been maximised, participation is fully inclusive and post-event actions are driven to achieve success. The whole spectrum of good and bad has made him passionate about helping to make meetings matter for everyone.

His early years of experiential learning focussed on using the outdoors where he developed and perfected many of his facilitation skills and crafted his approach. Planks and barrels, spiders' webs and ropes courses were at the heart of his programmes. Martin is also a committed volunteer youth leader and more recently has been supporting and training other youth leaders to provide great development for today's young people. In his volunteer roles, he has facilitated conferences, events, courses, and meetings where he has tried out many of the ideas in this book to great effect.

Martin loves travelling, running (though not as much as he used to) and spending time in the beautiful mountains of the UK's wild country areas. For him to be at his best, Martin admits that "this must include trips on his own, with friends and with his beautiful family in equal measure."

Also by the Successfactory

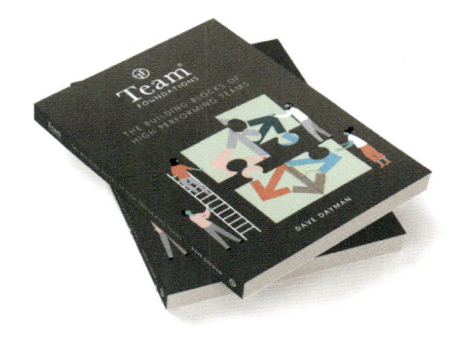

Leadership Laid Bare
Graham Wilson

Team Foundations
Dave Dayman

Wabisugi
Jenny Sutton &
Graham Wilson

Recommended Reading

There are so many great books out there that could be put on this page, but I've tried to select a range that can build on the contents of this book and further help in the reader's quest to make meetings matter.

Building a Better Business Using the LEGO Serious Play Method
Rasmussen and Kristiansen

Will There Be Donuts
David Pearl

Facilitating Breakthrough
Adam Kahane

Meeting by Design
Michael Clargo

Visual Meetings
David Sibbett

Death By Meeting
Patrick Lencioni